"What if the Psalter's 150 psalms were arranged in a strategic order to tell an epic story? What if these psalms speak of Jesus? What if they also guide us in our worship of God? In *Treasuring the Psalms*, Ian Vaillancourt offers the church an accessible, theologically rich introduction to reading Psalms as an epic story centered around a Torah-observant king. Many will treasure the Psalms more as a result of this book."

Andrew T. Abernethy, professor of Old Testament at Wheaton College and author of *Savoring Scripture*

"Ian Vaillancourt has written a delightful guide to the Psalms. Judiciously anchored in the latest scholarship, enthusiastically christological, and written with a pastoral heart, this warmly recommended book will indeed enable readers to treasure the Psalms and to sing afresh the glories of the Messiah."

L. Michael Morales, professor of biblical studies at Greenville Presbyterian Theological Seminary

"Psalms is one of the most beloved books in the Bible, yet many are unsure how the psalms can be applied to the Christian life in a legitimate and faithful way. In this accessible, focused, and winsomely written book, Vaillancourt's theological conviction and expertise shine. The first part, on the structure and shape of Psalms, is particularly compelling since it explains a complex topic so clearly and demonstrates its relevance for interpretation."

Eric Tully, associate professor of Old Testament and Semitic languages at Trinity Evangelical Divinity School

"Unfortunately, for much of the Christian church today, the book of Psalms is like a 'treasure hidden in a field.' The author of this volume has, however, performed an invaluable service in taking his readers on a 'treasure hunt' to rediscover this buried trove. With academic skill, literary flair, and yet wonderful clarity, Vaillancourt proves himself to be a reliable guide. My advice: sell all you have, buy the book, and join the author as he shows you how to read, pray, and treasure the book of Psalms in all its canonical and christological fullness."

Jerry Shepherd, emeritus professor of Old Testament, Taylor Seminary

"Ian Vaillancourt's *Treasuring the Psalms* not only provides a clear and comprehensive introduction to recent Psalms scholarship, it uses the best of that scholarship to show that the Psalter looks forward to the climax of Israel's history—a climax fulfilled in the story of Jesus Christ. Christian readers will resonate strongly with Vaillancourt's rich christological readings of the Psalms, while the applications he draws from them will encourage increasing praise and thankfulness to God."

Douglas J. Green, senior lecturer in Old Testament and Hebrew exegesis at Queensland Theological College

"This compelling book encourages readers to treasure the Psalms as history, as part of the whole Word of God, as a link to Christ, and as valuable for our very souls. By weaving together personal stories with solid academic study, Vaillancourt inspires as he enlightens with this accessible book. He creates a meaningful reading experience of the Psalms for students, pastors, and interested people alike."

Beth Stovell, professor of Old Testament at Ambrose University

"*Treasuring the Psalms* provides an excellent entry point for students of the book of Psalms. Vaillancourt introduces helpful ways to approach the book of Psalms as well as providing rich insights that aid in understanding the Psalms. Vaillancourt's work will aid anyone who desires a deeper understanding of this 'little Bible.'"

Michael Snearly, scholar in residence at Grace Church of Marin in San Anselmo, California

TREASURING
THE
PSALMS

HOW TO READ THE SONGS THAT
SHAPE THE SOUL OF THE CHURCH

IAN J. VAILLANCOURT

IVP
Academic
An imprint of InterVarsity Press
Downers Grove, Illinois

InterVarsity Press
P.O. Box 1400 | Downers Grove, IL 60515-1426
ivpress.com | email@ivpress.com

InterVarsity Press® is the publishing division of InterVarsity Christian Fellowship/USA®. For more information, visit intervarsity.org.

Scripture quotations, unless otherwise noted, are from The Holy Bible, English Standard Version, copyright © 2001 by Crossway Bibles, a division of Good News Publishers. Used by permission. All rights reserved.

While any stories in this book are true, some names and identifying information may have been changed to protect the privacy of individuals.

The publisher cannot verify the accuracy or functionality of website URLs used in this book beyond the date of publication.

Cover design: Cindy Kiple
Interior design: Jeanna Wiggins

ISBN 978-1-5140-0510-1 (print) | ISBN 978-1-5140-0511-8 (digital)

Printed in the United States of America ♾

Library of Congress Cataloging-in-Publication Data
A catalog record for this book is available from the Library of Congress.

29   28   27   26   25   24   23 | 13   12   11   10   9   8   7   6   5   4   3   2   1

DEDICATION

To Gregory John Vaillancourt

We are brothers by birth,

brothers in Christ by new birth,

and close companions because

we couldn't imagine it any other way.

I thank God for you, brother!

Contents

APPENDIXES: Digging Deeper
(Available as a Free PDF Download on
www.ivpress.com/treasuring-the-psalms)

Appendix A.
Digging Deeper: The Canonical Approach to the Book of
Psalms Through Two Thousand Years of Church History

Appendix B.
Digging Deeper: Psalm Superscriptions Through the Centuries

Appendix C.
Digging Deeper: Questions Remain About the
Psalm Superscriptions

Appendix D.
Digging Deeper: A Thematic Approach to
the Individual Psalms

Appendix E.
Digging Deeper: Bruce Waltke on the Imprecatory Psalms

Appendix F.
Digging Deeper: The Language of Praise

Bibliography for Appendixes

Preface

BEFORE WE DIVE INTO OUR STUDY of the Psalms, a few explanations will help us to read with greater understanding. Unless otherwise indicated, Scripture quotations are taken from the English Standard Version (ESV). Even where the English and Hebrew verses slightly differ, I have only included the English verse numbers. This includes the psalm superscriptions (or titles): while the Hebrew Old Testament includes them as part (or all) of verse 1 (or sometimes verses 1 and 2), I have cited them as "verse 0," to line up with the ESV. For short quotations of the psalms, I have placed slash marks in the text to mark off poetic lines (for example, "Truly God is good to Israel, / to those who are pure in heart," Ps 73:1). In the case of longer quotes, the poetic lines have been retained, so slash marks were not required.

Since I will explain their meaning as the book progresses, the Hebrew words "YHWH," *torah*, and *hesed* are left transliterated throughout, except when I am citing directly from the ESV Bible. This will help readers to remember the meaning of these words, and to identify them in their reading of the ESV, where YHWH is translated as "the LORD," *torah*, as "law," and *hesed* as "steadfast love." Readers are encouraged to supply these Hebrew words when they encounter my citations of the ESV.

Because some readers will be familiar with Hebrew, I have included the simple transliteration of some key Hebrew words, along with the actual Hebrew script in parentheses. This way, those who work with Hebrew will be able to identify the words with greater clarity, and those who are not will be able to skip over them. A knowledge of Hebrew is *not* required in order to understand this book.

Finally, it is important that readers understand when I capitalize (or not) the word *Psalms* in this book. When referring to the entire book, the word is capitalized, as in "book of Psalms" or "Psalms." When referring to individual psalms, the word is written in lower case, as in "psalm" or "psalms." However, when written along with a specific psalm number, the word is capitalized, as in "Psalm 73." I hope this helps to explain my uses of "book of Psalms," "Psalms," "psalm," "psalms," and "Psalm 73," throughout this book.

Acknowledgments

THE INITIAL IDEAS FOR THIS BOOK were born during my doctoral studies at the University of Toronto in 2012–2017. As I researched for seminar papers, comprehensive exams, and then my dissertation on the portrayal of the savior in book 5 (with a focus on Ps 110 and 118), the seeds of this book were germinating in my mind. Lectures on the Psalms to my students at Heritage Theological Seminary in Cambridge, Ontario, have sharpened my thinking. The opportunity to teach a course on the Psalms at both Tyndale University in Toronto, and Millar Graduate School in Saskatchewan, crystallized my thinking even further. Thanks to my very perceptive students from all these schools; their questions and comments have deepened my understanding in more ways than they could imagine.

This book was also shaped by a rich community of Christian friends. I am thankful that the following people gave feedback on a few early chapters: Darren and Andrea Thom, Steve and Sarah Dobrenski, Brigette VanHuistede, Andrew W. Hall, Wyatt Graham, J. Ryan Fullerton, Stephen G. Dempster, David Barker, Jerry Shepherd, Tim Challies, and Natalie Vaillancourt. Their feedback not only strengthened those chapters but helped me to find my voice for the material that followed. I am also thankful to my wife, Natalie Vaillancourt, and my friends, Andrew W. Hall and Cristian Rata, for reading and giving feedback on an early manuscript in its entirety.

This work is much stronger and much more coherent because of their labors. Any shortcomings are, of course, my own.

The team at IVP Academic has been a great blessing to this project. I am thankful for their interest in it, and the way they shepherded it toward completion with much more excellence than I could have achieved on my own. In particular, Anna Moseley Gissing (early in the process), along with Jon Boyd and Rachel Hastings (later in the process), were wonderful sources of insight and encouragement.

As always, my amazing wife, Natalie Vaillancourt, has been my best friend, helper, support, and encourager, throughout the writing of this book and in every aspect of my life. Along with Natalie, our two kids, Caleb (17) and Emily (15), were sources of fun (playing Catan or Ticket to Ride or Dominion) and exercise (going for hikes or bike rides) after writing sessions were completed. I pray that as we continue to immerse ourselves in our local church, in God's Word, and in prayer, each member of our family would grow in their vision of the glory of the God of the Psalms in such a way that we are propelled to love and serve him with all our heart, soul, mind, and strength.

Introduction

Getting Oriented to the Book of Psalms

THE BOOK OF PSALMS is a treasure: these 150 Holy Spirit–inspired poems, originally written in Hebrew, have shaped the songs, prayers, and theology of God's people for thousands of years. Imagine a treasure hunter on a new expedition. Although they are equipped with the best digging and locating equipment available, they don't need it for this venture: as soon as they arrive at their destination, they find masses of treasure *on the surface of the ground*. This is a little bit like encountering the book of Psalms for the first time: even an initial reading turns up glorious, surface-level gospel treasure for the taking. For example, in the Psalms,

> We are instructed in the life that is blessed by YHWH (e.g., Ps 1).[1]

> We encounter the anointed one who is YHWH's means of bringing salvation to his people (e.g., Ps 2).[2]

---

[1]Old Testament scholars often spell the personal name of God as *YHWH* (יְהוָה) in English and pronounce it as "Yahweh." English Bibles, however, tend to translate this name as "the LORD." But since this is a title and not a name, I prefer to use YHWH, to emphasize the personal, intimate connection a believer has with their God. Note too that earlier Christians tended to translate YHWH as "Jehovah," based on an older idea about how to pronounce the name most accurately.

[2]The Hebrew word for "anointed" is *mashiah* (מָשִׁיחַ). In the Old Testament, prophets were anointed (e.g., 1 Kings 19:16), priests were anointed (e.g., Ex 28:41), and kings were anointed (e.g., 1 Sam 16:13; Ps 2), all for special service to YHWH. The New Testament identifies Jesus as the ultimate Anointed One to come, who is the fulfillment of the prophet like Moses (Deut 18:15, 18; cf. Acts 3:22, etc.), the priest like Melchizedek (Ps 110:4; cf. Heb 6:20), and the royal son of David to come (2 Sam 7:12-13; cf. Mt 21:9). In fact, the Greek New Testament

We are given comfort by the God who always shepherds his people well (e.g., Ps 23).

We are humbled with reminders of how glorious it is to be forgiven by God (e.g., Ps 32).

We are blessed with words of security as we encounter our God as the best refuge imaginable (e.g., Ps 46).

We are led in self-forgetful praise of God (e.g., Ps 150).

It is for good reason, then, that the book of Psalms is among the most cited Old Testament books in the New Testament. Along with countless believers through the ages, it is also one of my favorite books of the Bible. In the Psalms we find the theology of the Old Testament put into poetry and expressed in worship to YHWH. This book is clearly Godward, practical, and encouraging.

Even better, the book of Psalms is not only a treasure when life is easy, but it is also precious when life is hard. In this book,

We are given words to express our sorrow in faith, for times when life is deeply painful (e.g., Ps 3).

We are given words to express our yearning to gather with God's people when we have been kept from fellowship (e.g., Ps 42).

We are helped with words of confession and repentance for times when we have committed a horrible sin (e.g., Ps 51).

We are blessed with a heavenly perspective for times when following Christ is hard, and when all but the godly seem to be doing well (e.g., Ps 73).

We are given vocabulary to express our longing for God's presence when he feels distant from us (e.g., Ps 84).

We even encounter the very words Jesus used to express his agony as he hung on the cross (e.g., Ps 22).

---

translates the Hebrew *mashiah* (מָשִׁיחַ) as *Christos* (χριστός). This explains the origin of the English words "Messiah" and "Christ," as they are used in reference to Jesus.

How awesome is this book that helps us express our own tears and also gives us a peek into the words and emotions of our Savior.

On the other hand, in our initial encounter with the book of Psalms, we not only find surface treasures but also some puzzling, seemingly impractical, and even deeply disturbing content. For example,

> What are we to make of God-the-judge laughing at his enemies (e.g., Ps 2:4)?

> Is it right to speak boldly and directly to YHWH, asking him why he stands far away and hides himself in times of trouble (e.g., Ps 10:1)?

> Did the psalmist exaggerate the depth of his suffering at times, or did his words always express his exact personal experience (e.g., "all my bones are out of joint," Ps 22:14)?

> Is a psalm that celebrates an ancient Israelite king (e.g., Ps 45) or Zion (e.g., Ps 87) even mildly relevant for us today?

> Should believers ever complain to God (e.g., Ps 64:1)?

> Can it possibly be right to call "blessed" those who smash the heads of children against "the rock" (Ps 137:9)?

An initial reading of the book of Psalms turns up just as much puzzling, seemingly impractical, and disturbing content as it does surface treasure.

As we continue in the book of Psalms, the questions also continue. For example,

> What is a *Shiggaion* or a *Maskil*?

> What does "according to The *Sheminith*," or "according to *Muth-labben*" mean?

> What about *Selah*?

To be sure, there are many terms in the book of Psalms that seem far removed from our understanding. And then there are the psalm titles in general: "To the choirmaster. Of David" (e.g., Ps 11:0). Does this accurately reflect the poem's original authorship? If so, why was it written in the third person? Why do our English Bibles set these titles in a different font and place them *prior* to verse 1? What about the so-called historical psalm superscriptions? Did David really write poems for occasions of his own desperation (e.g., Ps 3) or repentance (e.g., Ps 51)?

Further, is the book of Psalms a random assortment of 150 poems arranged in no particular order, or is there anything significant about the book's shape? Is there a message to be found in the flow of the psalms? If so, why is it out of chronological order, with a psalm of Moses (approximately 1400 BC) appearing in the middle (Ps 90), and many psalms of David (approximately 1000 BC) appearing before (e.g., almost all of Ps 3–41) and long after it (e.g., Ps 138–145)? And why is the larger book of Psalms separated into five smaller books, or sections? Was this a part of the original shape of the book, or was it a later addition?

Finally, we may also have questions about specific content. For example, if Psalm 72:20 marks the end of the prayers of David, son of Jesse, why do other prayers of David appear in Psalms 86 and 142? Or why does the name of YHWH all but disappear in Psalms 42–83? Is there a reason for the temporary switch to *Elohim* (אֱלֹהִים, "God") in this section, and then the switch back to YHWH in Psalms 84–150? An initial encounter with the book of Psalms certainly turns up questions that need to be answered.

TWO KEY WORDS

Although the focus of this book will be on reading the Psalms as a purposefully shaped collection of poems ("reading canonically") that points to Christ ("reading christologically") and applies directly to the Christian life ("reading personally and corporately"), in the rest of this introduction we will consider two key words and three helpful insights about the book of Psalms. These will equip us to navigate the particulars through the rest of our study. As we begin to dig a little deeper in search of even more gospel treasure from the book of Psalms, we find that noticing a bit about its use of words will help us to read with understanding. For now we'll look at two brief but important examples: YHWH (יְהוָה, "Yahweh," or "the LORD") and *hesed* (חֶסֶד, "steadfast love").

YHWH. First, the name YHWH (most commonly pronounced "Yahweh") stands out.[3] Isn't it telling that in this intimate book of praise and prayer, the most common way that the poets addressed their God was by his personal, covenant name? This name had been used in praise of God since the earliest days of his people (e.g., Gen 4:26b), by the patriarchs when they spoke to God (e.g., Gen 15:2), and by God when he revealed himself to the patriarchs (e.g., Gen 15:7). However, the full significance of this name was revealed in the exodus from Egypt, when YHWH *redeemed* his people from slavery (e.g., Ex 3:14-16; 6:2-3).[4] Therefore, the name YHWH is wrapped up in the

---

[3]See this book's preface for an explanation of the name YHWH.

[4]Waltke helpfully explains these texts on a grammatical basis. For Waltke, an analysis of the Hebrew text of Exodus 3:12-13 and Exodus 6:2-3 offers helpful insights into the meaning of these important passages. First, in Exodus 3:13, when Moses asked for God's name, he clearly could have used a Hebrew word with the connotation "What is the name you go by?," but instead he used a Hebrew word to ask, "What is the meaning of your name?" (see Bruce K. Waltke and Charles Yu, *An Old Testament Theology: An Exegetical, Canonical, and Thematic Approach* [Grand Rapids, MI: Zondervan, 2007], 365). In other words, even though it may not be clear in English, Waltke argues that in the Hebrew it is clear that *Moses was asking for an explanation of what the name YHWH means*. In this place, YHWH's answer was "I am who I am" (*ehye asher ehye* [אֶהְיֶה אֲשֶׁר אֶהְיֶה]), or "I will be who I will be." The same name in Hebrew in the third person "he is," is pronounced "Yahweh." The sense of the name here is that YHWH is always the same: he is unchanging, consistent. And the sense from this explanation by YHWH is something like this: "you can count on me" (see Waltke and Yu, *An Old Testament Theology*, 366-67). Then, in Exodus 6 for Waltke, YHWH was getting ready for the plagues on Egypt, and he began in v. 2, "I am YHWH." Then in v. 3, "I appeared to Abraham, to Isaac, and to Jacob, as God Almighty, but by my name, YHWH, I did not make myself known to them." While the Hebrew of Exodus 3:13-14 emphasizes the *meaning* of the name YHWH, Exodus 6:2-3 emphasizes its *significance* (see Waltke and Yu, *An Old Testament Theology*, 367-69). And it all comes down to the verb "to know," or "to make known" in the Hebrew text. So in Exodus 3, the *meaning* of YHWH is being stressed (consistent, never changing, covenant God), and in Exodus 6 the *significance* of the name YHWH is being stressed ("this is what YHWH is like"). And in both cases the context is the redemption of YHWH's people from Egypt. In other words, the meaning and the significance of the name YHWH cannot be fully known unless one has personally experienced redemption by him.

covenant commitment God made with his people: *it is the personal name of God that reminds us of his personal commitment to his people's salvation.*

There are 150 individual psalms, and the name YHWH occurs 695 times in the book.[5] That is an average of almost five occurrences per psalm. The first of these is found in the second verse of the book, Psalm 1:2: "Blessed is the [one] / who walks not in the counsel of the wicked, / nor stands in the way of sinners, / nor sits in the seat of scoffers; / but [this person's] delight is in the law of the LORD" (Ps 1:1-2). And the last time the personal name of God occurs is in the very last verse of the book, where we encounter it twice: "Let everything that has breath praise the LORD! / Praise the LORD!" (Ps 150:6). The psalmists had a boldness to come to their God personally and intimately, and by including the book of Psalms in the Bible, God invites us to enjoy this same kind of intimate, personal access.

Before we move on, a little bit of simple translation information will help transform our reading of the book of Psalms (and the entire Old Testament, for that matter). Our English Bibles almost universally translate the name YHWH with the title "the LORD."[6] While this is common convention, the use of a *title* is far less personal than is warranted by the *name* YHWH in the original Hebrew. If the psalmists lead us to employ the personal, covenant name of God that is especially wrapped up in our redemption, would it not seem logical to use this *name* in favor of an *impersonal title*? A strategy I use in my own reading is simple: when I encounter the title "the LORD"

---

[5]As a short form for YHWH, the Hebrew YH (יָהּ) occurs an additional 43 times in the book of Psalms. This increases the total occurrences of the personal name of God from 695 to 738 in the book.

[6]Martin Luther was the first to employ the use of capital letters to distinguish Hebrew names for God in the Old Testament. In Luther's case, he employed the German words "HErr" for *adonay* (אֲדֹנָי) and "HERR" for YHWH. See Martin Luther, *Luther's Works*, 69 vols., ed. Jaroslav Pelikan, Helmut T. Lehmann, and Christopher Boyd Brown (St. Louis, MO: Concordia, 1955), 35:248. Most English translations follow this convention by translating "the Lord" for *adonay* (אֲדֹנָי) and "the LORD" for YHWH.

in my English Bible, I read it as "YHWH." Over the years, I have found that this transforms my reading of the book of Psalms, and even the entire Old Testament: it constantly reminds me of the personal, intimate way I can and should relate to YHWH. Whether you follow my strategy or not, it is important to at least understand the significance of this Hebrew name, and to know when it is used in our reading of the book of Psalms (or the entire Old Testament).

Hesed (חֶסֶד). Our second key word is *hesed* (חֶסֶד). This is a Hebrew word that our English Bibles translate in various ways, including "mercy," "love," and "kindness," while the English Standard Version (ESV) translates it uniformly as "steadfast love." The word *hesed* occurs 256 times in the Hebrew Old Testament, and 130 of these are found in the book of Psalms. According to Baer and Gordon, this word has a strong relational sense, as well as an emphasis on a prior commitment or bond.[7] In the context of YHWH's *hesed* toward his people, we can say that it is relational (e.g., "love"), and that it expresses his covenant commitment to his people (e.g., "steadfast").

In its Old Testament context, this great covenant word reminds us that the God who purchased his people out of slavery is tender toward them, faithful to them, and will never let them go. The ESV has translated this word in a helpful way, because "love" emphasizes God's tenderness, and "steadfast" emphasizes his covenant faithfulness. A few examples:

> Have mercy on me, O God,
> > according to your steadfast love;
> > according to your abundant mercy
> > blot out my transgressions. (Ps 51:1)
> For as high as the heavens are above the earth,
> > so great is his steadfast love toward those who fear him (Ps 103:11)

So YHWH and *hesed* are two key words that will help us find even more treasure below the surface in the book of Psalms.

---

[7]See D. A. Baer and R. P. Gordon, "חָסַד," NIDOTTE 2:206-13.

THREE HELPFUL INSIGHTS

As we continue our initial excavation, it would be helpful to ask the question, "What *is* the book of Psalms?" In this section we will learn three helpful insights: one from the Hebrew Old Testament, and two from the early Reformers.

The book of praises. What comes to your mind when you hear reference to "praising God"? Some of us think of organs and hymns like "A Mighty Fortress Is Our God." Some of us think of guitars and songs like "10,000 Reasons." Some of us think of hand clapping and maybe even dancing. Sadly, some of us think of sharp disagreements we've had with other Christians about music styles at church. When we come to the Bible, we find an entire book, 150 chapters, devoted to praising God. The book of Psalms contains 150 songs/prayers of worship to YHWH. As we get looking at this book, we find that it mentions body posture like clapping, dancing, and bowing; it mentions instruments like lyres, harps, and cymbals; but its focus is on God and a believer's relationship with him. According to the book of Psalms, posture and instruments matter, but most important are the words we sing and the God to whom we sing them.

In the original Hebrew, the title of the book of Psalms is *Tehillim* (תְּהִלִּים), "Praises." This is related to *hallelujah*, a frequently occurring word in the Psalms that means "praise YHWH." The Psalms is a book of *Praises*, 150 of them, and for thousands of years it has been the song book and the prayer book of God's people. This means that if we want to learn to give expression to our praises (in song or prayer), we should come to the book of Psalms for guidance. And in this book we find words to praise God in every season of life, whether we are in the heights of joy or the depths of gloom, whether we feel close to God or far from him, whether we are healthy or sick, whether we are happy or sad or angry or anything in between. The book of Psalms teaches us to praise God in all of life.

A little Bible. When I was a new Christian, I heard a professor tell his class that whenever he had focused on the book of Psalms in his personal Bible reading and prayer time, he went through a dry spell in his walk with God. His conclusion (and his recommendation) was that Christians should never sit down to read from the book of Psalms exclusively but should add a psalm to their reading from other parts of the Bible. As a new Christian, this comment seemed out of step with my view of the Bible. After all, the book of Psalms is a part of the Word of God. So I set out to investigate whether this was helpful advice. Having studied the Bible for a few decades, I remain thankful for the impact of this man's teaching in most areas, but I disagree with this particular counsel.

Martin Luther's description of the book of Psalms gave me clarity about my uneasiness with this professor's advice. In his *Preface to the Book of Psalms*, Luther said that it

> might well be called a little Bible. In it is comprehended most beautifully and briefly everything that is in the entire Bible. . . . In fact, I have a notion that the Holy Spirit wanted to take the trouble himself to compile a short Bible and book of examples of all Christendom or all saints, so that anyone who could not read the whole Bible would here have anyway almost an entire summary of it, comprised in one little book.[8]

After a few decades of studying the Psalms, I can offer my hearty "amen" to the great Reformer's description. The book of Psalms is indeed a little Bible, containing a summary of the Bible's teaching about God, humanity, sin, and salvation. This is awesome when we think about it: a book that began its life as a collection of *responses* of people to God (in song and prayer) was later gathered into a book and recognized as *God's Word* to his people. These songs/prayers are deeply theological, even a little Bible!

---

[8]Luther, *Luther's Works*, 35:254.

An anatomy of all the parts of the soul. A third insight into the nature of the book of Psalms comes from the great theologian and biblical interpreter John Calvin. In his *Preface to the Book of Psalms*, Calvin noticed the elevated language and the varied nature of its content, and he concluded:

> The varied and [resplendent]. . . riches which are contained in this treasury it is no easy matter to express in words . . . I have been accustomed to call this book, I think not inappropriately, "An Anatomy of all the Parts of the Soul"; for there is not an emotion of which any one can be conscious that is not here represented as in a mirror. Or rather, the Holy Spirit has here drawn to the life all the griefs, sorrows, fears, doubts, hopes, cares, perplexities, in short, all the distracting emotions with which the minds of men are wont to be agitated. . . . In a word, whatever may serve to encourage us when we are about to pray to God, is taught us in this book.[9]

If the book of Psalms may fairly be called "the book of Praises" and "a little Bible," it may also be called "an anatomy of all the parts of the soul."

To summarize our findings so far, in the book of Psalms we learn that praises (*Tehillim*) consist in deeply theological ("a little Bible") and deeply emotive words from every season of life ("an anatomy of all the parts of the soul"), expressed in songs/prayers to YHWH, the great covenant God who has shown his *hesed* ("steadfast love") to his people. What an incredible book! What a treasure!

THE PATH AHEAD

This book was written to help equip college or seminary students, pastors, and church study groups to read and study the book of Psalms. In terms of reading level, I have kept the technical discussions

---

[9]John Calvin, *Commentary on the Book of Psalms*, vol. 1, trans. James Anderson, Calvin's Commentaries (Grand Rapids, MI: Baker, 1979), xxxvi-xxxvii. Original source has "resplendid."

to the footnotes and appendixes—the latter of which is available as a free PDF download on the IVP website (www.ivpress.com/treasuring -the-psalms). This way, church groups can focus on the heart of the book, while pastors and students can read these other items for a more academic study. In keeping with our treasure-hunting analogy, this book is meant to give Christian readers some tools in their tool-belts for a lifetime of digging deeply in the book of Psalms. This is not a book that *exhausts* everything everyone needs to know about the book of Psalms, but it focuses on some key areas that will equip readers to study deeply on their own.[10]

If this biblical book exhibits surface-level gospel treasure for the taking, it also contains many questions in need of answers before we can gain a deeper benefit from this book of praises, this little Bible, and this anatomy of all the parts of the soul. The Puritans likened the Bible to a bottomless gold mine, and none of us should be content with surface gold (or treasure!) when there is a depth of gospel riches to be mined. So this is a book about how to read the Psalms. Along the way, I will dig up some treasures and display them, and then invite readers to take the tools found in this book and to mine for themselves.

The chapters in this book are clustered into three sections. After this introduction, which has *generally* oriented us to the book of Psalms, in part one, "The Story: Reading the Psalms Canonically," we will ask if there are any implications in the fact that the individual psalms have been gathered into a *book*. In part two, "The Savior: Reading the Psalms Christologically," we will explore how to read the book of Psalms in light of the person and work of Christ, and with a desire for rich gospel application to the Christian life. In part three, "The Soul: Reading the Psalms Personally and

---

[10]For an accessible book that complements this one, see Tremper Longman III, *How to Read the Psalms* (Downers Grove, IL: InterVarsity, 1988).

Corporately," we will pick up on a key lesson from a previous chapter on the Psalms and the Christian: although the book of Psalms points to the person and work of Christ (i.e., "the gospel"), it also applies immediately and directly to the Christian (what we will refer to as "direct application").

The last bit of reading will actually come as bonus material available as a free PDF download from the IVP website (www.ivpress.com /treasuring-the-psalms). As I wrote this book with my broad list of readers in mind, I found that there were certain places—six to be exact—where offering a bit of advanced information would be helpful to readers in more academic settings. In these places, I did two things: in the book itself, I provided six "Did You Know?" sections that are marked off in text boxes. Each of these sections introduce and sum-marize the essence of the teaching in a way that most readers will understand. For each "Did You Know?" section within the book, I then offer a corresponding "Digging Deeper" appendix on the IVP website (www.ivpress.com/treasuring-the-psalms) so that interested readers can turn there to learn more about the subject. Whether you are a pastor or a person in the pew, a student or a layperson who wants to grow in your ability to read God's Word in a deeper way, you may choose to give these appendixes a try. If you are a pastor or a seminary student, these appendixes are targeted at your reading level, so I especially encourage you to read them.

Before we conclude this initial orientation to the book of Psalms, I return to the question of who should read this book and how they should use it. In my experience, any study of God's Word is deepened when a person with the gift of teaching leads Christians in group study. As I have written, I have had two such group settings in mind: a college or seminary classroom, and a group Bible study in local churches. For this reason, I have included questions for group dis-cussion at the end of each chapter. If everyone in the class or small group has read the chapter in question, I suggest that discussion, with the questions as a guide, has the potential to deepen everyone's understanding. Of course, individuals—pastors or students or laypeople—who read this book on their own could very much benefit from these questions too by using them to reflect more on the material. I conclude this introduction, then, with the first set of questions for further reflection.

DISCUSSION QUESTIONS

1. Early in the chapter, the author shared many examples of "surface treasure" found in the Psalms. Which ones stood out to you as particularly precious?

2. Did any of the author's examples of puzzling, seemingly impractical, and even deeply disturbing content in the Psalms leave you feeling particularly uneasy or confused? Why?

3. In light of your new understanding of the words YHWH and *hesed,* read Psalm 103 (ESV) aloud in your group, replacing the English "the LORD" with YHWH, and the English "steadfast love" with *hesed.*[11] What are your initial impressions about how understanding these two key words, and how being able to identify them in your reading of the Psalms in English, will impact your future study of this biblical book?

4. Of the three insights on the character of the book of Psalms as a whole—a book of praises, a little Bible, and an anatomy of the soul—which one seemed most insightful or helpful? Why?

---

[11]I suggest that readers use the English Standard Version (ESV) for this exercise because this translation uniformly translates *hesed* as "steadfast love." In other words, it is easier to identify in this translation.

PART ONE

THE
STORY

READING THE PSALMS CANONICALLY

IN PART ONE, WE FOCUS ON answering a key question from this book's introduction: Is the book of Psalms a hodgepodge collection of poems set in no particular order, or have these poems been intentionally arranged to communicate a larger message? If so, is it possible that this message conveys something greater than the sum of the book's parts—its individual psalms?

Spoiler alert: I do believe that the order of the individual psalms is significant. As you read this, you may remain unconvinced, or perhaps just skeptical. That's okay. I was unconvinced and skeptical before I considered the evidence within the book of Psalms.

The first two chapters of part one focus on root issues. In chapter one, I argue that the Holy Spirit's inspiration extended from the original composition of the individual psalms, through the gathering of psalms into collections, all the way to shaping them into a book. Then in chapter two we examine the superscriptions (or titles) of the psalms, with a special focus on how they are relevant to our reading of the book from beginning to end.

This will set us up to gain a sense of the whole in chapters three, four, and five. In chapter three we will approach Psalms 1 and 2 as a gateway to the book as a whole, and in chapter four we will overview the broad narrative of the book of Psalms. Finally, in chapter five we will look at the portrayal of the king across the book and ask if this has anything to teach us about its broader message.

1

From Individual Psalms to the Book of Psalms

IN APRIL OF 2001, forty-nine-year-old Jeffrey Ross Hyman lay dying of lymphoma at New York-Presbyterian Hospital. Previous to his seven-year illness, Hyman was not used to this kind of frailty. Better known by his stage name, Joey Ramone, he had been the lead vocalist of The Ramones, a pioneer band in the punk rock movement. Mikal Gilmore of *Rolling Stone* magazine describes the scene:

> On April 15, 2001, Joey's family and a few friends gathered at his bedside. Doctors turned off his respirator. Mickey played a song on a boombox that Joey liked, U2's "In a Little While" ("In a little while / This hurt will hurt no more / I'll be home, love"). By the time the song finished, Joey Ramone had closed his eyes. He was 49.[1]

When Bono—the lead singer of U2 and a life-long fan of The Ramones—reflected on this deathbed scene, he said, "Joe turned this song about a hangover into a gospel song I think cos that's the way I always hear it now through Joey Ramone's ears."[2]

How did a song about something so unwholesome turn into a gospel song, even in the mind of its author? Bono wrote about one thing, and now when he sings it, the entire "meaning" of the song has

---

[1] Mikal Gilmore, "The Curse of the Ramones," *Rolling Stone*, May 19, 2016, www.rollingstone .com/feature/the-curse-of-the-ramones-165741/.

[2] "U2 Elevation 2001 Boston Show Two 6 June," U2, June 6, 2001, www.u2.com/news/title/u2 -elevation-2001-boston-show-two-6-june/.

shifted.[3] We see from this that new life experiences can alter the way a song is received, even in the mind of its author.[4]

As we come to the book of Psalms, we notice some similarities with the way Bono now hears "In a Little While," but also some differences. Just like "In a Little While," all of the psalms have a history in which they have been "heard." Unlike "In a Little While," the ultimate author of the various psalms foresaw the entire panorama of that history.[5] If the human author of each psalm wrote in their own style and from their own perspective, the divine author was—and is—all-knowing. Therefore, if a psalm was written by King David in 1000 BC, and then "heard" differently by postexilic Jews who read it in its book of Psalms context in 300 BC, both of these "hearings" were intended by the divine author from its time of composition.[6]

---

[3]To access the song's full lyrics, see "In a Little While," U2.com, n.d., www.u2.com/lyrics/68.

[4]I first heard this illustration—about Bono and Joey Ramone—from my friend Paul S. Evans. The research, references, and retelling are my own.

[5]Darrell L. Bock helpfully distinguishes between a historical-exegetical reading of a biblical text—one that is focused on the original author's intention as he wrote in his own historical context—and a theological-canonical reading—one that pays attention to the progress of revelation, in which "the force of the earlier passage is clarified or developed beyond what the original author could have grasped." Darrell L. Bock, "Single Meaning, Multiple Contexts and Referents: The New Testament's Legitimate, Accurate, and Multifaceted Use of the Old Testament," in *Three Views on the New Testament Use of the Old Testament*, ed. Kenneth Berding and Jonathan Lunde, Counterpoints: Bible and Theology (Grand Rapids, MI: Zondervan, 2008), 116.

[6]One way of expressing this "deeper meaning" that was intended by the divine author is with the Latin *sensus plenior*, which means "fuller sense." Baker cites the classic work: "Raymond Brown defines it as 'the deeper meaning, intended by God but not clearly intended by the human author, that is seen to exist in the words of Scripture when they are studied in the light of further revelation or of development in the understanding of revelation.'" David L. Baker, *Two Testaments, One Bible: A Study of the Theological Relationship Between the Old and New Testaments*, 3rd ed. (Downers Grove, IL: InterVarsity, 2010), 184. As an evangelical interpreter, Oss explains further: "Since the canon of Scripture is a unified literary work, the *sensus plenior* of a given text is simply that which emerges when the text is subjected to the light of all of biblical revelation . . . discerning in a text all the strata of meaning that the canonical context warrants. The progress of revelation dictates that the meaning of scriptural texts became deeper and clearer as the canon unfolded. The exegete, by considering the Bible as an integrated whole, reaches a fuller understanding of individual texts of Scripture. That fuller understanding involves strata of meaning, all of which the author expressed, whether or not he intended to express them." Douglas A. Oss, "Canon as Context: The Function of *Sensus Plenior* in Evangelical Hermeneutics," *Grace Theological Journal* 9 (1988): 105. Oss then helpfully reflects on this concept in light of the interplay between the meaning intended by the human

This chapter is about the history of the book of Psalms, and the way that history impacts the way we are intended to "hear" each psalm. Sometimes it was a new life situation that would impact the way a psalm was "heard" (e.g., the way Bono now hears "In a Little While"). And sometimes the major factor was the setting of a given psalm in its new context in a collected book of Psalms. By way of analogy, think of the way a church's music leader chooses the songs and readings and order of material so that the various elements of the service flow into one another and also prepare the worshiper's heart for the sermon. These songs and readings were not written with reference to one another but can be given new depth in the mind of the worshiper when they are heard and sung together. In a similar way, we will be able to grasp the meaning of the Psalms best if we begin by considering the big-picture process, from the time each psalm was first penned to the "final form" of the book we now have in our Bibles. (This way of studying the Psalms as a well-ordered book is often referred to as "the canonical approach" to the book of Psalms.)

FROM INDIVIDUAL PSALMS TO THE BOOK OF PSALMS

As we approach the book of Psalms, we can begin with a simple observation: it was not originally *written* as a book. We can picture the poet—including Moses (Ps 90), King David (seventy-three times,

---

and the divine authors, as it relates to the emerging shape of the canon: "When applied to biblical interpretation there should be no hesitation in affirming that what the human author intended to say is also part of God's meaning. But it is another matter to ask whether the full meaning of the text is restricted to human intent. Is it possible that God intended what the human author expressed as well as something more? In particular, God has known from the beginning his entire plan for redemptive history. Moreover, God has always known the final shape of the canon." Douglas A. Oss, "Canon as Context," 114. For another helpful treatment of this subject, see Matthew Barrett, *Canon, Covenant and Christology: Rethinking Jesus and The Scriptures of Israel*, NSBT 51, ed. D. A. Carson (Downers Grove, IL: IVP Academic, 2020), 26-30. Since the book of Psalms was clearly completed in stages, from the original composition of the individual psalms to the final form of the book as a whole, this concept seems to especially apply.

Ps 3–145), Asaph (twelve times, Ps 50–83), or the Sons of Korah (eleven times, Ps 42–88), and others—emerging from their desk with the ink still wet.[7] Excited, the author would have run to the temple (or tabernacle) to personally hand their song to the worship leader (notice the note "for the choir director" in fifty-five psalms [Ps 4–140]). We can picture them working with the musician to find the perfect tune to accompany the lyrics (e.g., "according to The Doe of the Dawn," Ps 22), and then testing it out with the Levitical choir. Finally, we can picture the worship leader assigning a scribe to make some copies of the psalm, and then storing the original with the others in the temple.

The point I am making is that the various psalms started out as *individual compositions*. And then at some point, these began to be gathered into "mini collections." For example, it is possible that the Songs of Ascents (Ps 120–134) were gathered as a mini collection *well before* the book of Psalms received its final shape. This is logical, because these fifteen poems were sung by Jews at festival time as they walked in pilgrimage to Jerusalem. Since Jerusalem is set at the highest point in the land, with the temple "mount" as its pinnacle, the faithful had to "go up" or "ascend" to Jerusalem. As they walked, they sang these fifteen psalms, and this is the reason they are referred to as "Songs of Ascents."

Did you notice, however, that in my Songs of Ascents example I said that *it is possible* that they were gathered as a mini collection before the book of Psalms took its final shape? Although it is certain that the various psalms were written as individual compositions over about a seven-hundred- to one-thousand-year period,[8] and although it is probable that groups of psalms formed early mini collections that

---

[7] For more on the authorship of the various psalms, see chapter 2. See chapter 4 for an argument in favor of Psalm 72 as penned by David "for Solomon."

[8] Note that Psalm 90 is a psalm of Moses, and Psalm 137 reflects on the exile. Moses led the exodus from Egypt in around 1444 BC, and the Babylonian exile occurred in 587/586 BC. Since it is possible that the exodus occurred a few hundred years after this estimated date, and it is

were associated with worship during the late-tabernacle and early first-temple periods, any theories beyond this are simply conjecture. Instead of spending our time theorizing about which psalms formed early mini collections, I suggest that it is better spent by recognizing something of the process of formation for the book, and then moving on to more sure avenues of inquiry.

What did the process of shaping the book of Psalms look like? Being careful to guard against building elaborate theories about its history, we can still make the following observations:

- Each psalm was penned by an author, who consciously wrote a poem as a response of worship to YHWH.

- The various psalms were meant to be sung and/or prayed. For example, Psalm 120 is explicitly called "A Song of Ascents" and Psalm 86 "A Prayer of David." Most, if not all, of the psalms, however, can do double duty, and be employed as songs and/ or prayers.

- The various psalms were meant to be sung and/or prayed by individuals and/or the community as a whole. For example, Psalm 3 is an individual lament. It was written about the personal suffering of King David and is full of first person singular pronouns: "I," "me," and "my." Since David was king over Israel, however, his solitary experience would have impacted the community as a whole. Because of this "corporate solidarity" between the king and his people, the psalms of the individual could have been employed by the community as well.[9] Psalm 137, on the other hand, is a community lament. It was written about the community's experience of living in exile and begins with a

---

also possible that many psalms were written hundreds of years after the exile, a 700-1,000 year spread for their authorship seems like the most accurate estimate.

[9]See chapter 5 for an introduction to the concept of corporate solidarity. I also discuss the issue of corporate solidarity in Ian J. Vaillancourt, *The Multifaceted Saviour of Psalms 110 and 118: A Canonical Exegesis*, Hebrew Bible Monographs 86 (Sheffield, UK: Sheffield Phoenix, 2019), 68n228.

string of plural pronouns: "we," "our," and "us." Since the psalm also includes singular pronouns, however, we see that the experience of the community was also radically personal for every individual. As a final example, Psalm 118 was written as a responsive song for a leader and a congregation. We see evidence for this in lines such as "Let Israel say, / 'his steadfast love endures forever'" (Ps 118:2).

- The psalms were almost certainly used and kept by the song leader and stored in the tabernacle or temple. For example, fifty-five psalms (Ps 4–140) begin with the line, "for the choir director" (*lamnatseah* [לַמְנַצֵּחַ]).[10] This song leader would have led the people in the singing and praying of the various psalms.

- Over time, certain psalms became associated with one another. For example, it is possible that the song leader collected most of the psalms marked "*Miktam*" (מִכְתָּם, Ps 56–60) and had them written on a small scroll.[11] The same possibility holds true for the Songs of Ascents, and other clusters throughout the book of Psalms.[12]

- All the while, scribes would have been copying the individual psalms and the mini collections of psalms in order to preserve them for future generations. (Remember that there were no printing presses, computers, e-ink readers, or cloud-syncing services.) This copying was also done to distribute psalms to the various communities inside and outside of Jerusalem for personal, and especially corporate, use.[13]

---

[10]In the ESV, this phrase is translated "To the choirmaster."

[11]Note that Psalm 16 is also a *miktam*, and this case in point helps to emphasize the slippery nature of theories of the pre-history of the book of Psalms.

[12]For a more detailed (and very plausible) theory about this process, see James M. Hamilton Jr., *Psalms Volume 1: Psalms 1-72*, Evangelical Biblical Theological Commentary (Bellingham, WA: Lexham, 2021), 50-52.

[13]I say "especially" for corporate use because (1) the high illiteracy rate would have meant that few people could read anything, much less the Psalms; and (2) a lack of printing press and the need to employ scribes to copy books resulted in a very high price tag on any written material, and this would have alienated most of the common people from "scroll ownership."

- Somewhere along the line, the various psalms—which began their life as responses of worshipers to YHWH—were also recognized as God's Word to his people. In other words, these songs and prayers to God were also Holy Scripture, and so God's Word to us.

- As time continued to pass and the collection of psalms continued to expand, they would have been transcribed in clusters that became associated with one another. So larger mini collections were born.

- As still more time passed, it is likely that Psalms 3–72—or most of them—were formed into a larger "book." This is evidenced by the Dead Sea Scrolls.[14] Tellingly in this regard, the last verse of Psalm 72 reads, "The prayers of David, son of Jesse, are ended" (Ps 72:20). However, between Psalms 73 and 150, a further nineteen psalms are said to be "Of David" (*ledavid* [לְדָוִד]), and Psalms 86 and 142 are explicitly prayers of David. It is most probable, therefore, that Psalm 72:20 was intended as a conclusion to Psalms 3–72 as a whole.

- As still even more time passed, Psalms 73–150 took on something resembling its final "shape," and Psalms 1–2 were set as an introduction to the book as a whole. We cannot be certain when each of these steps took place. For example, Psalms 1–2 may have been set as an introduction early or late in the process.[15]

- At some point in the history of the book of Psalms, five "doxologies" were placed throughout in order to form "books." For example, Psalm 41:13 concludes book 1 with the following

---

[14]In the Dead Sea Scrolls, books 1 and 2 of the Psalms are fairly uniformly presented as a single unit, on a single scroll, and they line up well with these psalms as they appear in our Hebrew Bibles today.

[15]Some scholars theorize that Psalms 1-2 were added later, because of the wisdom theme of Psalm 1, and a perceived wisdom theme in Psalms 73-150, over against Psalms 3-72, which are said to focus more on the king. However, I suggest that this is conjecture; we cannot be certain it is accurate.

doxological refrain: "Blessed be the LORD, the God of Israel, /
from everlasting to everlasting! / Amen and Amen." And so the
five books of psalms were born,[16] mirroring the five books of the
Torah, or Pentateuch.[17] It is possible that these doxologies were
added to pre-existing psalms, but it is also possible that these
particular psalms were chosen to conclude a given "book," because they already concluded with doxologies.[18]

These are some of the most important points to bear in mind in the
process of the formation of the book of Psalms.

As an evangelical Christian, I also think it is important to emphasize that if the shaping of the book of Psalms bears evidence
of intentionality, and if the placement of a psalm in the larger
book of Psalms can add to its interpretive depth, we must recognize the sovereignty of God throughout this process. If we want
to call this a "canonical" approach to the book of Psalms, we may
even refer to an individual "canonicler," or group of "canoniclers,"[19]
as the one(s) responsible for the final shape of the book of Psalms.
In fact, I suggest that it is important to speak of the Holy Spirit's
inspiration of the original author *as well as the individual(s)* who
brought about the final form of the book as a whole. Although
we will flesh out some of the particulars in later chapters, for now

---

[16]Book 1: Psalms 1-41; book 2: Psalms 42-72; book 3: Psalms 73-89; book 4: Psalms 90-106; book 5: Psalms 107-150.

[17]Genesis, Exodus, Leviticus, Numbers, Deuteronomy.

[18]Although it is possible that doxologies were added to pre-existing psalms, the fact that they differ from one another seems to be evidence in favor of their pre-existence as a part of the psalm. This would mean that a given psalm was chosen to conclude a "book" because it concluded with a doxology. Hamilton adds that "the doxology at the end of Ps 41 is an integral piece of the psalm, standing as the closing statement in the psalm's chiastic structure. . . . The same point can be made about the chiastic structures of Pss 72 and 106. . . . Note also that the doxology that closes Book 4, Ps 106:48, is quoted with the verse that precedes it (106:47) in 1 Chr 16:35-36—the Chronicler quotes the last two verses from Ps 106, which includes Book 4's doxology" (Hamilton, *Psalms Volume 1*, 22).

[19]To my knowledge, this term was first coined by John Sailhamer, and was made with reference to the final shape of the Old Testament canon as a whole. I employ it here for the book of Psalms. See John H. Sailhamer, *Introduction to Old Testament Theology: A Canonical Approach* (Grand Rapids, MI: Zondervan, 1995), 240.

we see that the "canonical approach" to the book of Psalms takes all these points into consideration. Most important, from this angle of inquiry the book of Psalms is not treated as a ragbag of unrelated elements but as a purposefully shaped book that bears evidence of care and intentionality—even theology—in its final shape.

DID YOU KNOW?
The Canonical Approach to the Book of Psalms Through Two Thousand Years of Church History

Over the past two thousand years of church history, many interpreters have approached the Psalms as a book with at least some measure of intentional structure and overall message. These include: Augustine (AD 354–430), Cassiodorus (490–583), Thomas Aquinas (1225–1274), Franz Delitzsch (1813–1890), and Alexander MacLaren (1826–1910). Although this approach largely fell out of fashion during the 1800s and 1900s, the work of Brevard S. Childs (1923–2007) and Gerald H. Wilson (1945–2005) revived interest in the Psalms as a purposefully shaped book. In fact, since the work of Childs and Wilson, many have followed who have built on and refined their ideas. For those who would like to dig deeper into this issue, appendix A is available as a free download on the IVP website (www.ivpress .com/treasuring-the-psalms).

UNPACKING THE CANONICAL APPROACH: PSALMS 118 AND 119

Although we will return to Psalm 118 later in this book, for now we notice that its placement beside Psalm 119 extended its meaning beyond what it originally conveyed on its own. In other words, the Holy Spirit's authorial intention—with its later placement in the book of Psalms in full view—went beyond what the human author could have foreseen.[20] To set up our observations, it is essential to notice that the speaker of Psalm 118 was the king over God's people. For example, it was the king's role to lead the victory procession from the battlefield (Ps 118:19-20), and only the rescue of the king would have occasioned national thanksgiving (Ps 118:1-4, 29).

Although its 176 verses make Psalm 119 the longest psalm in the book of Psalms, we do not need to quote all of it in order to make our point. If we turn to Psalm 119 in our Bible, we will notice that it is broken up into twenty-two sections, with eight verses in each section. Set as a heading above each eight-verse cluster is the name of a different Hebrew letter, from the beginning to the end of the alphabet. For example, above verses 1-8 is the title "Aleph," and above verses 9-16 is "Beth." The Hebrew language has twenty-two letters,[21] and Psalm 119 is an alphabetic acrostic: in each eight-verse section, the first word of each line begins with the same Hebrew letter. If the theme of Psalm 119 is clearly "the *torah*" (תּוֹרָה), or "instruction" of YHWH, we can say that this psalm poetically sets forth the beauty and glory of the *torah*, from A to Z (or from "aleph" to "taw," in this case).

In order to get a sense of this great psalm, let's simply quote its first part: the "aleph" section, in verses 1-8:

> 1 Blessed are those whose way is blameless,
>
>   who walk in the law of the LORD!

---

[20]In the categories of Bock, a theological-canonical reading of Psalm 118 offers insights beyond an exegetical-historical reading. And in Bock's view, both of these readings are entirely appropriate, because both of them are witnessed in the New Testament authors' use of the Old Testament. See Bock, "Single Meaning, Multiple Contexts and Referents,"115-18.

[21]In this reckoning, "*sin*" and "*shin*" are counted as one letter; otherwise Hebrew would have twenty-three letters in its alphabet. This twenty-two letter reckoning is in line with ancient Hebrew practice, and is because "*sin*" and "*shin*" look and sound nearly identical in Hebrew: "*sin*" makes an "s" sound and looks like this: שׂ. And "*shin*" makes an "sh" sound and looks like this: שׁ. Whether readers are familiar with Hebrew or not, they will likely notice that the only difference between them is the placement of the "dot," either on the left or right side of the consonant. Since ancient Hebrew was unpointed, it simply appeared this way: ש (whether representing a sin or a shin), hence the twenty-two letter reckoning.

2 Blessed are those who keep his testimonies,
  who seek him with their whole heart,
3 who also do no wrong,
  but walk in his ways!
4 You have commanded your precepts
  to be kept diligently.
5 Oh that my ways may be steadfast
  in keeping your statutes!
6 Then I shall not be put to shame,
  having my eyes fixed on all your commandments.
7 I will praise you with an upright heart,
  when I learn your righteous rules.
8 I will keep your statutes;
  do not utterly forsake me! (Ps 119:1-8)

Notice that the psalm begins with the word "blessed" (*ashre* [אַשְׁרֵי]). This is the same word used at the beginning of Psalm 1, and the same concept (in a different language) that heads the Sermon on the Mount. The idea is that those who follow the advice of this psalm are blessed by YHWH, in the sense of being happy.

The rest of the psalm reveals that the "blessed one" has a life steeped in and shaped by the *torah* of YHWH. The word *torah* in Hebrew is often translated as "law" in our English Bibles, but the fullness of this word's meaning needs to be fleshed out in a longer explanation. I don't know about you, but when I hear the word "law," I think of a bunch of dos and don'ts that I need to dutifully follow. Actually, the Hebrew word *torah* in this context simply speaks of the "instruction" of YHWH in covenant living. The sense is this: "now that you are the people of YHWH—because he has redeemed you and graciously made you his people—here is instruction on how to live with YHWH as your God." Maybe this helps to explain why Psalm 119 delights so much in the *torah*, because it is a joy to follow and serve the one who has made us his own.

In the first eight verses of Psalm 119, notice the *torah*-synonyms that are used: testimonies, ways, precepts, statutes, commandments, and rules. Each of these represents a different Hebrew word that carries its own unique thrust, but when the meaning of all of them is combined, they can be summed up as the comprehensive, covenantal instruction of YHWH. The psalm also talks about having a blameless way (v. 1), of seeking YHWH with one's whole heart (v. 2), of one who does no wrong (v. 3), of keeping diligently (v. 4), of steadfast ways (v. 5), of not being put to shame (v. 6), of an upright heart (v. 7), and of not being utterly forsaken by YHWH (v. 8). These blessings will be attained by "walking" in the *torah* of YHWH (v. 1), keeping his testimonies (v. 2), walking in his ways (v. 3), keeping YHWH's precepts diligently (v. 4), steadfastly keeping his statutes (v. 5), having one's eyes fixed on his commandments (v. 6), learning his righteous rules (v. 7), and keeping his statutes (v. 8). Psalm 119 goes on like this for 176 verses. It truly is a delight-filled expression of the blessedness of living out the *torah* of YHWH.

We have seen that the speaker of Psalm 118 is the king, and that the theme of Psalm 119 is the *torah* of YHWH. Jamie Grant is a Psalms scholar who has shed light on the meaning of these two psalms, not on their own, but in their side-by-side placement in the book of Psalms. Grant steps back and notices an important passage from Deuteronomy that gives clear instruction about the kind of king Israel was to set over themselves (Deut 17:14-20). In short, Israel was to choose a king whose life was shaped by the *torah* of YHWH, who even wrote out a personal copy of Deuteronomy so he could read from it every day and have it impact the way he lived and governed. As the king did this, he would be leading the people in righteousness, in blessing. However, when we turn to the books of Samuel and Kings, we see something horrible: it didn't happen! Although there were some bright spots during the reigns of a few kings, the general trajectory was downward, away from the *torah* of YHWH, and therefore away from YHWH's blessing.

By the time the book of Psalms received its final shape, there was no king on the throne of Israel. As a clear result of national sin, and led by a series of sinful kings, the kingdom had initially split in two, and each of these kingdoms eventually lost its king and its land, and the temple in Jerusalem was also destroyed. The people were carried away into exile, and they were left with their hopes dashed. Second Samuel 7 had promised that a descendant of David would always reign on his throne, and now there was no king to lead the people in living out the *torah* of YHWH, and no land or temple with YHWH dwelling in their midst. It was tragic, and it was their own fault.

As the book of Psalms was assembled, it is perhaps surprising that the psalms about the king were not eliminated. Actually, they were put into prominent positions. Although we will explore the theme of the king more in a later chapter, for now we can notice with Jamie Grant that in the book of Psalms, royal psalms (about the king) and *torah* psalms (that delight in YHWH's instruction) are paired together in three places: Psalms 1–2, Psalms 18–21, and Psalms 118–119. In Grant's view, these kingship and *torah* psalms were placed side by side in order to convey hope in the midst of tragedy: although the history of Israel's kings witnessed a downward spiral of sin, and although this resulted in the loss of a king for Israel, the people could read (or sing or pray) the book of Psalms and be encouraged with "eschatological hope in a monarch who will be the true 'keeper' of the torah of Yahweh."[22] In short, the pairing of Psalms 118 and 119 points us to the Messiah, who would be the perfect, *torah*-keeping king. From this we see that although Psalms 118 and 119 were originally written as separate compositions, their pairing in the final form of the

---

[22]Jamie A. Grant, *The King as Exemplar: The Function of Deuteronomy's Kingship Law in the Shaping of the Book of Psalms*, ed. Adele Berlin, Society of Biblical Literature Academia Biblica Series 17 (Atlanta: Society of Biblical Literature, 2004), 9.

book of Psalms communicates a message that is greater than the sum of their parts—a Holy Spirit–inspired message about hope in a *torah*-steeped royal Savior to come.

DISCUSSION QUESTIONS

1. The author began this chapter with a story about the impact of Joey Ramone's death on the meaning of a U2 song. Can you think of any other songs—Christian or secular—that have taken on a new significance when they were "heard" in light of later circumstances? (These new circumstances could include a later event or the placement of a song in a larger album.)

2. Have you ever heard someone suggest that the book of Psalms is to be read as a well-ordered book, and that theology can be gleaned from its individual compositions as well as its overall message?

3. In the section titled, "From Individual Psalms to the Book of Psalms," the author reflected at length about the historical process from the original penning of each psalm to the well-ordered book we now have in our Bibles. Share an insight with your group that you had not previously considered, and that you found particularly helpful. Are there any additional insights that you would like to suggest?

4. Why is it important that a consideration of the "canonical shape" of the book of Psalms is not a completely new invention of the late-twentieth century?

5. What is the major theme of Psalm 119? Give some examples to support your answer.

6. If the speaker of Psalm 118 is the king, how does its pairing with Psalm 119 impact the way this king is portrayed?

2

Superscriptions

WHAT IS IN A PSALM TITLE?

AS OUR CHURCH FAMILY was going through the Covid-19 lockdown in the spring of 2020, our senior pastor had a great idea: everyone would memorize Psalm 46 at home, and then on a future in-person Sunday, we would all recite it from memory. This would mean that during a very uncertain time in our world, our church family would be soaking in the truths of an incredible psalm as we worked to commit it to memory. The news about suffering in the world would be watched through the lens of God as our refuge and strength. The volatile financial markets would be viewed through the lens of God as a very present help in trouble. As the world was at a standstill, we would be constantly exhorted not to fear. And then, when it was all over and we could worship together again, we would recite the psalm together as we looked back on God's grace during quarantine. It would be a great faith-building affirmation of who God is for us, his people.

During the first live-streamed worship service after this announcement, our music pastor led us in a virtual dry run: "Let's recite as much of it as we remember, together, from our homes." He looked at the camera and began, "God is our refuge and strength, a very present help in trouble." At the same time—from my couch at home—I began, "To the choirmaster. Of the Sons of Korah. According to *Alamoth*. A Song." Do you see the difference? Our church music pastor—who is a very godly and wise Christian man—began at the "start" of Psalm 46, at least from his perspective. In our English Bibles, the part I recited comes before verse one, and is printed in a different font than the rest. It *appears* to be the unimportant ancient title that has nothing to do with the rest of the psalm. In this chapter we are going to challenge this assumption. We'll see that a disregard of the superscriptions (or titles) of the psalms has more to do with an approach to biblical interpretation that has been popular for the past few hundred years, and less to do with the way the church through the ages has approached the book of Psalms.

It may surprise some people that in Hebrew, Psalm 46 begins *in verse one* just as I recited: "For the director of music. Of the sons of Korah. On the alamoth. A song" (author's own translation). Then, *verse two* continues: "God is our refuge and strength, a very present help in trouble." In our English Bibles, the psalm superscriptions *appear* to be a less important part of the psalm because they come *before* verse one and are written in a different font. In the Hebrew Old Testament, the psalm superscriptions *are* verse one,[1] and the lens through which we are to read the rest of the psalm. As we read our English Bibles, it seems as though we should skip over the "unimportant" superscription and get to the important content: the body of the psalm. If we read the Hebrew Old Testament, or an English Bible translated by Jewish scholars—for example, the *Jewish Publication Society Tanak* (Old Testament)—we are led to begin by reflecting on the superscription, and then move to think through the rest of the psalm in light of it.[2]

In the following pages, we'll consider what the psalm superscriptions mean and why they are important. And we will see that even in

---

[1] Depending on its length, the superscription is sometimes verse 1 in its entirety (e.g., Ps 46), verses 1 and 2 in their entirety (e.g., Ps 51), or the first few words of verse 1 (e.g., Ps 110).

[2] The consonants in *Tanak* form a Hebrew acronym used as short form for the three sections of the Old Testament in its Hebrew Bible order: *Torah* (תּוֹרָה, Law), *Navi'im* (נְבִיאִים, Prophets), and *Ketuvim* (כְּתוּבִים, Writings). Vowels are then supplied, and "TNK" becomes "Tanak."

cases where we aren't sure what a given musical term means, there is a lot in the superscription that helps us to understand the psalm, and there is a lot in the superscription that helps us to read each individual psalm in light of its place in the larger book of Psalms. We will begin with a short history lesson, as we summarize a few thousand years of interpreting psalm superscriptions in a "Did You Know" text box. This new understanding will then allow us to zero in on the various kinds of information found in the superscriptions. As we consider the various terms, we will also notice which ones we can understand, and which ones we can (surprisingly) still benefit from, *even if we don't know their meaning*. This will involve another "Did You Know" text box. Finally, we will unpack the things we have learned in this chapter by considering the way the superscription of Psalm 110 transforms the way we read the rest of the psalm.[3]

DID YOU KNOW?
Psalm Superscriptions Through the Centuries

Although many readers instinctively ignore the psalm superscriptions, this trend has only been popular for the past few hundred years. During the first eighteen hundred years of church history, interpreters greatly valued the superscriptions. This is because they appear in every single ancient Psalms manuscript, and these types of titles were also common in the (non-canonical) poetic works of Israel and its neighbors. In fact, 126 out of 150 psalms in the book of Psalms include some sort of superscription. The New Testament authors interpreted the psalms through the lens of the superscriptions (e.g., Jesus in Lk 20:42-43), and so did the early church fathers. In fact, Gregory of Nyssa (AD 335–395) wrote an entire book on them.

---

[3]For more information on superscriptions, at a slightly more academic level than this chapter or even this book's online appendixes, see the following article: Ian J. Vaillancourt, "Reading Psalm Superscriptions Through the Centuries," *Themelios* (forthcoming, 2023).

Why are they so important? First, when a psalm indicates its author, it is meant to be heard from the perspective of that author's "voice." Second, when a psalm indicates the historical context for its composition, it is meant to be heard from that perspective as well. While the larger story (usually from 1 and 2 Samuel) will tell us what was going on in that person's life *externally*, the psalm will tell us what was going on in that person's *inner life*.[4] For those who would like to dig deeper into this issue, appendix B is available as a free download on the IVP website (www.ivpress.com/treasuring-the-psalms).

WHAT THEY SAY: THE INFORMATION IN THE SUPERSCRIPTIONS

With Peter Craigie, observe that five kinds of information is found in the psalm superscriptions: (1) claims of authorship (e.g., "Of David" seventy-three times); (2) historical occasion (thirteen times, e.g., Ps 51); (3) musical information (e.g., Ps 4); (4) liturgical information (e.g., Ps 100); (5) type of psalm (e.g., Ps 46 as a "song").[5]

To flesh out these categories further, the following information appears in psalm superscriptions:

Authorship (seven different authors listed).

- David (seventy-three times, most highly concentrated in book 1, and also prominently in books 2 and 5)
- The Sons of Korah (eleven times, all in books 2 and 3)
- Asaph (twelve times; once in book 2, and the rest in book 3)

---

[4]For more on the psalms as a window into the poet's soul, see the final few pages of chapter 9.
[5]See Peter C. Craigie, *Psalms 1-50*, WBC 19 (Waco, TX: Word, 1983), 32. For one scholar's summary of terms, along with explanations of them, see Samuel Terrien, *The Psalms: Strophic Structure and Theological Commentary* (Grand Rapids, MI: Eerdmans, 2003), 28-32. While I appreciate Terrien's work here, I would be more convinced if he had shared the *grounds* for his claims. For example, he argues that *Miktam* denotes either a chant of expiation or a secret prayer, and *Maskil* is an individual meditation, hummed as a private introspection, but he does this without explanation.

- Solomon (twice)[6]
- Heman the Ezrahite (once)
- Ethan the Ezrahite (once)
- Moses (once)
- Anonymous (about forty-nine times)[7]

Historical notices (thirteen times).[8]

- Psalm 3: "A Psalm of David, when he fled from the face of Absalom, his son."
- Psalm 7: "A *Shiggaion* of David which he sang to YHWH concerning the words of Cush, a Benjamite."
- Psalm 18: "For the choir director. Of the servant of YHWH, David, who spoke to YHWH the words of this song on the day YHWH delivered him from the hand of all his enemies, and from the hand of Saul."
- Psalm 34: "Of David, when he changed his countenance before Abimelech, who drove him out, and he went."
- Psalm 51: "For the choir director. A Psalm of David. When the prophet Nathan came to him after he had gone in to Bathsheba."
- Psalm 52: "For the choir director. A *Maskil* of David. When Doeg the Edomite went and reported to Saul, 'David has gone to the house of Ahimelech.'"
- Psalm 54: "For the choir director. With stringed instruments. A *Maskil* of David. When the Ziphites came and said to Saul, 'Is not David hiding among us?'"

---

[6]As I will argue in a later chapter, however, Psalm 72 may more properly be a prayer of David "for Solomon." If this is correct, there would only be one psalm authored by Solomon, and seventy-four by David.

[7]Note that Psalm 88 has two different authors listed in its superscription. This is why 102 different authorial notices occur in the book of Psalms, but only 101 psalms have reported authors.

[8]All translations of the historical superscriptions in this section are my own.

- Psalm 56: "For the choir director. According to silent dove, distant ones. Of David. A *Miktam*. When the Philistines seized him in Gath."
- Psalm 57: "For the choir director. Do not destroy. Of David. A *Miktam*. When he fled from the face of Saul into the cave."
- Psalm 59: "For the choir director. Do not destroy. Of David. A *Miktam*. When Saul sent and said to the house to kill him."
- Psalm 60: "For the choir director. To [the tune of] 'The Lily of the Covenant.' A *Miktam* of David. For teaching. When he fought with Aram Naharaim and Aram Zobah and Joab returned and struck down twelve thousand of Edom in the Valley of Salt."
- Psalm 63: "A Psalm of David, when he was in the desert of Judah."
- Psalm 142: "A *Maskil* of David. When he was in the cave. A prayer."

Musical, liturgical, and type-of-psalm terms.

- *Mizmor* (usually translated as "psalm"), *Miktam*, *Maskil*, *Tephillah* (usually translated as "prayer"), *Negina*, *Higgayon*, *Shiggayon*, *Lehazkir*. For the choir director (fifty-five times in the book of Psalms), *Selah* (not in headings, but the term occurs seventy-one times in the body of various Psalms), *Teruea*, Ruberics prefaced by "*al*" ("upon") that apparently designate well-known popular airs or melodies: "On the eighth," "On death," "Upon the *gittith*," "On the air of lilies," "On the air of *Mahalath*," "On the air of do not destroy."[9]

---

[9]This summary list was adapted from Terrien, *The Psalms*, 28-32.

DID YOU KNOW?
Questions Remain About the Superscriptions

My hope is that by briefly orienting ourselves to the history of interpreting the psalm superscriptions, and by overviewing some of the information found in them, these neglected portions of God's Word will get back onto the collective radar of the church. In the very least, I hope that we will stop ignoring them, and at best I hope they will play an important role in our interpretation. Practically speaking, when we are called to read a psalm during a Sunday worship service, I hope that we will begin to include the superscription in our reading so that our congregations are invited to "hear" the rest of the psalm through its lens. At this point, however, we also need to recognize that some questions still remain. First, we are not sure when the various pieces of information in the superscriptions were added. Did the author assign all of the information? Did the director of music add some of it? Someone else? What about the musical information? Was the tune assigned much later? Second, we can notice that there are some differences in the superscriptions between the Hebrew, Greek, Latin, and other Psalms manuscripts. For example, where the Hebrew reads, "for the director of music," the Greek reads, "for the end." This means that the early church fathers, who were reading the Psalms in Greek, *were sometimes working with different superscription information* than the sixteenth-century Reformers, who were working from the Hebrew. For those who would like to dig deeper into this issue, appendix C is available as a free download on the IVP website (www.ivpress.com/treasuring-the-psalms).[10]

---

[10]In addition to appendix C, readers will find conservative conclusions about the superscriptions, along with a very thorough exploration of these issues, in James M. Hamilton Jr., *Psalms Volume 1: Psalms 1-72*, Evangelical Biblical Theology Commentary (Bellingham, WA: Lexham, 2021), 25-52.

EITHER WAY, THEY STILL MATTER

In his *Old Testament Theology*, Paul R. House argues that the canonical approach to biblical interpretation has resulted in a productive exchange between critical and evangelical scholars.[11] For our purposes, notice that this also applies to the psalm superscriptions. For example, while many critical scholars debate whether the "Of David" notice in a psalm is historically accurate, canonical interpreters from critical *and* conservative schools of thought will agree that the psalms were *meant* to be read in light of their superscriptions. Further still, even when we do not know what a given musical or liturgical term means, a canonical approach can lead us to consider whether those terms have any part to play in the clustering of psalms and their ordering in the book. We can say that on a grand scale, the nineteenth century witnessed a shift, and for the first time in history, the psalm superscriptions were widely ignored. But as we have seen, canonical interpreters have revived interest in them. Therefore, a canonical reading of the psalms—a reading that pays attention to the structure and overall message of the book of Psalms in its final form—should take the superscriptions seriously.

UNPACKING THE SIGNIFICANCE OF SUPERSCRIPTIONS: PSALM 110

In a later chapter, we are going to unpack Psalm 110 in more detail. For now, I am simply going to summarize its key features and show how its superscription is an essential lens for interpreting the rest of the psalm. It simply reads: "Of David. A Psalm." That's it. But that little bit of information changes everything because it tells us who the author was: King David. In other words, we are meant to read Psalm 110 as the voice of David.

---

[11]See Paul R. House, *Old Testament Theology* (Downers Grove, IL: InterVarsity, 1998), 273.

Davidic authorship of Psalm 110 transforms the way we read the rest of the psalm, because—and this is where I'll summarize what I will explain more in a later chapter—it is presented as a prophetic oracle, and its author (David) is presented as a prophet. Technical Hebrew words are used in verse 1 that clearly mark this as a prophetic oracle. My own translation of Psalm 110:0-1 is: "Of David. A Psalm. / A [prophetic] declaration of YHWH to my lord: / 'Sit at my right hand / until I place your enemies as a footstool for your feet.'"[12] Just like Isaiah, Jeremiah, Ezekiel, and the other Old Testament prophets were the mouthpieces of YHWH, in Psalm 110, so was David. And the psalm is about a word of YHWH to David's lord who would sit at YHWH's right hand until YHWH made his enemies a footstool for his feet.

The psalm continues by painting a portrait of the Savior to come: he would be the cosmic king at the right hand of YHWH (v. 1), and he would be a priest in the manner of Melchizedek (v. 4). And there is a coming day when all of his enemies will be defeated (vv. 1, 5-7). We could say more, but for now we notice that since this is a psalm of David, its prophecy about the coming Messiah is a look ahead at one who would be *David's* lord—he would be greater than the greatest king in Israel's history. While David reigned on the throne in Jerusalem, this Savior would reign on the throne of the cosmos. While David acted in a priestly manner at times (e.g., 2 Sam 21:4-6), this Savior would be a king *and* a priest (Ps 110:1, 4).

Do you see the massive significance of having the coming Savior as *David's* lord? Second Samuel 7 had taught God's people to expect an eternal reign of kings in the line of David. When David penned the words of Psalm 110, he would have seen its portrait of the Savior as the ultimate fulfillment of that promise. But by the time the book

---

[12]This translation also appears in Ian J. Vaillancourt, *The Multifaceted Saviour of Psalms 110 and 118: A Canonical Exegesis*, Hebrew Bible Monographs 86 (Sheffield, UK: Sheffield Phoenix, 2019), 86.

of Psalms received its final shape—likely about seven to eight hundred years later—the exile had happened, and there was no king on David's throne. At that later time, it would have been all the more meaningful to read Psalm 110 as the prophetic word of David about his coming lord. The black velvet of Israel's historical situation would have made the diamond of this psalm's teaching about the Messiah shine all the more brightly.

As Christians, we can look back on Psalm 110 and see that it is clearly about Jesus. In fact, Psalm 110:1 is the most quoted verse in the New Testament. It bears witness to the enthronement of Jesus after his ascension (e.g., Heb 12:2). But it was also quoted by Jesus himself:

> Now while the Pharisees were gathered together, Jesus asked them a question, saying, "What do you think about the Christ? Whose son is he?" They said to him, "The son of David." He said to them, "How is it then that David, in the Spirit, calls him Lord, saying, 'The Lord said to my Lord, / Sit at my right hand, / until I put your enemies under your feet?' / If then David calls him Lord, how is he his son?" And no one was able to answer him a word, nor from that day did anyone dare to ask him any more questions. (Mt 22:41-46)

In other words, *Jesus* was reading the psalm superscriptions. In Jesus' view, the superscription for Psalm 110 contained an essential piece of information: it was the lens through which the psalm was to be read. Based on the teaching of 2 Samuel 7 *and* the superscription for Psalm 110, Jesus taught that the Messiah would be *both* the Son (i.e., descendant) of David *and* the Lord of David (i.e., greater than the great King David). Without the superscription Psalm 110 would read as an anonymous prophetic word about a lord to come, but with the superscription it is about one greater than the greatest king in Israel's history, one to whom David would bow as his lord.

But there is still another way the superscriptions add depth to our reading. This time the depth-reading comes *beyond the individual psalm*. In the next few chapters, we are going to paint a picture of the grand narrative presented in an intentionally structured book of Psalms. As preparation for this, let's notice that in book 5 (Ps 107–150), clusters of Davidic psalms are found at the beginning and the end (Ps 108–110; 138–145), with a few others mixed in between (Ps 122, 124, 131, 133). This is a clue that David envelops and permeates the entire fifth and final book of the Psalms. We can also notice that while Psalms 108–110 are all said to be "psalms" that are also "of David" (written by David), each of these three superscriptions is written with a slight variation from the others. This suggests that David likely wrote each of these psalms at different times in his life, and that they were *later* gathered together into a cluster. This also suggests that the later editor was linking previously existing psalms according to theme. Further to the Davidic psalms in book 5, the one psalm of David we have looked at speaks of the greater lord of David to come (Ps 110:1). Could it be that the high concentration of Davidic psalms in book 5 point collectively to the Messiah? We will explore this more in a later chapter.

We could say so much more about Psalm 110, but for now, we have seen that reading it in light of its superscription transforms our understanding of the individual psalm (i.e., the great King David was speaking prophetically about his coming lord), about the way Jesus and the New Testament authors read the psalm (i.e., about Jesus as this greater Son of David), and about the way we read the placement of Psalm 110 in the last portion of the book of Psalms.

DISCUSSION QUESTIONS

1. Take a survey of your group: previous to reading this chapter, how many of you (a) read the superscriptions as part of your personal Bible reading; and (b) go to a church where the superscriptions are included in corporate Bible reading?

2. Did it surprise you to learn that the superscriptions have been viewed as an essential part of each psalm for most of church history? Did it also surprise you to learn that the tendency to disregard the psalm superscriptions is fairly recent when compared to the two thousand year history of the Christian church? Discuss.

3. What are some of the questions you still have about superscriptions? Share them with your group.

4. The author noticed that canonical interpreters—those who believe in an intentionally arranged book of Psalms—most often take the superscriptions into consideration. Restate the author's point in your own words.

5. How does reading Psalm 110 in light of its superscription transform the way we read the psalm as a whole? The psalm in light of the New Testament? The psalm in light of its placement in the book of Psalms?

6. Has this chapter (and perhaps the online appendixes) changed your view of the importance of superscriptions? Or has it at least given you food for thought before you decide your position on this issue? If so, which factors are leading you to reconsider your former position?

3

The Shape of the Book, Part One

PSALMS 1–2 AS GATEWAY

LET'S PICTURE THE SCENE TOGETHER: an ancient worshiper has made the pilgrimage to Jerusalem for one of the annual feasts. As he enters the city, he continues walking, because his ultimate destination is not a city, a house, or even a hotel. It is the temple courts. Jerusalem is set on the highest ground in the area, so he has been walking "up" to Jerusalem and singing the Songs of Ascents along the way. And the temple sits on the highest point in Jerusalem, so as he enters the city, he continues his ascent. In the distance he can now see it. And he can see the other pilgrims walking in a long line toward it. As he gets closer, he can see the gate with a pillar on either side. He will enter into the temple courts and worship YHWH with the other pilgrims.

Just as the physical temple courts in Jerusalem had two pillars through which the pilgrims walked as they entered to worship YHWH, in this chapter we will explore the two pillars of the book of Psalms—two psalms that act as the gateway into the life of praise that is played out in the rest of the book.[1] In fact, if we find

---

[1] Many others have used "gateway" language regarding the relationship between Psalms 1 and 2 and the rest of the book. For example, see J. Glen Taylor, "Psalms 1 and 2: A Gateway into the Psalter and Messianic Images for the Restoration of David's Dynasty," in *Interpreting the Psalms for Teaching and Preaching*, ed. Herbert W. Bateman and D. Brent Sandy (St. Louis, MO:

clear evidence that the first two psalms were *intentionally* set as a gateway to the book, this would warrant looking beyond them to evidence of shaping in the rest of the book. As we dig into the details, we will see that the themes of the Word of God (Ps 1), and the anointed king as Son of God (Ps 2), form a dual perspective. To switch analogies, just like those of us who wear glasses view the world through a set of corrective lenses, those who gave the book of Psalms its final shape intended Psalms 1 and 2 as the dual lenses through which we are to read the rest of the book.

BOUNDED BY BLESSING, WITH OTHER LINKS IN-BETWEEN

Later in this chapter, we will walk through these psalms in turn. This will allow us to understand the respective message of each and also the sum of their parts: the message they communicate *together* as the dual gateway for the book of Psalms. But first we can notice some links between the two, just so we get a sense of the way they were *intended* to be read together.

As we dive into the book of Psalms, the first word we encounter is "blessed" (*ashre* [אַשְׁרֵי], Ps 1:1). And as we read on through Psalm 2, the last line of the last verse reads, "blessed (*ashre* [אַשְׁרֵי]) are all who take refuge in him" (Ps 2:12b). Although we'll see that the sources of blessing are very different, the fact that blessing *envelops*, or *bounds* the first two psalms hints that they may form a unit. While they were likely composed on different occasions and by different authors, the editors seem to have linked them together to communicate a message: if we follow the teachings of these two psalms, we will find blessing in covenant with YHWH.

Chalice, 2010), 47-62; Robert Cole, *Psalms 1-2: Gateway to the Psalter*, Hebrew Bible Monographs 37, ed. David J. A. Clines, J. Cheryl Exum, and Keith W. Whitelam (Sheffield, UK: Sheffield Phoenix, 2013).

Something else that links the two psalms together is what they *do not* have: superscriptions. It is true that numerous other psalms do not include a superscription, but early in the book, this is extremely rare. Other than Psalms 1 and 2, superscriptions are only lacking in Psalms 10 and 33 for book 1 (Ps 1–41) and Psalms 43 and 71 for book 2 (Ps 42–72). Since a lack of superscription is so uncommon in books 1 and 2, we can conclude that Psalms 1 and 2 are not only bounded by blessing but also linked by lack of superscription.

As we continue to look closely at Psalms 1 and 2, we find that there are numerous word links that bind them together. Many of these are not noticeable in English because they are translated with different English words, even though exactly the same Hebrew word is used. My favorite example of this is found in Psalms 1:2 and 2:1, with the Hebrew verb *hagah* (הָגָה). In Psalm 1:2 it is translated "to meditate", and in Psalm 2:1 it is translated "to plot." Van Pelt and Kaiser list the range of meanings for this Hebrew word as "[to] groan, moan, sigh, utter, speak, meditate, muse, imagine, devise."[2] This word has a broad range of meanings, therefore, and some of them can be positive and some negative. However, when we understand that in the ancient world, people didn't "meditate" as we do, we are helped.

These days, when Christians think of meditating on Scripture, they envisage "repeating it silently, in their minds." In the ancient world, though, meditation was audible, and done under the breath. People "murmured" words quietly as they meditated on them. The picture in Psalm 1, then, is of a wise person who repeats the content of the *torah* of YHWH under their breath as a way of having it on their minds and applying it to the various aspects of their day. But in Psalm 2:1, the term is used negatively, as people "murmured" in complaint against YHWH and his anointed king. This murmuring was the kind of thing

---

[2]Miles V. Van Pelt and Walter C. Kaiser Jr., "הָגָה," NIDOTTE 1:984. This is the usage range for the Qal stem; both occurrences of the term in Psalms 1:2 and 2:1 are in this stem.

that was done against a ruler with whom the general public was not happy. It was the kind of murmuring one did when they complained to their friend or to themselves, but they didn't want to get caught. They did, however, want to wallow in their anger, and they wanted to draw others into it with them.

When we hear this explanation of *hagah* (הָגָה) in each of these psalms, it is easy to see why the translations use different English words, even though the same Hebrew word is used. A word's meaning depends on its context, and the best English word is not always the same in each case.[3] In Psalm 1:2, the meaning of *hagah* (הָגָה) is positive, as the wise person *meditates* on the *torah* of YHWH day and night. And in Psalm 2:1, the meaning of *hagah* (הָגָה) is negative, as the nations *complained under their breath*, or *murmured about* the authority of YHWH and his anointed king. But in both cases, *hagah* (הָגָה) was used, and a Hebrew reader would have seen this and made the link between Psalms 1 and 2.

In our growing collection of links, therefore, we have found that these psalms are bounded by blessing, they are linked by lack of superscription, and they are also linked by a verb which carries the meaning of "talking under one's breath." But that is not all. In fact, entire books have been written about the way these two psalms fit together, and interested readers can study them.[4] In closing, we will notice just one more similarity: in the concluding verse of each psalm (Ps 1:6; 2:12) the "way" (*derek* [דֶּרֶךְ]) of the wicked will lead them to "perish" (*abad* [אָבַד]).[5] The Hebrew words I have placed in brackets

---

[3] I appreciate the way the English Standard Version (ESV) describes itself as an "essentially literal" translation. Wherever possible, the translators use the same English word to translate a given Hebrew word. But in so doing they recognize it is not always possible. In the end, the most detailed work of exegesis can only be done by those who take the time to learn Hebrew and Greek.

[4] I think especially of the following excellent, very detailed work: Cole, *Psalms 1-2: Gateway to the Psalter.*

[5] I was first alerted to this link between the words "way" (*derek* [דֶּרֶךְ]) and "perish" (*abad* [אָבַד]) in Psalms 1:6 and 2:12 in Robert Cole, "An Integrated Reading of Psalms 1 and 2," *Journal for the Study of the Old Testament* 26, no. 4 (2002): 77.

are the same in each psalm, and the theme of the perishing of the wicked is also the same.

Now that we have established some clear links between Psalms 1 and 2, we can dive into each of them in turn. As we do so, we'll notice that the teaching of each contributes to the gateway to the book of Psalms.

PSALM 1: THE *TORAH* OF YHWH

Psalm 1 is a wisdom psalm, one that teaches us how to live skillfully in covenant with YHWH, something that results in his blessing. And as we have seen, the particular focus of this lesson is on living a life that is shaped by the *torah* of YHWH. Let's read together:

> 1 Blessed is the man [or woman]
>   who walks not in the counsel of the wicked,
>   nor stands in the way of sinners,
>   nor sits in the seat of scoffers;
> 2 but [this person's] delight is in the law of the Lord,
>   and on his law [this person] meditates day and night.
> 3 [This person] is like a tree
>   planted by streams of water
>   that yields its fruit in its season,
>   and its leaf does not wither.
>   In all that [this person] does, [they prosper].
> 4 The wicked are not so,
>   but are like chaff that the wind drives away.
> 5 Therefore the wicked will not stand in the judgment,
>   nor sinners in the congregation of the righteous;
> 6 for the Lord knows the way of the righteous,
>   but the way of the wicked will perish. (Ps 1:1-6)

The psalm begins in a similar way as the Sermon on the Mount. Or maybe we should say that the Sermon on the Mount—which was delivered hundreds of years after Psalm 1 was written—was shaped by this great psalm. In other words, as Jesus began his most famous sermon, he echoed the beginning of Psalm 1.

Although the psalm begins with a positive word—"blessed"—it continues in verse 1 with the negative side of blessing. Before it tells us how *to* live, it tells us how *not* to live: if we want to live under YHWH's blessing, we need to know what *not* to do, as much as we need to know what *to* do. When we looked at Psalm 119 in an earlier chapter, we noticed that it is filled with near synonyms—words that mean almost the same thing. This is a common feature of Hebrew poetry, so it is not surprising that in Psalm 1:1 we discover three lines that are replete with words that carry similar meanings. After the statement "blessed is the man [or woman]," the psalm continues: (1) "who walks not in the counsel of the wicked," (2) "nor stands in the way of sinners," (3) "nor sits in the seat of scoffers." In these three lines we notice three verbs: "to walk," "to stand," and "to sit." And we notice three kinds of unwise people: "wicked," "sinners," and "scoffers." By using these similar words, the author is communicating a broader concept than any of the terms could convey on their own. A short summary of the teaching is this: it is completely wise to never, ever get in the path of these kinds of people. Whatever you are doing, whether you are walking along, standing, or sitting, do not follow the lead of the wicked, sinners, or scoffers.

The next verse transitions to the positive side of blessing. It begins with the word "but," and this signals a contrast. It is not enough to "not do the don'ts," but in order to be under YHWH's blessing, we also have to "do the dos." The blessed person does not follow the behavior of sinful people on the one hand (v. 1), and on the other hand, the blessed person *does* delight in the *torah* of YHWH (v. 2). This is something of what John Piper refers to as "the duty of delight."[6] Isn't

---

[6]See, for example, John Piper, *Desiring God: Meditations of a Christian Hedonist*, rev. and exp. ed. (Colorado Springs, CO: Multnomah, 2011).

it wonderful that our God is not calling us to do the right thing in a way that is detached from our heart, our emotions? He is not calling us to external obedience or unfeeling duty. He is calling us to *delight* in his *torah*, his instruction. And isn't it wonderful that this *torah*, this instruction, is not something we need to figure out on our own? In fact, in the Hebrew Old Testament, the first five books are grouped under the broad heading of *Torah*. The call of Psalm 1:2 is to immerse ourselves with delight in Genesis, Exodus, Leviticus, Numbers, and Deuteronomy, with a view to encountering God, having our day-to-day lives shaped, and living under his continuous blessing.

What will this delight in the *torah* of YHWH look like? The same way it looks for anything we delight in. When I first started to get to know my wife, I was smitten. No one had to tell me to think about her. Actually, sometimes people had to tell me to stop thinking about her. I planned out ways to surprise her, thought through fun things to do on dates, threw caution to the wind, and stayed up way later than was healthy as we spent hours on the phone. When a person delights in someone or something, they think about that person or thing all the time. So when the psalmist was fleshing out what it looks like to delight in the *torah* of YHWH, he said, "And on his *torah* [this person] meditates day and night." The call here is for delight-induced, day and night, reading and thinking and applying and soaking in the precious Word of God. *Do not* follow the logic of sinful people, and *do* steep your mind in the Word of God.

In verse 3, we are given an image that explains the reason for the call to a *torah*-steeped life. When I worked in landscape construction as a summer student, sometimes I would have to dig out a dead tree that the company had planted in the previous year. It was not a lot of work. As soon as we began digging, the ball of roots and the metal cage would emerge, and we could easily pull the dead tree out of the ground. The roots were in a cluster at the farm, and they never made it out of that cluster after the tree was planted. And so it died. This is the opposite of what the *torah*-steeped life looks like. The person who lives a *torah*-steeped life "is like a tree / planted by streams of water / that yields its fruit in its season, / and its leaf does not wither." In short, "in all that [this person] does [they prosper]." Just as fruit and healthy leaves evidence a tree with roots in rich, moist soil, so it is with the *torah*-steeped life: there is a holistic health to our lives and our fruitfulness, and this evidences our rootedness in the *torah* of YHWH.

Verses 4 and 5 contrast this with the *now* and the *then* for the wicked. *Now,* the wicked are like chaff that the wind drives away. And *then*, on the day of judgment that is coming, "the wicked will not stand," nor will sinners stand "in the congregation of the righteous." Notice that the blessing for the believer is not only "on that future day" but also "today and every day until then." And notice that the horrible outcome of a wicked life is not simply reserved for the day of judgment but is also experienced "today and every day until then." And so the psalm ends in verse 6 with a summary statement: "for the LORD knows the way of the righteous, / but the way of the wicked will perish." YHWH *knows*, he pays attention to, he is conscious of the way of the righteous, the way of the one with a *torah*-steeped life. But the way of the wicked will perish.

The first pillar in the gateway to the book of Psalms is the pillar of the *torah* of YHWH and the *torah*-steeped life. The message of Psalm 1 is *not* to "do the right thing even though the wrong thing is more fun." The message is "fill your mind with the Word of God: delight in it, and live every day under God's blessing. And as you do this, you can also anticipate the future day when you will stand firm in the judgment."

PSALM 2: THE ANOINTED KING AS SON OF YHWH

The first pillar of the gateway to the book of Psalms flows immediately into the second, with the call in Psalm 2 to submit to the leadership of the anointed king of YHWH. Let's read together:

1 Why do the nations rage
    and the peoples plot in vain?
2 The kings of the earth set themselves,
    and the rulers take counsel together,
    against the LORD and against his Anointed, saying,
3 "Let us burst their bonds apart
    and cast away their cords from us."
4 He who sits in the heavens laughs;
    the Lord holds them in derision.
5 Then he will speak to them in his wrath,
    and terrify them in his fury, saying,
6 "As for me, I have set my King
    on Zion, my holy hill."
7 I will tell of the decree:
    The LORD said to me, "You are my Son;
    today I have begotten you.
8 Ask of me, and I will make the nations your heritage,
    and the ends of the earth your possession.
9 You shall break them with a rod of iron
    and dash them in pieces like a potter's vessel."
10 Now therefore, O kings, be wise;
    be warned, O rulers of the earth.
11 Serve the LORD with fear,
    and rejoice with trembling.
12 Kiss the Son,
    lest he be angry, and you perish in the way,
    for his wrath is quickly kindled.
    Blessed are all who take refuge in him. (Ps 2:1-12)

In some ways, Psalm 2 is very different from Psalm 1. The first psalm is focused on living the *torah*-steeped life, and the second psalm is focused on submitting to the leadership of YHWH and his anointed king. But in other ways the two psalms are similar, because they both ask the implicit question, "Why would anyone, ever, do something contrary to what this psalm teaches?"

The first three verses of Psalm 2 detail the response of "the nations," "the peoples," and "the kings of the earth" to YHWH and his anointed one. If Israel was God's Old Testament people, the nations, peoples, and kings of the earth are meant to stand for "everyone but Israel." And the psalm begins with the word "Why?," in the sense of, "Why would anyone ever do this?" Why would anyone ever rage against YHWH and his anointed one? Why would anyone ever set themselves and take counsel together against YHWH and his anointed one? In summary, they did not want the bonds or cords of the rule of YHWH and his anointed one plaguing their lives. They wanted to do whatever they wanted to do. Just like the wicked, the sinners, and the scoffers from Psalm 1 did not want to live out the *torah* of YHWH, the nations, the peoples, and the kings of the earth from Psalm 2 did not want to be under the rule of YHWH and his anointed king. Instead, they wanted to break free from the chains of that rule.

In verses 4-9, the response comes from "he who sits in the heavens," also called *adonay* (אֲדֹנָי, "Lord"): he laughs, and then he speaks. Notice that "he who sits in the heavens" emphasizes God as ruler over the entire earth. He is not a localized deity worshiped by Israel alone. And notice that the word "*adonay*" emphasizes the fact that YHWH is also the divine Lord and master. And his laughter is in response to the desire of the nations—even their rulers—to throw off the shackles of the rule of YHWH and his anointed king. But this laughter is not light-hearted, it is derision. It is a laugh of mockery.

And then YHWH speaks. The words are words of wrath and fury that are meant to terrify the nations, the peoples, the kings of the earth. But as we will see, the words are also words of *invitation to blessing*. More on that later. For now, let's soak these verses in again:

6 "As for me, I have set my King
   on Zion, my holy hill."
7 I will tell of the decree:
   The LORD said to me, "You are my Son;
   today I have begotten you.
8 Ask of me, and I will make the nations your heritage,
   and the ends of the earth your possession.
9 You shall break them with a rod of iron
   and dash them in pieces like a potter's vessel." (Ps 2:6-9)

The message can be summarized: (1) YHWH has set his king on Zion; (2) YHWH has called his king his son whom he has begotten; (3) YHWH will make the nations the inheritance of his king; (4) the anointed king of YHWH will obliterate the nations just like an iron rod smashes a piece of pottery.

The first word spoken to the nations is that YHWH has set his king on Zion, his holy hill. As we read this in light of the sweep of the Old Testament, we notice that Psalm 2 was written with a focus on the promised king from David's lineage. According to Deuteronomy 17:14-20, the king was to lead the people in *torah* living, in the *torah*-steeped life. And as he led in this manner, the people as a whole would live under the blessing of YHWH.

In the Hebrew text of Psalm 2:6, an interesting word appears that is not immediately evident in our English translations. While our English Bibles usually have something like, "I have *set* my King on Zion, my holy hill," the Hebrew literally reads, "I have *poured out* my King on Zion, my holy hill." Notice first that the translators of our English Bibles have not made a mistake. Their job is to understand the ancient text and also to understand the twenty-first-century culture and language. Through these dual understandings, they seek to communicate the ancient message in the best manner available. But in order to be completely clear about the language used in Psalm 2:6, an explanation is needed. In the Hebrew mindset, the message and the image would have been clear: "to pour out" a king was an image from his coronation ceremony, where anointing oil would have been poured onto his head. In the Old Testament, prophets were anointed (e.g., 1 Kings 19:16), priests were anointed (e.g., Ex 28:41), and kings were anointed (e.g., 1 Sam 16:13), all for special service to YHWH. In Psalm 2:6, YHWH has—no doubt through the agency of his prophet (cf. 1 Sam 16:13)— poured out, or anointed his specially chosen Davidic king to rule from the center of Jerusalem (Zion). This is why he has already been called YHWH's "anointed one" in Psalm 2:2: the anointing oil had been poured over his head at his coronation ceremony.

In verse 7, YHWH refers to his anointed king as his begotten son. If Israel as a whole was the son of YHWH (Ex 4:22), his king was their representative head. The call in verse 8 is for the king to ask, and YHWH will give the nations, the ends of the earth, into his hands. And the promise in verse 9 is that this king will shatter these peoples who live in rebellion against YHWH.

The psalm ends with three verses of invitation to non-Jews. If the first nine verses had a tone of mocking judgment, in his grace YHWH would not leave it there. In these verses, he addressed the rulers of the non-Jewish nations, and called on them to "be wise," and "be warned." From the beginning, YHWH had called Abram to "be a blessing" (Gen 12:2) and promised him that "I will bless those who bless you, and him who dishonors you I will curse, and in you all the families of the earth shall be blessed" (Gen 12:3). The invitation to the nations in Psalm 2:10-12 is in the vein of this promise. The specific call, in verses 11 and 12, is that they "serve YHWH with fear," that they "rejoice with trembling," and that they "kiss the son, lest he be angry, and you perish in the way." The reason: the wrath of the king/son is quickly kindled, and all who take refuge in him are blessed.

The second pillar in the gateway to the book of Psalms is the pillar of the anointed king as begotten son of YHWH. The message of

Psalm 2 is that this king will rule over the nations, and will be YHWH's instrument of judgment against all who oppose him by opposing his people. The message to the nations is, "submit to the rule of this king and be blessed." And the message to Israel is: "even if the nations are raging against YHWH today, you need to know that he will be victorious in the end. And you also need to know that this victory will come through the agency of his king. Do not compromise today because those foreign nations seem like superpowers who have you under their control; live today in light of YHWH's reign over those nations, and in light of the fact that YHWH's king will ultimately smash them like pottery."

THE KING AS IDEAL *TORAH*-KEEPER

In an earlier chapter, I mentioned the work of Jamie A. Grant. By way of reminder, he suggests that at various points in the book of Psalms, royal psalms (about the king) and *torah* psalms (that delight in YHWH's instruction) are paired together in three places: Psalms 1–2, 18–21, and 118–119. In Grant's view, these kingship and *torah* psalms were placed side by side in order to convey hope in the midst of tragedy: although the history of Israel's kings witnessed a downward spiral of sin, and although this resulted in the loss of a king for Israel, the people could read (or sing or pray) the book of Psalms, and be encouraged with "eschatological hope in a monarch who will be the true 'keeper' of the *torah* of Yahweh."[7] It is enormously significant that the first of these *torah*-kingship pairings occurs in the gateway to the book of Psalms. This is not merely a subtheme in the book; it is a lens through which the entire book of Psalms is to be read. In other words, a book of Psalms with Psalms 1 and 2 as its gateway emphasizes hope in a coming king who will be the perfect *torah*-keeper.

---

[7]Jamie A. Grant, *The King as Exemplar: The Function of Deuteronomy's Kingship Law in the Shaping of the Book of Psalms*, ed. Adele Berlin, Society of Biblical Literature Academia Biblica Series 17 (Atlanta: Society of Biblical Literature, 2004), 9.

As we will see in a later chapter, there was no king on David's throne after the Babylonian exile (587/586 BC). Therefore, after this time Israel's hope shifted to a coming messiah, who would exhibit all the ideal characteristics of the king from Deuteronomy 17:14-20. In light of this life situation for Israel, Psalms 1 and 2 were placed as a *messianic* gateway to the book of Psalms. In light of the clear New Testament teaching—that Jesus is the ultimate, messianic fulfilment of the Anointed Son from Psalm 2—we can look back and notice that from the very beginning of the book of Psalms, Christians should be looking for glimpses of Jesus as we read.[8]

From this perspective, we can go so far as to re-read Psalm 1 through the lens of the king in Psalm 2:

1 Blessed is [the ideal king]
   who walks not in the counsel of the wicked,
   nor stands in the way of sinners,
   nor sits in the seat of scoffers;
2 but [this ideal king's] delight is in the law of the Lord,
   and on his law he meditates day and night.
3 He is like a tree
   planted by streams of water
   that yields its fruit in its season,
   and its leaf does not wither.
   In all that he does, he prospers.
4 The wicked are not so,
   but are like chaff that the wind drives away.
5 Therefore the wicked will not stand in the judgment,
   nor sinners in the congregation of the righteous;
6 for the Lord knows the way of the righteous,
   but the way of the wicked will perish. (Ps 1:1-6)

---

[8]For example, see Acts 13:33.

PSALMS 1 AND 2 AS GATEWAY

In conclusion, we are meant to read Psalms 1 and 2 as the gateway for the entire book of Psalms. The themes of the *torah* of YHWH and the anointed king as son of YHWH are the dual lenses through which we are to read the rest of the book. In fact, the theme of the king as ideal *torah*-keeper is to be on our minds as we read from Psalms 3 to 150. But what does this look like, practically speaking? How does reading Psalms 1 and 2 as a gateway influence our reading of the rest of the book? We can begin to get a sense of this as soon as we enter through the "gateway" and encounter the very next psalm.

With the theme of the king as ideal *torah*-keeper in mind, we are immediately introduced in Psalm 3 to King David, and things seem hopeful. But we don't even get out of the superscription before our hopes are dashed. The psalm begins this way: "A Psalm of David, when he fled from Absalom his son." In a later chapter, we will notice more about Psalm 3 from another angle. For now, let's observe two things about its superscription. First, immediately after the gateway to the book of Psalms, we encounter King David on the run for his life and uttering words of *lament*. Second, we remember from the book of 2 Samuel that this difficulty in David's life was ultimately a consequence of his own sin with Bathsheba. Here are YHWH's exact words through the prophet Nathan:

> Nathan said to David, "You are the man! Thus says the LORD, the God of Israel, 'I anointed you king over Israel, and I delivered you out of the hand of Saul. And I gave you your master's house and your master's wives into your arms and gave you the house of Israel and of Judah. And if this were too little, I would add to you as much more. Why have you despised the word of the LORD, to do what is evil in his sight? You have struck down Uriah the Hittite with the sword and have taken his wife to be your wife and have killed him with the sword of the Ammonites. Now therefore the sword shall never depart from

your house, because you have despised me and have taken the wife of Uriah the Hittite to be your wife.' Thus says the LORD, 'Behold, I will raise up evil against you out of your own house. And I will take your wives before your eyes and give them to your neighbor, and he shall lie with your wives in the sight of this sun. For you did it secretly, but I will do this thing before all Israel and before the sun.'" David said to Nathan, "I have sinned against the LORD." And Nathan said to David, "The LORD also has put away your sin; you shall not die. Nevertheless, because by this deed you have utterly scorned the LORD, the child who is born to you shall die." (2 Sam 12:7-14)

In light of the teaching found in 2 Samuel 12:11-12, we can observe that the later trouble between David and Absalom (from 2 Sam 13-19) was ultimately a consequence of King David's sin. Therefore, the deep heart lament from Psalm 3 communicates that David was *not* the absolutely ideal *torah*-keeping king who is portrayed in Psalms 1–2.

In this way, Psalms 1–2 set the stage for tension in the rest of the book, as we encounter fifty psalms with a primarily lament theme. Deuteronomy portrays life in covenant with YHWH as one's "walk," and Psalms 1–2 have called all God's people—and particularly the king as head over God's people—to walk in the way of the *torah*. The message from Psalms 1–2 is that the one who lives this way will be blessed. And Psalm 3 signals for us, even in its superscription, that this blessing in covenant with YHWH may be coming, but it is not yet fully experienced. In this life we sin, and we are sinned against. In the life of the ancient Israelite who lived after the exile, there was no king on the throne, and they were still waiting for the full restoration that had been promised in the prophets. Once again, their hope would have been deflected away from David, and onto his greater Son, the coming Messiah.

DISCUSSION QUESTIONS

1. Previous to reading this chapter, had you ever heard it suggested that Psalms 1 and 2 were intentionally placed as the introduction to the book of Psalms?

2. What is the linguistic and thematic evidence that Psalms 1 and 2 are meant to be read together at the beginning of the book of Psalms?

3. What primary insight stuck out to you in our walk through Psalm 1?

4. What primary insight stuck out to you in our walk through Psalm 2?

5. How does reading Psalms 1–2 as the gateway impact the way we understand the rest of the book? Share examples from this chapter, or think of your own.

4

The Shape of the Book, Part Two

THE BROAD NARRATIVE OF BOOKS 1–5

Now that we have soaked in Psalms 1 and 2 as an intentionally placed gateway, we can move on to the rest of the book. We do so with a qualification: entire books could easily be written on this topic.[1] In what follows, we will walk through the various "books" within the larger book of Psalms and observe their contribution to the storyline of the whole.

BOOKS 1 AND 2 (PS 1–72): THE TEARS OF DAVID AS HE REIGNS IN TENSION

In light of our observations so far, I commend the practice of reading the book of Psalms from beginning to end and determining the major theme of each individual psalm.[2] Even in a cursory reading, this practice would reveal that roughly fifty out of 150 psalms contain a

---

[1] For a helpful and accessible introduction to reading the Psalms as an intentionally ordered book that communicates a message, see O. Palmer Robertson, *The Flow of the Psalms: Discovering Their Structure and Theology* (Phillipsburg, NJ: P&R, 2015). For a more scholarly book in this regard, see especially Adam D. Hensley, *Covenant Relationships and the Editing of the Hebrew Psalter*, Library of Hebrew Bible/Old Testament Studies 666, ed. Andrew Mein and Claudia V. Camp (London: T&T Clark, 2018).

[2] In addition to my own wrestling in this regard, I have been helped by the following seven-column summary of the form-critical categorizations of the psalms by various scholars: Philip S. Johnston, "Appendix 1: Index of Form-Critical Categorizations," in *Interpreting the Psalms: Issues and Approaches*, ed. David G. Firth and Philip S. Johnston (Downers Grove, IL: IVP Academic, 2005), 295-300.

dominant lament theme, and that these are much more heavily clustered in Psalms 1–72. For example, William H. Bellinger classes forty-two out of the seventy-two psalms in books 1 and 2 as laments, either of an individual or the community.[3]

As we continue to read, it also becomes clear that book 1 (Ps 1–41) and book 2 (Ps 42–72) are dominated by the voice of David. In book 1, thirty-seven psalms are listed as Davidic (Ps 3–9; 11–32; 34–41). In book 2, the authors listed include the Sons of Korah (Ps 42; 44–49), Asaph (Ps 50), David (Ps 51–65; 68–70), and Solomon (Ps 72).[4] Therefore, with one psalm by Solomon, one by Asaph, seven by the Sons of Korah, and eighteen by David, David's is the dominant voice in book 2 as well. This means that fifty-five out of seventy-two psalms in books 1 and 2 are Davidic.

Next, we notice that with few exceptions, the psalms in books 1 and 2 contain superscriptions. In fact, in book 1 only Psalms 1, 2, 10, and 33 lack a superscription. In book 2, only Psalms 43 and 71 lack a superscription. This is significant in light of what we learned in our previous chapter on superscriptions: as readers, we are meant to interpret books 1 and 2 through the lens of the superscriptions and their reported authors.

Finally, we notice something about the historical occasions for the composition of various psalms: twelve of the thirteen historical superscriptions occur in books 1 and 2 (Ps 3, 7, 18, 34, 51, 52, 54, 56, 57, 59, 60, 63). These are meant to recall to our minds the narrative of 1 and 2 Samuel. This means that we are meant to read Psalms 1–72 with the narrative of David's life in the back of our minds.

As we put all of this together and consider the broad-strokes theme of books 1 and 2, I suggest something along these lines: *the tears of David as he reigns in tension.* We know this because these psalms are

---

[3]See Johnston, "Appendix 1," 296-98.
[4]As we will see later in this chapter, however, Psalm 72 may be a prayer of David *for* Solomon, rather than a psalm authored by Solomon.

so dominantly laments; they are so dominantly the voice of David; they are almost universally superscripted; and on a dozen occasions, we are pointed to the story of David's life from 1 and 2 Samuel. In the narratives of 1 and 2 Samuel, we find two broad reasons for the tension in David's reign: the sin of the community and his own sin. For example, as the anointed king in place of Saul (1 Sam 16), David had to endure constant threats to his life from Saul *before* his reign could officially begin. Even after Saul died and David's reign finally began, it was at first limited to Hebron. So his career began in tension, and this is reflected in the voice of weeping King David in Psalms 1–72.

However, David was also the cause of his own suffering at times. As we saw in a previous chapter, his sin of adultery and murder (2 Sam 11) resulted in conflict within his family and threats to his life (2 Sam 12-19). The suffering part of these sins was the explicit occasion for his writing of Psalm 3. And the repentance part of these sins was the explicit occasion for his writing of Psalm 51.

As we consider these things again through the lens of Psalms 1 and 2, we find that David was *not* the ideal *torah*-keeping king who would obliterate all of his enemies (Ps 2:9). His reign in tension meant that he *awaited* the day when the sin of the community would not hamper his rightful reign, and when his own sin would not do the same. In short, he reigned in tension because he lived in a fallen world in which he was sinned against, and in which he sinned.

Although much more could be said about books 1 and 2, in this overview of the material we need to consider one more thing. The second-to-last verse of book 2 reads: "Blessed be his glorious name forever; / may the whole earth be filled with his glory! / Amen and Amen!" (Ps 72:19). In a previous chapter, we saw that each "book" within the larger book of Psalms concludes with a doxology, which signals the end of the section. But in book 2, the doxology is the second-to-last element. The very last element comes in Psalm 72:20:

"The prayers of David, the son of Jesse, are ended." What does this mean? Notice from its superscription that Psalm 72 is an "Of Solomon" (*lishlomoh* [לִשְׁלֹמֹה]) psalm. While this Hebrew construction usually communicates authorship, the last verse in the psalm seems to indicate that it is a "prayer of David" (v. 20) "*for* Solomon" (v. 0, emphasis added). This is certainly a valid translation option for the Hebrew. In fact, several ancient sources agree with this reading.[5] This interpretation also has the benefit of being guided by the context of the psalm as a whole. Notice further that "prayers" in Psalm 72:20 is a plural noun. Therefore, the (plural) *collection* of prayers of David are ended in Psalm 72:20. All of this seems to indicate that Psalm 72:20 performs double duty, indicating that Psalm 72 is a prayer of David *for* Solomon, and also indicating that Psalms 1–72 as a whole should be labeled as "the prayers of David."

This is reinforced when we turn to Psalm 86 and read its superscription: "A prayer of David."[6] If the prayers of David, son of Jesse were ended in Psalm 72:20, then why does another prayer of David appear later? First, it would seem as though Psalms 1–72 made up an earlier collection that was a unit before the latter portion of the book of Psalms was shaped into its present form. Second, it would seem as though this early collection was broadly titled, "the prayers of David," with a primary emphasis on the historical David, son of Jesse. This makes sense: we have seen that David was the author of fifty-five out of seventy-two psalms in books 1 and 2, and around forty-two out of

---

[5]While the LXX most often translates *lamed* + proper name as "τῷ + proper name" in Greek (referring to the authorship "Of . . ."), in light of the note about the prayers of David in Psalm 72:20, the superscription is translated as "Εἰς Σαλωμων" ("for Solomon"). For a helpful overview of this issue, along with a convincing argument in favor of reading Psalm 72 as a prayer of the aged David for his son and successor, see Adam D. Hensley, "David, Once and Future King? A Closer Look at the Postscript of Psalm 72:20," *Journal for the Study of the Old Testament* 46, no. 1 (2020): 24-43.

[6]See also the superscription of Psalm 142: "A *Maskil* of David, when he was in the cave. A Prayer."

these seventy-two are laments. It is easy to see why this collection as a whole would be labeled "the prayers of David."

BOOK 3 (PS 73–89): THE EXILE AND LOSS OF KINGSHIP

In the literature on the shape of the book of Psalms, it is almost universally recognized that book 3 (Ps 73–89) reflects the exile and the loss of kingship. Scholars who take this position are not suggesting that every psalm in this section was *composed* in light of the exile. Instead, they are suggesting that this cluster of psalms was *employed* in reflection on the exile.

Let's begin with an illustration: April 15, 2013, began like most other days at that time of year for the people of Boston. It was Boston Marathon day, and thousands of runners were ready to participate in this annual race. But this year would be different. As the nation watched the event, double bombs near the finish line killed three people and injured at least 264.[7] As I was watching news coverage of this tragedy, one station compiled photos from the scene and set it to the song "Timshel," by Mumford and Sons. This song was not written *for* the Boston Marathon bombings. It first appeared on the *Sigh No More* album, which was released in the UK in late 2009, and in the USA in early 2010, over three-and-a-half years *before* this tragedy. The news feature I watched, though, was extremely powerful. When I heard the song's opening lines about cold water that "freezes your already cold mind," I felt the chill of death that, according to the song, is "at your doorstep" and "will steal your innocence." And as I heard the song's promise that "you are not alone in this," I felt a sense of solidarity with those who had experienced loss on that day. As the images flashed across the screen, this song helped me to feel the gravity of the tragedy.

---

[7]See CNN Editorial Research, "Boston Marathon Terror Attack Fast Facts," CNN.com, May 4, 2020, www.cnn.com/2013/06/03/us/boston-marathon-terror-attack-fast-facts/index.html.

If a previously written secular song helped me to feel the weight of this tragedy, how much more of a blessing are the biblical psalms. As we will unpack more thoroughly in part three of this book, psalms of lament help us with language for our aching. But they also do not stop there. They point the same weeper to hope in the God who is there for the broken-hearted. He sees and he hears. Therefore, the lament-dominated book 3 would have been powerful for those who had experienced the exile firsthand.

The book begins with Psalm 73, and this sets the reading direction for book 3 as a whole. If the psalmist grieved the prosperity of the wicked, a heavenly perspective would reveal the end of the ungodly, and it would not be pretty. Through the rest of book 3, lament psalms dominate and then culminate at Psalms 88 and 89. As a lament of an individual, Psalm 88 is the bleakest psalm in the book of Psalms. Contrary to the other laments, it does not conclude with hope, but with darkness as the psalmist's closest friend. It is followed by Psalm 89, which seems to point the reader to words of hope in its beginning—"I will sing of the steadfast love of the LORD, forever" (Ps 89:1a)—but by the end, the crown of David was in the dust and the psalmist was in anguish:

46 How long, O LORD? Will you hide yourself forever?
    How long will your wrath burn like fire?
47 Remember how short my time is!
    For what vanity you have created all the children of man!
48 What man can live and never see death?
    Who can deliver his soul from the power of Sheol? *Selah*
49 Lord, where is your steadfast love of old,
    which by your faithfulness you swore to David?
50 Remember, O Lord, how your servants are mocked,
    and how I bear in my heart the insults of all the many nations,
51 with which your enemies mock, O LORD,
    with which they mock the footsteps of your anointed.
    (Ps 89:46-51)

Once again, the psalm concludes with darkness. Specifically, it concludes with a lament over the loss of Davidic kingship.

Although the loss of kingship sounds horrible to our twenty-first-century ears, it was an absolute *spiritual* tragedy for the Israelites. Not only was a king in David's lineage to reign forever (cf. 2 Sam 7), but he was also the earthly expression of YHWH's reign among his people. And from the history recorded in the books of Samuel and Kings, we know that this tragedy was brought on by the sin of Israel, Judah, and their kings. At the very center of this tragedy was the loss of the temple. Even if God's people had their land (which they did not), they no longer had the land with YHWH dwelling in their midst.

This reality drives us back into book 3 to see that even its psalms that mention Zion could have been read as laments in this context (for examples of psalms that mention Zion in book 3, see Ps 74, 76, 78, 84, and 87). What had been celebrated in these psalms was now lost in the exile. And since these psalms with a Zion theme were surrounded by laments, this reinforces the loss surrounding the place where YHWH had dwelled most personally and powerfully.

BOOK 4 (PS 90–106): YHWH REIGNS EVEN WHEN DAVID DOES NOT

As we have discussed in a previous chapter, the recent scholar who has contributed most to the shape of the book of Psalms discussion is Gerald H. Wilson (1945–2005).[8] And among his most helpful insights is his work on book 4 (Ps 90–106). In the context of book 3 and its reflection on the exile, Wilson noticed that book 4 begins with a psalm of Moses, includes the "YHWH reigns" psalms, and concludes with a plea for restoration. Each of these features is worth unpacking.

---

[8]See especially Gerald H. Wilson, *The Editing of the Hebrew Psalter*, Society of Biblical Literature Dissertation Series 76 (Chico, CA: Scholars Press, 1985).

The first important feature of book 4 is its beginning in Psalm 90, with a psalm of Moses. We know this from the psalm's superscription: "A Prayer of Moses, the Man of God." Although this makes Psalm 90 one of the oldest psalms in the book of Psalms—since the exodus from Egypt occurred in either the twelfth or fourteenth century BC—the placement of this Mosaic psalm communicates an important message when it is read in the context of the book of Psalms as a whole.[9] While book 3 laments the fact that there was no longer a king on David's throne (cf. Ps 89 and 2 Sam 7), the introduction of book 4 as a psalm of Moses reminds us that the covenant stretches back before David, all the way to Moses (and earlier). The psalm then begins by reflecting on *adonay* as his people's dwelling place throughout all generations. Once again, in the context of the exile, Israel could take refuge in their God. Finally, in verse 4, Moses wrote that "a thousand years in your sight are like a day" (NIV). This would also have been precious in the context of Israel's experience of exile, because although it seemed to be taking forever, even a thousand years are like a day in the sight of their God. From the lips of Moses—who led God's people through the wilderness wanderings—Psalm 90 reminds them that their God would also lead them through the "new wilderness" of exile.[10] The implied answer to Moses' question, "How

---

[9]Miles Van Pelt has shown that in the English Old Testament, which reflects the order of the LXX, the book of Ruth follows Judges. This reflects the importance of *chronology* in the Greek mindset of the LXX translators. However, in the *BHS* Hebrew Old Testament, the book of Ruth follows Proverbs. This reflects the importance of *theme* in the Hebrew mindset of those who shaped this arrangement. While the book of Proverbs concludes with a reflection on the excellent wife (*esheth hayil* [אֵשֶׁת־חַיִל]), the only woman in the entire Old Testament who is called this is Ruth (3:11). According to the order of the English (and Greek) Old Testament, Ruth follows Judges because it "comes next" chronologically. According to the order of the *BHS* Hebrew Old Testament, Ruth follows Proverbs because of theme: "I have told you about the kind of woman you should marry, and now I'm going to show her to you." See Miles V. Van Pelt, "Introduction," in *A Biblical-Theological Introduction to the Old Testament: The Gospel Promised*, ed. Miles V. Van Pelt (Wheaton, IL: Crossway, 2016), 23-42. Along with other shape of the Psalms scholars, I suggest that this same principle holds true for the ordering of the various psalms in the book of Psalms: theme is more important than chronology. This is especially on display in the placement of Psalm 90.

[10]Although space will not allow me to trace a theme of Moses and the exodus from Egypt through book 4 as a whole, interested readers can consult the following works: Michael G.

long, O YHWH?" is, "In his perfect time; just trust that he is working, even in the midst of your suffering."

The next distinctive feature of book 4 is its high concentration of "YHWH reigns" psalms (Ps 93, 97, 99).[11] In fact, book 4 is the only place these occur. Each of them begins with the phrase "YHWH reigns," and then lists what he reigns over. In the context of book 3 and the loss of Davidic kingship, these psalms communicate the message, "YHWH reigns, even when David does not; even when there is no earthly king on the throne of Israel, our covenant God reigns over all." Therefore, there was hope in exile and the loss of the earthly king.

The last distinctive feature of book 4 is its ending. Psalm 106 is a long, forty-eight-verse psalm that begins with the exclamation: "Praise the LORD! / Oh give thanks to the LORD, for he is good, / for his steadfast love endures forever!" (Ps 106:1). This psalm references a time in the future when YHWH would save his people (v. 4), and it confesses that "both we and our fathers have sinned" (v. 6). It then reflects on Israel's sins in the exodus from Egypt (v. 7), and YHWH's decision to save them for his name's sake (v. 8). The psalm continues with Israel forgetting God's works (v. 13), and as a result, sinning (e.g., vv. 14-18). In fact, much of the psalm reflects on YHWH's response of discipline in the face of his people's sin after the exodus. This ultimately leads to a reflection on the exile as the expression of YHWH's anger toward his sinful people (vv. 40-43). Even in the face of this, however, YHWH looked on their distress, heard their cry, remembered his covenant, and relented according to his *hesed* (vv. 44-46). The psalm concludes with a plea by the exiles—"Save us, O LORD our God, / and gather us from among the nations, / that we may give

---

McKelvey, *Moses, David and the High Kingship of Yahweh: A Canonical Study of Book IV of the Psalter* (Piscataway, NJ: Gorgias, 2013); Robert E. Wallace, *The Narrative Effect of Book 4 of the Hebrew Psalter*, Studies in Biblical Literature 112, ed. Hemchand Gossai (New York: Peter Lang, 2007).

[11]Psalm 96:10 also contains the phrase, "YHWH reigns."

thanks to your holy name / and glory in your praise" (v. 47)—before a doxology closes book 4 as a whole (v. 48). In this context, a plea for restoration from the exile closes out book 4.

In book 4 overall, we have seen that the covenant stretches back before David, a thousand years is like a day in YHWH's sight, YHWH reigns even when David does not, and we have also heard the exiles crying out for deliverance. When we remember the teachings of Leviticus 26 and Deuteronomy 28, 30:1-10, we are taught to read these things with optimism. In those chapters, God's people were told of blessings for covenant keeping (Lev 26:3-13; Deut 28:1-14), curses for covenant breaking (Lev 26:14-39; Deut 28:15-68), and restoration for covenant repentance (Lev 26:40-45; Deut 30:1-10). These chapters were addressed to a people YHWH *had rescued* from slavery in Egypt. This means that they were not about how to *become* God's people but how to *live* as God's people. They were meant as a means of grace, to warn God's people to be faithful to him. If they did so, they would be blessed, but if they broke the covenant, they would be cursed. This curse would include being driven from the land of Israel and no longer having YHWH dwell in their midst.

It is the last feature of these chapters—the promise of restoration for covenant repentance (Lev 26:40-45; Deut 30:1-10)—that would have been especially precious for those in exile. Imagine an entire nation torn from their land and people, and knowing that they were driven away because of their own sin. What would they do when they only had themselves to blame for their suffering? What would they do when it was clear that they were bearing the curse of YHWH for covenant breaking (Lev 26:14-39; Deut 28:15-68)? Well, their God told them clearly: they should cry out to *him*, and he would restore them (Lev 26:40-45; Deut 30:1-10). It was an incredible promise to be able to approach their covenant God, YHWH, in the midst of their suffering, *which was caused by YHWH's anger at their sin*. The very

One whose anger punished their sin would restore them if they turned back to him. If this is not gospel in the Old Testament, I don't know what is. In light of this, by concluding book 4 with Psalm 106, the editors created a note of optimism that God's people would experience his gracious restoration. Could it be that this would happen in book 5?

BOOK 5 (PS 107–150): THE RETURN OF A NEW AND BETTER DAVID

In the context of this cry for restoration by the exiles that closes out book 4 (Ps 106:47), book 5 opens with a psalm of thanksgiving for redemption from exile. Although psalms were often written in one context and then redeployed for a new one as they were placed in their new "book of Psalms context," Psalm 107 appears to have been written specifically in response to a return from exile. The psalm begins with a call for the community to "give thanks to the LORD, for he is good, / for his steadfast love endures forever!" (Ps 107:1; cf. Ps 118:1, 29). In verse 2, there is a call for the redeemed of YHWH to say that his *hesed* (steadfast love) is eternal. To this point, the reader can see that the psalm would fit a return-from-exile context, but there has been nothing unique about the language that would tie the psalm to that specific experience. In the second half of verse 2, however, those links become clear.

In Psalm 107:2b, the psalmist began to rehearse the kind of redemption that these people had experienced. They had been redeemed from trouble (v. 2b) and gathered in from the lands, east, west, north, and south (v. 3); from desert wastes with no city to dwell in (v. 4); and from hunger and thirst (v. 5). If we were reading this psalm on its own, the images would be vivid but unremarkable. However, in the context of Leviticus 26 and Deuteronomy 28 and 30:1-10, these images are incredible, because they are direct reversals of the specific curses for covenant breaking outlined in those texts. If the land had been desolate (Lev 26:33), they had now been gathered from desert wastes (Ps 107:4). If their cities had been laid waste (Lev 26:33), they had now been gathered from the horrible position of having no city to dwell in and finally being given one (Ps 107:4, 7). If their supply of bread had been broken (Lev 26:26), they had now been redeemed from hunger (Ps 107:5). And this is just a sampling. If we had more space, we could read Psalm 107 alongside these texts from the Pentateuch and see clearly that the psalm as a whole was written as the direct fulfillment of the promise of restoration for covenant repentance. In the return from exile, the curse was reversed— the covenant breaking that caused the exile was forgiven for the repentant community!

One last feature of Psalm 107 emphasizes the return-from-exile theme: its repeated sayings. Throughout the psalm, a summary statement is repeated four times: "then they cried to the LORD in their trouble, / and he delivered them from their distress" (Ps 107:6, 13, 19, 28). And each time, a refrain follows closely on the heels of the summary statement: "let them thank the LORD for his steadfast love, / for his wondrous works to the children of man!" (Ps 107:8, 15, 21, 31). The return from exile was indeed wonderful.

Book 5 then continues with a cluster of Davidic psalms (Ps 108– 110). If a psalm of Moses is the lens through which we are to read book 4 (cf. Ps 90), the re-emergence of David in book 5 seems to signal his return. This first Davidic cluster of book 5 climaxes in Psalm 110, in which David acted as a prophet of YHWH; he spoke of his (David's) lord who would sit at the right hand of YHWH on the throne of the cosmos *until* his enemies were made a footstool for his feet (Ps 110:1). The psalm offers images of victory by this messianic figure who was both royal (v. 1) and priestly (v. 4), and who was clearly greater than David (v. 1). This is the first hint in book 5 that a new and better David was coming, one who would be supremely victorious and who would also mediate as a priest between YHWH and his people.

Next, a cluster of psalms reflects back on the exodus from Egypt (Ps 113–118). The climax of this grouping is the great Psalm 118. If Psalm 110:1 is the most quoted verse in the New Testament, Psalm 118 is the most quoted psalm: it is referenced in twenty to sixty New Testament texts, with quotations or allusions from up to eighteen of its verses.[12] While Psalm 107 celebrates the redemption of the community as a whole, Psalm 118 celebrates the deliverance of an individual. While this individual was distinct from the community—notice the way he acted as the leader in a responsive song of thanks (Ps 118:19-28)—his deliverance was also cause for national celebration. This hints that the figure was a king, and this is strengthened when we recall that it was the role of the king to lead the victory procession from the battlefield (cf. Ps 118:19-28). But with his words, this royal savior echoed Moses' words in the Song of the Sea (cf. for example, Ps 118:14 with Ex 15:2a).[13] Finally, the link between Psalms 107 and 118 is made even stronger with the repeated invitation to "give thanks to the LORD, for he his good, / for his steadfast love endures forever" (Ps 107:1; 118:1, 29).

If the people had been looking for a coming king to sit on David's throne (cf. 2 Sam 7 and the promise of an eternal dominion for

---

[12]Of course, the broad range of twenty to sixty references is because it depends on one's views of allusions and echoes. See Frank-Lothar Hossfeld and Erich Zenger, *Psalms 3: A Commentary on Psalms 101-150*, ed. Klaus Baltzer, trans. Linda M. Maloney, Hermeneia (Minneapolis, MN: Fortress, 2011), 245. See also Andrew C. Brunson, *Psalm 118 in the Gospel of John: An Intertextual Study on the New Exodus Pattern in the Theology of John* (Tübingen, Germany: Mohr Siebeck, 2003), 4. For other relatively recent works in this regard, see especially Hyukjung Kwon, "The Reception of Psalm 118 in the New Testament: Application of a 'New Exodus Motif'?" (PhD diss., University of Pretoria, 2007); Jutta Schröten, *Entstehung, Komposition und Wirkungsgeschichte Des 118. Psalms*, Bonner Biblische Beiträge 95 (Weinheim, Germany: Beltz Athenäum, 1995), 154-70. See also Hans-Joachim Kraus, *Theology of the Psalms*, trans. Keith R. Crim (Minneapolis, MN: Augsburg, 1986), 193-94. This sentence first appeared in Ian J. Vaillancourt, *The Multifaceted Saviour of Psalms 110 and 118: A Canonical Exegesis*, Hebrew Bible Monographs 86 (Sheffield, UK: Sheffield Phoenix, 2019), 188.

[13]For a list of numerous other references in this regard, see Vaillancourt, *The Multifaceted Saviour of Psalms 110 and 118*, 151-54; 171-75.

David's seed), they had also been waiting for the coming of a prophet like Moses (cf. Deut 18:15-18; 34:10-12). By acting like a king and echoing the words of Moses, the messianic figure in Psalm 118 embodied both roles in one person. When we combine this with Psalm 110, we find Old Testament hints at something that is made even more clear in the New Testament: Jesus would be the ultimate messianic prophet, priest, and king; he was the ultimate fulfillment of all three roles.

This exalted portrait of the coming Savior sheds further light on the postscript for books 1 and 2. We have seen that Psalm 72:20 communicates that books 1 and 2 are primarily focused on the David of history—the son of Jesse who was the king of Israel. Could it be that appearances of David *after* this point in the book of Psalms are intentionally meant to trigger hope in a new and better David to come? The Messiah? Appearances of David, and even a specific prayer of David (cf. Ps 86) in books 3–5, would certainly hint in this direction, and the exalted portrait of the Savior in the first part of book 5 seems to confirm it. According to Psalms 110 and 118, the coming Savior would be David's lord who would sit enthroned at the right hand of YHWH (Ps 110:1); he would gain ultimate victory (Ps 110); he would mediate as priest between God and his people (Ps 110:4); his deliverance would be the cause of national celebration (Ps 118:19-28); and he would lead the people to sing the words of Moses in celebration of a new exodus (Ps 118:14, 19-28), even suggesting that he would be the hoped-for, new, and better Moses to come (cf. Deut 18:15-18; 34:10-12).

Book 5 continues with a psalm that celebrates the *torah* (Ps 119), and we have seen that since it is coupled with Psalm 118, together they paint a portrait of the ideal *torah*-keeping king of Deuteronomy 17:14-20. This is followed by fifteen Songs of Ascents (Ps 120-134), which were sung by the pilgrims as they ascended to Jerusalem for the various annual feasts. In the context of the themes we have been noticing in book 5, however, the ascent up to Jerusalem in these songs could have also signaled the celebration of the return to Jerusalem from Babylonian exile. Imagine the joy of the returnees as they sang their old song in this new life situation: "I lift up my eyes to the hills. / From where does my help come? / My help comes from the LORD, / who made heaven and earth" (Ps 121:1-2). In the mouths of the returnees, this expression of trust would have become a cry of thanksgiving for YHWH's faithful deliverance.

Near the end of the Songs of Ascents we encounter Psalm 132, which celebrates David. Imagine how the following words would have been heard by those returning from exile: "Remember, O LORD, in David's favor, / all the hardships he endured" (Ps 132:1). This psalm highlights David's yearning to build a temple for YHWH's dwelling, so the covenant God could make a permanent residence in the center of his people. While the original context of this psalm may have been a reflection on what David went through to set Solomon up for success in the construction of the temple, the new postexilic readers would have heard it as an expression of yearning for full restoration. Consider these words: "Arise, O LORD, and go to your resting place, / you and the ark of your might. / Let your priests be clothed with righteousness, / and let your saints shout for joy. / For the sake of your servant David, / do not turn away the face of your anointed one" (Ps 132:8-10). In light of this psalm's context in the book of Psalms, it is nothing less than a prayer for YHWH to re-inhabit his people in the new temple that had been promised in the prophets (cf. Ezek 40–48).

Psalm 132 then continues with a recollection of YHWH's covenant with David, and in particular the promise that one of David's sons would always be on the throne, so long as he was faithful to the covenant (Ps 132:11-12). In the contexts of Israel's history, and of Leviticus 26 and Deuteronomy 28, 30:1-10, this would have been heard by the returnees as an expression of hope in the restoration of the Davidic kingship (cf. Lev 26:40-45; Deut 30:1-10). If this kingship had been lost because of the people's (and the king's) sin (cf. Lev 26:14-39; Deut 28:15-68), an expectation of restoration was equally rooted in Old Testament promises.

Following the Songs of Ascents (Ps 120–134) are a *hallelujah* psalm (Ps 135), a thanksgiving psalm (Ps 136), and a psalm that vividly laments the Babylonian exile (Ps 137). We have seen that the psalms of lament tend to be more concentrated near the beginning of the book of Psalms, and the psalms of praise near the end. But this is a general pattern, not a rule. In fact, Psalm 137 sounds more in line with the dominant themes of book 3 rather than book 5:

> 1 By the waters of Babylon,
>> there we sat down and wept,
>> when we remembered Zion.
> 2 On the willows there
>> we hung up our lyres.
> 3 For there our captors
>> required of us songs,
>> and our tormentors, mirth, saying,
>> "Sing us one of the songs of Zion!"
> 4 How shall we sing the LORD's song
>> in a foreign land? (Ps 137:1-4)

The psalm closes on a note of vengeance against Babylon: "Blessed shall he be who takes your little ones / and dashes them against the rock!" (Ps 137:9). How would this psalm have been heard by the returnees? It would have been a bitter reminder of the real suffering they had endured, and it would have pointed them to the urgency of the project of rebuilding Jerusalem: "If I forget you, O Jerusalem, / let my right hand forget its skill!" (Ps 137:5). It would have also been an appropriate cry as they lived in tension: they had experienced a measure of restoration, but the full restoration that had been promised in Leviticus 26:40-45 and Deuteronomy 30:1-10 was yet to come. For example, the foundation of the Second Temple was so much smaller than the first that those who remembered its former glory cried (Ezra 3:12). If Ezekiel had promised that the new temple would be *better* than the first (cf. Ezek 40–48), then these older men had reason to weep. Psalm 137 would have given the returnees words to express their yearning.

I also do not want to gloss over the expression of vengeance at the end of Psalm 137. Once again: "Blessed shall he be who takes your little ones / and dashes them against the rock!" (Ps 137:9). Bruce Waltke has written a very helpful, brief explanation of expressions of vengeance in the book of Psalms, and I quote him at length in appendix E (available as a free PDF download on the IVP website at www.ivpress.com/treasuring-the-psalms). I encourage you to read and consider his very balanced understanding and application of these difficult texts. In this place, I will simply observe that this verse was written by a person who had watched the Babylonian soldiers do exactly this to the Israelite children: these enemy soldiers had dashed the Israelite children's heads against "the rock" (i.e., the Temple Mount). The very locale of greatest blessing had become the place of a horrible enactment of curses for covenant breaking. The tone of vengeance in this verse communicates, therefore, "as you have done to the people of YHWH, may it be done to you."

Book 5 continues with a cluster of Davidic psalms (Ps 138–145), and one of these is a prayer of David (Ps 142). We have seen that following Psalm 72:20, these would likely signal hope in a new and better David to come. David Howard has suggested that Psalms 1 and 2 make the themes of the sovereignty of YHWH and of his anointed king keynotes for the entire book of Psalms.[14] He then adds that the

---

[14]See David M. Howard Jr., "The Psalms and Current Study," in *Interpreting the Psalms: Issues and Approaches*, ed. David G. Firth and Philip Johnston (Leicester: Apollos, 2005), 27.

placement of the royal Davidic Psalm 144 alongside the kingship-of-YHWH Psalm 145 "signals that the earthly and the heavenly expressions of Yahweh's kingdom stand together as messages of hope at the end of the Psalter as at the beginning."[15]

The book of Psalms then concludes with five *hallelujah* psalms (Ps 146–150). Each of these begins and ends with the Hebrew word *hallu-yah* (הַלְלוּ־יָהּ). If each of the previous four books concluded with a verse of doxology (Ps 41:13; 72:19; 89:52; 106:48), book 5 concludes the book of Psalms with five entire psalms of praise. The last of these is a self-forgetful call on all of creation to praise YHWH with body posture, voices, and instruments (Ps 150). As the book of psalms ends with all of creation in worship of YHWH, it is nothing less than a foretaste of the final consummation.

DISCUSSION QUESTIONS

1. The author suggested that the broad theme of books 1 and 2 (Ps 1–72) is the tears of David as he reigns in tension. What evidence did he offer to support this suggestion?

2. What does a news station's use of the song "Timshel," by Mumford and Sons, after the Boston Marathon bombing model for us about the way a poem that was written in one context can be reappropriated for a new context?

3. What did the author suggest as the broad theme for book 3 (Ps 73–89)? What main features of this section lend support for this proposed theme?

4. What did the author suggest as the broad theme of book 4 (Ps 90–106)? What main features of this section lend support for this proposed theme?

---

[15]Howard Jr., "The Psalms and Current Study," 27. This argument, along with the references to the work of Howard, also appears in Vaillancourt, *The Multifaceted Saviour of Psalms 110 and 118*, 58.

5. Read through Psalm 107, Leviticus 26, Deuteronomy 28, and Deuteronomy 30:1-10. Along the way, record as many thematic and verbal parallels as you can between the psalm and the Pentateuch chapters. What do these parallels indicate about the compositional context of Psalm 107?

6. The author suggested that book 5 (Ps 107–150) sketches a portrait of the coming messianic Savior as a prophet better than Moses, a king greater than David, and the ultimate priestly mediator between God and his people. What evidence did he offer in support of this?

5

The Shape of the Book, Part Three

THE PORTRAIT OF THE KING

ON JUNE 2, 1953, twenty-seven million people in the UK alone tuned in on their televisions. Video cameras and news crews were set up at Westminster Abbey, so that for the first time in British history, people could watch a coronation ceremony from home. On that day, Queen Elizabeth II was crowned. She had been just twenty-five when she was proclaimed Queen by her dying father, but now at twenty-seven, she officially wore the crown. Princess Elizabeth was now Queen Elizabeth II.

When Western readers approach the Bible, it is difficult to avoid reading references to kings through the lens of British monarchs. But it is important for us to notice that there are some major differences. (To give one example, the power of the king in antiquity was not balanced by a prime minister who was put into office through a democratic process.) In this chapter, we will consider the broad Old Testament teaching about Israel's king, and then apply that teaching to our reading of the Psalms. We will do this under four broad headings: the Old Testament teaching about the king, the corporate solidarity between the king and his people, the royal psalms as messianic, and the royal psalms and the shape of the book of Psalms.

THE OLD TESTAMENT TEACHING
ABOUT THE KING

If the panorama of the Old Testament offers a gradual unveiling of God's plan of redemption, the theme of God's king is also gradually revealed as central to his purposes.

Genesis is a book that charts the genealogy of the coming messianic Savior, from the promise of a seed of the woman who will crush the head of the seed of the serpent (Gen 3:15), through ten family lineage statements that give structure to the book.[1] In this context, Jacob blessed his twelve sons at the end of Genesis. All twelve were clearly special and would make up the twelve tribes of Israel. However, one of the twelve was especially centered out, because kings would follow in his lineage: "The scepter shall not depart from Judah, nor the ruler's staff from between his feet, until tribute comes to him; and to him shall be the obedience of the peoples" (Gen 49:10). In this verse, we are introduced to something essential in God's unfolding plan of redemption: the tribe of Judah would produce a king (i.e., one who carries a scepter/ruler's staff), and this kingship would be perpetual (i.e., it would not depart from [the tribe of] Judah). This is the first Old Testament hint that God would work especially through the agency of a king.[2]

As the Old Testament story continued to unfold, it would speak once again about the king. After a miraculous preservation from famine (Gen 50:20) and a subsequent four hundred years of slavery (Gen 15:13), YHWH redeemed his people out of Egypt. He instructed

---

[1] Genesis 2:4; 5:1; 6:9; 10:1; 11:10; 11:27; 25:12; 25:19; 36:1, 9; 37:2. For a more thorough explanation of this theme, see Ian J. Vaillancourt, *The Dawning of Redemption: The Story of the Pentateuch and the Hope of the Gospel* (Wheaton, IL: Crossway, 2022), chap. 3.

[2] For another hint in Genesis about a king, see Gen 27:27-29. As Sailhamer put it, "Isaac's blessing foreshadows Jacob's later prophecy concerning the kingship of the house of Judah. . . . Thus the words of Isaac are a crucial link in the development of the theme of the blessing of Abraham's seed." John H. Sailhamer, *The Pentateuch as Narrative: A Biblical-Theological Commentary*, Library of Biblical Interpretation (Grand Rapids, MI: Zondervan, 1992), 191. Readers may also want to consider Gen 37:5-11 and Sailhamer's comments on it in Sailhamer, *The Pentateuch as Narrative*, 206-7. For the insights in this footnote, I am indebted to comments by the anonymous peer reviewer of my initial manuscript submission to IVP.

them about how to live as his people (Ex 19–24); he dwelled among them in the tabernacle (Ex 25–40); and after a forty-year hiatus in the wilderness (see the book of Numbers), Moses readied the next generation to enter the Promised Land (see the book of Deuteronomy). Among these preparations was some clear teaching about the king:

> When you come to the land that the LORD your God is giving you, and you possess it and dwell in it and then say, "I will set a king over me, like all the nations that are around me," you may indeed set a king over you whom the LORD your God will choose. One from among your brothers you shall set as king over you. You may not put a foreigner over you, who is not your brother. Only he must not acquire many horses for himself or cause the people to return to Egypt in order to acquire many horses, since the LORD has said to you, "You shall never return that way again." And he shall not acquire many wives for himself, lest his heart turn away, nor shall he acquire for himself excessive silver and gold. And when he sits on the throne of his kingdom, he shall write for himself in a book a copy of this law, approved by the Levitical priests. And it shall be with him, and he shall read in it all the days of his life, that he may learn to fear the LORD his God by keeping all the words of this law and these statutes, and doing them, that his heart may not be lifted up above his brothers, and that he may not turn aside from the commandment, either to the right hand or to the left, so that he may continue long in his kingdom, he and his children, in Israel. (Deut 17:14-20)

In this passage—long before the first king of Israel, and even before Israel conquered the Promised Land—YHWH told them what kind of *king* they should set over themselves. If Genesis 49:10 was clear that he would be a descendant of Judah, Deuteronomy 17:14-20 taught that he must be an Israelite (v. 15), and he must not accumulate excessive wealth or wives (vv. 16-17). This king also needed to have a reign that was steeped in the *torah* of YHWH, so much so that he would write out his own copy by hand and read from it every day. This was done so that the precious *torah* would inform and shape his reign (vv. 18-20).

As we approach the books of Samuel and Kings, the promise of a king from the tribe of Judah (Gen 49:10), who would reign with a *torah*-shaped righteousness (Deut 17:14-20) is on our minds. When a baby was miraculously born to a barren woman (1 Sam 1–2), our attention is alerted: just as YHWH had raised up miracle children for barren women in the book of Genesis, he was doing it again. But in the song of Hannah, where she celebrated the birth and coming accomplishments of her newborn, Samuel, we read something surprising: "The LORD will judge the ends of the earth; / he will give strength to his *king* / and exalt the horn of his anointed" (1 Sam 2:10b, emphasis added). In the story that follows, baby Samuel would grow up to be a priest (1 Sam 2:35) and a prophet (1 Sam 3:19-21), but not a king. From the beginning of the book, however, we are told to expect that YHWH would raise up a king.

Near the end of Samuel's life, the people of Israel asked him to appoint a king over them (1 Sam 8:4-5), and they chose Saul for his physical, not his spiritual attributes (1 Sam 9:2). What is more, he was from the tribe of Benjamin, *not* Judah. Saul lacked courage from the beginning (1 Sam 10:22), but he was still anointed as king in response to the people's request. Saul's reign started out well as he led battles against the Philistine enemy (1 Sam 13:4), but he also sinned against YHWH, so his days as king were numbered (1 Sam 13:8-15).

By this point in the story, YHWH has revealed a great deal about the coming king who would be his instrument of salvation. We have encountered Samuel, who was a great man, priest, and prophet but not the promised king. Saul had been anointed as king, but he had also proved to not ultimately be God's man. What would God do? After YHWH definitively rejected Saul as king (1 Sam 15), YHWH then sent

Samuel to the house of Jesse, to anoint one of his sons as his chosen king (1 Sam 16). And Jesse was from the tribe of *Judah*! As the youngest and smallest, David was at first overlooked but was then chosen because YHWH looks on the heart (16:7). David was anointed as king by Samuel, but his official reign would not begin until the death of Saul. In the meantime, David entered into service for Saul as his personal musician and armor-bearer (1 Sam 16:14-23). All the while, though, we as readers are beginning to think that David could be the promised king who would save God's people. In light of these events, it is significant that the very next chapter of the Bible—1 Samuel 17—tells the story of a great victory for a young King David (over Goliath!), along with its effects on the people of Israel as a whole.[3]

This ultimately leads to 2 Samuel 7, and YHWH's covenant with David.[4] Although David wanted to build a house for YHWH to dwell in, YHWH would build a house for him instead:

> When your days are fulfilled and you lie down with your fathers, I will raise up your offspring after you, who shall come from your body, and I will establish his kingdom. He shall build a house for my name, and I will establish the throne of his kingdom forever. I will be to him a father, and he shall be to me a son. When he commits iniquity, I will discipline him with the rod of men, with the stripes of the sons of men, but my steadfast love will not depart from him, as I took it from Saul, whom I put away from before you. And your house and your kingdom shall be made sure forever before me. Your throne shall be established forever. (2 Sam 7:12-16)

From this we see that the reign of David would be perpetual: he was from the tribe of Judah (cf. Gen 49:10), and his descendants would reign on this throne forever.

---

[3]This paragraph and the previous one first appeared in Ian J. Vaillancourt, *David, Goliath, and the Gospel: Living in Light of Our Savior's Victory*, Discovery Series (Grand Rapids, MI: Our Daily Bread Ministries, 2021), https://discoveryseries.org/courses/david-goliath-and-the-gospel/.

[4]Although the word *covenant* is not used in these verses, the theme is certainly present. Also, this is retrospectively referred to as a covenant in Psalms 89:3 and 132:12.

If the story ended on this high note, we would have every reason to rejoice. But from this point forward, things quickly deteriorated. Beginning with David, the sins of Israel's kings were horrible. But through the lens of Leviticus 26 and Deuteronomy 28, they were disastrous. In this light, they were nothing less than spiritual treason against YHWH, and a sure path to the entire nation enduring the curses for covenant breaking (cf. Lev 26:14-39; Deut 28:15-68).

The downward spiral among Israel's kings began with David, who committed adultery and murder (2 Sam 11). His son Solomon acquired riches and power and wives (e.g., 1 Kings 11:4) in direct contrast to the portrait of the ideal king of Deuteronomy 17:14-20. After the death of Solomon, the kingdom was divided in two, with Israel in the north and Judah in the south. The book of Kings then offered pronouncements on the covenant faithfulness or unfaithfulness of each successive monarch. None of the kings of Israel received a positive assessment, and only some of the kings of Judah were deemed faithful to the covenant. Ahaz serves as an example of a bad report: "Ahaz was twenty years old when he began to reign, and he reigned sixteen years in Jerusalem. And he did not do what was right in the eyes of the LORD his God, as his father David had done" (2 Kings 16:2). Jehoash serves as a representative positive example: "And Jehoash did what was right in the eyes of the LORD all his days, because Jehoiada the priest instructed him" (2 Kings 12:2).

As the king's heart went, so went the people. The downward spiral away from covenant faithfulness to YHWH went on uninterrupted in the northern kingdom of Israel until they were finally conquered by the Assyrians and taken into exile in 722 BC. Although the downward spiral of covenant breaking was not as universal in the southern kingdom of Judah, the reforms of various faithful kings were ultimately overshadowed by an overall pattern of unfaithfulness. So, in 587/586 BC, the southern kingdom of Judah was exiled to Babylon.

As the kings of Israel and Judah led the nation into spiritual treason, the long-suffering YHWH had finally responded with the curses for covenant breaking. The books of Samuel and Kings, therefore, must be read in light of Leviticus 26 and Deuteronomy 28, 30:1-10.

As we return to God's covenant with David in 2 Samuel 7, we can see how much this decline and exile was an absolute tragedy. The most relevant portion is spoken in relation to the son of David:

> I will establish the throne of his [i.e., David's] kingdom *forever*. I will be to him a father, and he shall be to me a son. When he commits iniquity, I will discipline him with the rod of men, with the stripes of the sons of men, but my steadfast love will not depart from him, as I took it from Saul, whom I put away from before you. And your house and your kingdom shall be made sure *forever* before me. Your throne shall be established *forever*. (2 Sam 7:13b-16, emphasis added)

In contrast to the promise of a "forever" reign by the Davidic kings, by the end of the books of Kings, no one sat on Israel's throne. In fact, in the panorama of Israel's history, the title "king of the Jews" would not be properly used until it was given to Jesus, and that as a sign on the instrument of his crucifixion (Mt 27:37).[5]

CORPORATE SOLIDARITY

At this point, we need to notice one more way that the Bible's concept of kingship is likely foreign to us: the corporate solidarity between the king and his people. Walter Kaiser points out that in this way of thinking, "the whole group is able to function as a single individual through one of its members."[6] Put another way, although the king was still accountable as an individual before YHWH, his life also represented his people before YHWH. As Peter Gentry put

---

[5]Previous to the cross, various oral confessions of Jesus' kingship were also made. See, for example, Matthew 2:2; 27:11.
[6]Walter Kaiser, *The Christian and the Old Testament* (Pasadena, CA: William Carey Library, 2012), 175.

it, only Israel's king could say, "I am Israel" and also be distinguished from Israel.[7]

This insight helps make sense of many Old Testament passages that may have previously confused us. For example, when David took a census of Israel, YHWH responded by putting to death seventy thousand men from the community (2 Sam 24:15). To our individualistic Western ears, this sounds very unfair, but when we understand that the king represented the people in his actions, we see that the entire community was in fact guilty because *they had sinned in the actions of their king*. This same principle holds true for the narratives of Samuel and Kings: not only did the king lead Israel into or out of sinful patterns, but his personal behavior also impacted YHWH's disposition toward the entire community (e.g., 2 Kings 24:18-20; Is 39:5-7).

This concept of corporate solidarity should lead Christians to treasure Jesus all the more. I praise God that I *never* have to worry about being punished for the sins of my covenant head, because Jesus *never* sinned (e.g., 1 Pet 2:22). Far to the contrary, Jesus lived the perfect life that I failed to live and died the death under God's wrath that I deserved to die.[8] This also enables a believer's union with Christ to be effective—think of all the New Testament occurrences of the phrase "in Christ" (e.g., Rom 3:24). When a person turns from their sin and then trusts and follows Christ, they experience a union with him as their covenant head, and the Father looks on the Christian with all the delight he has in his perfect Son. So this Old Testament idea of the corporate solidarity between the king and his people is gloriously fulfilled in Jesus, the perfect king, and Christians, his grateful subjects.

---

[7]See Peter J. Gentry and Stephen J. Wellum, *Kingdom Through Covenant: A Biblical-Theological Understanding of the Covenants*, 2nd ed. (Wheaton, IL: Crossway, 2018), 495.

[8]I first heard this turn of phrase from the ministry of Timothy Keller. What an awesome summary of the active obedience and atoning death of Christ!

Back to the Old Testament, this idea of corporate solidarity helps us to make sense of the relationship between the king and the people in the book of Psalms. As Michael Snearly reflects on the relationship between YHWH, the king, and the people in the book of Psalms, he points out that they work harmoniously, as YHWH appointed an earthly king, and the people identified closely with the king as their head, and vice versa: as the king represented the people, so the people reflected the king.[9] This also explains the psalms that celebrate the king, and the reason the people delighted in and prayed for the blessing of their king (e.g., Ps 72). Finally, this is why it made sense to the people that the Messiah would be cast in the light of a new and better David, even one to whom David bowed as his lord (cf. Ps 110:1). As the earthly (or messianic) king was lavished with YHWH's blessing, his subjects would also be the recipients of that blessing.

THE ROYAL PSALMS ARE MESSIANIC[10]

In this context, we can make an important observation: at the time most of the individual psalms were composed, there was a king reigning on the throne of David. In fact, David is listed as the author of seventy-three of the 150 psalms. However, by the time the book of Psalms was compiled into its present form, the tragedy of exile and its resulting loss of kingship hung over God's people like a dark cloud. Even the return from exile was only a partial restoration, for the Second Temple was less glorious than the first (cf. Ezra 3:12), and the monarchy was not reestablished.

Would a new (and better?) David be raised up? If 2 Samuel 7 was the highest point in Israel's history to that period—when David finally reigned in peace, and he had not yet committed adultery and

---

[9]See Michael K. Snearly, *The Return of the King: Messianic Expectation in Book 5 of the Psalter*, Library of Hebrew Bible/Old Testament Studies 624 (London: T&T Clark, 2016), 183.

[10]Bellinger's list of royal psalms is as follows: 2, 18, 20, 21, 45, 72, 89, 101, 110, 132, 144. See William H. Bellinger Jr., *Psalms: Reading and Studying the Book of Praises* (Peabody, MA: Hendrickson, 2009), 23.

murder—would one come who could reestablish an even better time of blessing? In this context, it is telling that the royal psalms were even left in the book of Psalms. Obviously, to the compilers of the book they were not reminders of irreversible failure, nor were they out of date and impractical. Something else was going on. Bruce Waltke explains:

> The concept of Messiah was also developed in the editing of the Psalter. Israel draped the magnificent royal psalms as robes on each successive king, but generation after generation the shoulders of the reigning monarch proved too narrow and the robe slipped off to be draped on his successor. Finally, in the exile, Israel was left without a king and with a wardrobe of royal robes in their hymnody. On the basis of [YHWH's] unconditional covenants to Abraham and David, the faithful know that Israel's history ends in triumph, not in tragedy. The prophets, as noted, envisioned a coming king who would fulfill the promise of these covenants. Haggai and Zechariah, who prophesied about 520 BC when the returnees had no king, fuelled the prophetic expectation of the hoped-for king by applying it to Zerubbabel, son of David, and to Joshua, the high priest. When this hope fell through, Israel pinned their hope on a future Messiah. It was in that context, when Israel had no king, that the Psalter was edited with reference to the king. Accordingly, the editors of the Psalter must have resignified the Psalms from the historical king and draped them on the shoulders of the Messiah. Samuel Terrien, commenting on Psalm 21, agrees: "The theology of kingship and divine power had to be re-examined in the light of the historical events. Psalm 21 needed to be reinterpreted eschatologically. The Anointed One began to be viewed as the Messiah at the end of time." In short, in light of the exile and the loss of kingship, the editors colored the entire Psalter with a messianic hue.[11]

---

[11]Bruce K. Waltke and Charles Yu, *An Old Testament Theology: An Exegetical, Canonical, and Thematic Approach* (Grand Rapids, MI: Zondervan, 2007), 890.

If this is true of all the royal psalms, how much more those in book 5, as we have seen in a previous chapter. But in the context of the exile and the loss of kingship, coupled with the undying hope in YHWH's faithfulness to his promise in 2 Samuel 7, the postexilic Jews—including those who assembled the book of Psalms into its final shape—read all of the royal psalms in light of their hope in a coming Messiah. In light of their New Testament fulfillment, we can see that these psalms pointed directly to Jesus.

THE ROYAL PSALMS AND THE SHAPE OF THE BOOK OF PSALMS

We have already noticed that the book of Psalms was assembled in stages, and that while the individual psalms were *composed* in a certain historical context, they were *shaped into a book* at a time when Israel had no king. We can now build on this by noticing that the placement of the royal psalms in the context of the larger book of Psalms speaks to their prominence, and therefore, the conclusions we have been making in this chapter.

Yet another helpful contribution of Gerald H. Wilson is his work on the king. If books 1 and 2 are taken as a unit, we can notice that royal psalms occur at the beginning of this section (Ps 2) and its end (Ps 72), with others scattered in between (Ps 18, 20, 21, 45). With this climax, Stephen G. Dempster points out that the larger section ends on a note of hope, since Psalm 72 speaks of the day when the Davidic "son" will rule the earth, bring an end to injustice, renew nature, and reign from sea to sea. In addition, his enemies will lick the dust, kings will worship him (cf. Is 60:14), and all nations will be blessed in him (cf. Gen 12:1-3).[12]

---

[12]See Stephen G. Dempster, *Dominion and Dynasty: A Biblical Theology of the Hebrew Bible*, New Studies in Biblical Theology 15, ed. D. A. Carson (Downers Grove, IL: InterVarsity, 2003), 196. As previously noted in Ian J. Vaillancourt, "Formed in the Crucible of Messianic Angst: The Eschatological Shape of the Hebrew Psalter's Final Form," *Scottish Bulletin of Evangelical Theology* 31, no. 2 (2013): 142.

Although the portrait of the human king seems to have concluded with the notice of the end of the prayers of David, son of Jesse (Ps 72:20), book 3 also ends with a royal psalm, albeit a dark one (Ps 89). We have noticed that book 3 was likely appropriated as a means of mourning the exile and the loss of kingship, and that its concluding royal psalm ends with the covenant renounced[13] and the crown of David in the dust (Ps 89:39). In the context of Leviticus 26 and Deuteronomy 28, the king—who, we have seen, was the representative head of the people—was bearing the curses for covenant breaking. It is also important to notice that the name YHWH was used throughout this psalm. This means that the very God who was providentially bringing the calamity was also the personal covenant God—YHWH—to whom the psalmist could cry out. In light of these things, there is an implicit note of hope in this lament for the loss of kingship, because Leviticus 26:40-45 and Deuteronomy 30:1-10 also spoke of restoration for covenant repentance. The scene at the end of Psalm 89 is horrendous and tragic, but in this context it is not so dark as to be hopeless.

We have seen that in book 4 the emphasis is that YHWH reigns, even when his earthly king does not. But even in the midst of a cluster with this emphasis, Psalm 101 draws attention to the Davidic king once again. Dempster explains:

> But it is not as if the hopes in the Davidic covenant have been abandoned for a counsel to trust Yahweh alone. . . . A Davidic psalm stressing the ideal characteristics of a human king follows (Ps. 101), suggesting that this new world order will be presided over by a just Davidic monarch. David's role is not minimized in this new section—a just Davidide will one day rule.[14]

---

[13]The Hebrew verb *naar* (נָאַר) occurs only twice in the Hebrew Old Testament—here and in Lam 2:7—and its meaning is uncertain. However, Merrill notices that in both contexts, "Yahweh is the subject and the issue is his abandonment of his covenant with his chosen ones" (Eugene H. Merrill, "נָאַר," NIDOTTE 3:7).

[14]Dempster, *Dominion and Dynasty*, 199.

Then, near the beginning of book 5, Psalm 110 expands the vision of the coming king. He will be (1) David's lord (v. 1), (2) who will rule at the right hand of YHWH on the throne of the cosmos (v. 1), (3) who will lead a young and willing army to ultimate victory (vv. 2-3, 5-7), and (4) who will also be a priestly figure (v. 4).

The messianic Savior from Psalm 110 is not the only royal figure from book 5 who transcends the usual role of the Davidic king. Although Psalm 118 is usually classed as a psalm of thanksgiving, we have seen that its subject (and speaker) is also a king. This king led the victory procession from the battlefield and into the temple to sing a responsive song of thanks to YHWH for deliverance. By leading this song, the king assumed the usual position of the Levitical song leader (priest), and in the words of the song he echoed the words of Moses that celebrated the exodus from Egypt (e.g., Ps 118:14; Ex 15:2a). The psalm seems to point, therefore, to the end-times victory of a coming *king*, who would also exhibit characteristics of a *priest*, as well as a *prophet* greater than Moses (cf. Deut 18:15-18; 34:10-12). In the context of Psalm 72:20, it seems as though a new and better son of David was being portrayed in this last book of the Psalms.

But these are not the only royal references in book 5. Psalm 132 portrayed the king as well:

10 For the sake of your servant David,
    do not turn away the face of your anointed one.
11 The LORD swore to David a sure oath
    from which he will not turn back:
"One of the sons of your body
    I will set on your throne.
12 If your sons keep my covenant
    and my testimonies that I shall teach them,
    their sons also forever
    shall sit on your throne." (Ps 132:10-12)

This is clearly a reflection on the covenant with David in 2 Samuel 7, in light of the theology of Leviticus 26 and Deuteronomy 28 and 30:1-10. Once again, there is hope.

Finally, Psalm 144 concludes the book of Psalms with another portrait of the king. In this psalm, David the warrior (vv. 1-8) sang a new song to YHWH (v. 9). On the one hand, this was in line with David as "the sweet psalmist of Israel" (2 Sam 23:1), who wrote at least seventy-three of the 150 canonical psalms. On the other hand, the fact that it was a *new* song hearkens our minds back to the *old* song—the Song of the Sea that celebrated the greatest act of deliverance in the entire Old Testament (Ex 15). In this context, the *new* song sung by David was nothing less than the song of a new and great deliverance by YHWH, a second exodus. According to the latter portion of this psalm, God "gives victory to kings" and "rescues David his servant from the cruel sword" (v. 10) of foreigners (v. 11). The portrait is of a return from exile, and this is reinforced with echoes of restoration for covenant repentance (Lev 26:40-45; Deut 30:1-10):

> 12 May our sons in their youth
>   be like plants full grown,
>   our daughters like corner pillars
>   cut for the structure of a palace;
> 13 may our granaries be full,
>   providing all kinds of produce;
>   may our sheep bring forth thousands
>   and ten thousands in our fields;
> 14 may our cattle be heavy with young,
>   suffering no mishap or failure in bearing;
>   may there be no cry of distress in our streets!
> 15 Blessed are the people to whom such blessings fall!
>   Blessed are the people whose God is the LORD! (Ps 144:12-15)

In book 5, therefore, the portrait of the king is of David's lord, who would be a victorious warrior, a priest, and a prophet greater than

Moses. He would also accomplish a second exodus, and those under his reign would receive full restoration. In other words, the portrait is of the Messiah to come and the deliverance he would accomplish.

DISCUSSION QUESTIONS

1. What does Deuteronomy 17:14-20 teach about the kind of king Israel was to set on the throne?

2. How do Genesis 49:10 and 1 Samuel 2:10 combine to center out David (rather than, say, Saul) as YHWH's choice as king over Israel?

3. How does YHWH's covenant with David in 2 Samuel 7:12-16 impact our reading of the royal psalms, and in particular, of the psalms that lament the *loss* of kingship in Israel?

4. Explain the concept of corporate solidarity. How does this help our understanding of the Old Testament teaching on the king?

5. The author suggested that by the time the book of Psalms received its final shape, the royal psalms had been resignified (reinterpreted) with reference to the Messiah. Explain what he meant by this and share some examples.

6. What does the flow of the book of Psalms teach about the king, from the first royal psalm in book 1 (Ps 2), to the last royal psalm in book 5 (Ps 144)? As you discuss this, be sure to pay special attention to the shift in portrayal after Psalm 72:20.

PART TWO

THE
SAVIOR

READING THE PSALMS CHRISTOLOGICALLY

IN PART ONE OF THIS BOOK, we spent five chapters learning the overall structure and message of the book of Psalms. Now in part two, we are going to spend four chapters learning Christ-centered application of the Psalms. A Christian reading of the Old Testament is meant to build people up in Christ and to move them on to maturity. But how do we do this well? To begin, we will notice that the entire Old Testament—the book of Psalms included—is fulfilled in the person and work of Jesus Christ. Therefore, before we think about how the various psalms *apply* to the Christian (chap. 9), we will think through ways they are *fulfilled* in Christ (chaps. 6 through 8). The ultimate goal is that we gain some tools to find personal, life-changing, God-encountering, God-glorifying, Christ-exalting, satisfaction-producing application of the Psalms to the nitty gritty of our lives. In other words, we want the "living and active" (Heb 4:12) Word of God to do exactly what it was designed to do.

Over my years as a Christian, pastor, and professor, my thinking on this topic has been refined as I have read books by Sidney Greidanus,

Graeme Goldsworthy, and many others.[1] The rhythm of weekly preaching to people who yearn to experience gospel hope has been extremely formative for me. And regular classroom lecturing to pastors in training has been indispensable: there is nothing like the questions of perceptive students to expose flaws and to sharpen thought. The four chapters in part two are indebted to all of these shaping influences, but especially to the work of Greidanus and Goldsworthy, even as I build on their insights, reframe some of their terms, and outline many unique aspects of my own approach to this endeavor.

---

[1]See especially Graeme Goldsworthy, *Preaching the Whole Bible as Christian Scripture: The Application of Biblical Theology to Expository Preaching* (Grand Rapids, MI: Eerdmans, 2000); Sidney Greidanus, *Preaching Christ from the Old Testament: A Contemporary Hermeneutical Method* (Grand Rapids, MI: Eerdmans, 1999). Although Greidanus has written an entire volume on the Psalms, its focus is on preaching through the lectionary, so it lacks my focus on the Psalms as a book. In addition, I have reframed and refined many of his ideas. See Sidney Greidanus, *Preaching Christ from Psalms: Foundations for Expository Sermons in the Christian Year* (Grand Rapids, MI: Eerdmans, 2016). For a book that clearly lays out various positions on Christ in the Old Testament, see Brian J. Tabb and Andrew M. King, eds., *Five Views of Christ in the Old Testament: Genre, Authorial Intent, and the Nature of Scripture* (Grand Rapids, MI: Zondervan Academic, 2022).

6

The Psalms and Christ, Part One

THE TWO MEN WERE CONFUSED, perhaps even struggling with despair. As they walked toward the city ahead, they processed what had just happened. They had believed that Jesus was the Son of God, the Messiah, the fulfillment of the hope promised in the Scriptures, but now he was dead. As they continued their journey, a man drew near and walked along with them. It was Jesus, risen from the dead, but he kept them from recognizing him. The man asked them what they had been talking about, and they were surprised. To paraphrase, they said, "You are walking from Jerusalem to Emmaus just like we are. Don't you know what has just happened? We believed that Jesus was a prophet who was mighty in word and action, and three days ago the Jewish religious leaders condemned him to death and crucified him." And now to quote them: "But we had hoped that he was the one to redeem Israel" (Lk 24:21).

The two men continued by recounting rumors about his resurrection, but they remained confused and likely in doubt. So the man responded:

"O foolish ones, and slow of heart to believe all that the prophets have spoken! Was it not necessary that the Christ should suffer these things and enter into his glory?" And beginning with Moses and all the Prophets, he interpreted to them in all the Scriptures the things concerning himself. (Lk 24:25-27)

Later, after their eyes had been opened and they knew it was Jesus, he gave them another Bible lesson:

> Then he said to them, "These are my words that I spoke to you while I was still with you, that everything written about me in the Law of Moses and the Prophets and the Psalms must be fulfilled." Then he opened their minds to understand the Scriptures, and said to them, "Thus it is written, that the Christ should suffer and on the third day rise from the dead, and that repentance for the forgiveness of sins should be proclaimed in his name to all nations, beginning from Jerusalem." (Lk 24:44-47)

Can you imagine being present for this Bible lesson as the resurrected Jesus explained the Scriptures (i.e., the Old Testament) with himself as their fulfillment? For our purposes in this book, do you notice what parts of the Bible Jesus spoke from? Luke 24:44 tells us: "the Law of Moses and the Prophets and *the Psalms*" (emphasis added). In the Hebrew Old Testament, the Law of Moses (or the *torah* of Moses) refers to the first five books of the Old Testament. Next, "the Prophets" refer to the books of Joshua, Judges, Samuel, Kings, Isaiah, Jeremiah, Ezekiel, and the Twelve (Minor Prophets). The third and final section of the Hebrew Old Testament contains all the remaining books, and the first of these is the book of Psalms. In Hebrew thought, one way of referring to the whole is to name the first in a list. By referring to "the Psalms" in this context, it is most likely that Luke was referring to all the rest of the books of the Old Testament, beginning with the book of Psalms.

This passage tells us something incredible: the entire Old Testament, from beginning to end, is fulfilled in Jesus. And in case we were in doubt, the book of Psalms is explicitly listed as one of those books that find their fulfillment in him. *According to Jesus*, when we read the book of Psalms, we are meant to be looking for passages that point ahead *to Jesus* for their ultimate fulfillment.

In this chapter we will begin our journey from the Old Testament context of the book of Psalms, to their New Testament fulfillment in Christ (chaps. 6, 7, and 8), and their application to the Christian life (chap. 9). We have seen that Jesus taught his followers to do this, but so did Paul. Speaking of the Old Testament Scriptures, the great apostle put it like this: "All Scripture is breathed out by God and profitable for teaching, for reproof, for correction, and for training in righteousness, that the man [or woman] of God may be complete, equipped for every good work" (2 Tim 3:16-17). According to the apostle Paul, if we read a psalm (or any other portion of the Old Testament, for that matter) and conclude that it is impractical or outdated, the problem is not with the psalm, but with us.

To put it differently, the Old Testament is incomplete on its own. Therefore, it should never be read on its own. But this doesn't mean we can just be "quarter Bible Christians" (who abandon the Old Testament), because without the Old Testament, the New Testament wouldn't make sense. Dutch theologian Herman Bavinck put it like this: "The Gospel is the fulfillment of the promises of the Old Testament. Without it, the Gospel hangs suspended in the air. The Old Testament is the pedestal on which the Gospel rests, and the root out of which it came forth."[1] In keeping with our treasure-hunting illustration, in these chapters we will gain some tools for the task of mining the Old Testament for gospel treasure—as Scripture that leads us to exult in what God has done for us in Christ.

Under the broad umbrella of "the Psalms and Christ," in this chapter we will notice that the Bible is not a random assortment of verses. The Bible tells a grand story from Genesis to Revelation, and that grand story has a particular focus: on God and his plan to redeem

---

[1]Herman Bavinck, *The Wonderful Works of God: Instruction in the Christian Religion According to the Reformed Confession* (Glenside, PA: Westminster Seminary Press, 2020), chap. 8, "Scripture and Confession." I am thankful to Nick Mitchell, who first alerted me to this excellent quotation.

a people from sin and for himself. While a court stenographer's job is to *exhaustively* record every word that is spoken while the court is in session, each biblical author *selectively* recorded information that suited their purpose of telling the story of God's redemption (cf. Deut 29:29). Therefore, this chapter will begin the journey of moving from the book of Psalms to Christ and the Christian life, with a focus on the big picture. We will do this under three headings that I first learned from the writings of Sidney Greidanus: redemptive-historical progression, promise-fulfillment, and contrast.[2]

REDEMPTIVE-HISTORICAL PROGRESSION

Understanding redemptive-historical progression. If you were to step into an elevator, and someone asked you to explain what the Bible is about, what would you say? Instinctively, your mind might begin to formulate some ideas, but you would quickly realize that you have seconds, not hours to explain. Along with many others, I suggest that the message of the entire Bible can be summarized under four headings: (1) creation (Gen 1–2); (2) fall (Gen 3); (3) redemption (Gen 3:15–Rev 19); (4) new creation (or consummation, Rev 20–22). From this, we notice that the bulk of the Bible's grand story—all but its first few and last few chapters—fall under the umbrella of "the story of redemption." Therefore, the main focus of the Bible is to tell the story of God redeeming a people for himself.[3] This began with his word of promise in Genesis 3:15 (of a seed of the woman who would crush the serpent's head), it continued through the Old Testament as a whole, was fulfilled in the person and work of Jesus Christ, and will find its consummation in the new heavens and the new earth, set forth in the final chapters of Revelation.

---

[2]See Sidney Greidanus, *Preaching Christ from the Old Testament: A Contemporary Hermeneutical Method* (Grand Rapids, MI: Eerdmans, 1999), 203-78.

[3]For another explanation of redemptive-historical progression, see Greidanus, *Preaching Christ from the Old Testament*, 203-6.

As a first step, it is important to plot the Old Testament text on a timeline of redemptive history:

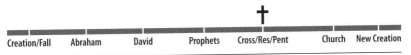

| Creation/Fall | Abraham | David | Prophets | Cross/Res/Pent | Church | New Creation |

Figure 6.1. Redemptive history

As we interpret the book of Psalms, we can notice that a given passage may fit in numerous places on our grid, but all of them will be prior to the cross. What do I mean? We have seen that seventy-three of the individual psalms were written by King David, so we can easily place them on our timeline. However, the book of Psalms received its final shape in the centuries leading up to Christ. Therefore, we also need to interpret with a sensitivity that the "canoniclers"—those who gave the book its final shape—may have intended meaning in the psalm's placement in the larger book. We saw earlier that this was done under the inspiration of the Holy Spirit. In this place, we can simply notice that the human author wrote at one point on this timeline, and the human compiler(s) did their work at a later point on this timeline, while the divine author was involved from start to finish.

After we have charted our passage on the biblical timeline, we can begin to move from the Old Testament to Christ. But as we do, we need to notice that redemptive history moves toward a fulfillment in Christ before its goal in consummation/new creation is realized. Specifically, if we were to read the Gospels with a focus on their timeline, we would find that a third to a half of each Gospel is focused on the last few weeks of Jesus' life. I would put it like this: the focal point of redemptive history consists in five key events: (1) the cross (and death) of Jesus; (2) the burial of Jesus; (3) the resurrection of Jesus; (4) the ascension of Jesus; and (5) the gift of the Holy Spirit on Pentecost. This is the fivefold fulfillment focus of the majority of the Old Testament hope.

This means that as we move on our timeline from the Old Testament passage to its application to the church and the individual Christian, we need to do so in light of the cross. Instead of an arched line that moves from the Old Testament context, over the cross, and to the Christian and the church, we need to think in terms of a straight line from the Old Testament context, to its fulfillment at the focal point of redemptive history (chaps. 6, 7, and 8 of this book), and then think about its application to the Christian (chap. 9 of this book).

Another way of thinking about the movement from the Old Testament passage, through Christ, to Christian application, is the following illustration of an hourglass:

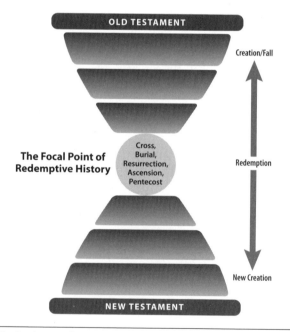

Figure 6.2. The focal point of redemptive history

When I go to the doctor, he sometimes sits me down, picks up a rubber mallet (the small ones that doctors use), and hits the tendon below my kneecap. My instant reaction is to kick. As whole-Bible

Christians, we need to develop a "knee-jerk" reaction: to think about how our Old Testament passage was fulfilled in the focal point of redemptive history (also called "salvation history") before we think about how it applies to our life, or the life of our local church.

Unpacking redemptive-historical progression: Psalms 90 and 136. Now that we have noticed that the biblical timeline can be summarized as the story of redemptive history, we can apply this to our study of the book of Psalms. For our purposes, I am going to model the interpretive tools we have learned by looking at two kinds of psalms. Because of space, for the first type we will return to Psalm 90 and simply notice that its speaker was Moses, and in it he reflected on the wilderness wanderings recorded in the book of Numbers. The hope of these wanderers was *adonay* (Ps 90:1-6), and the cause of these wanderings was also their God (Ps 90:7-12). The psalm ends with an imperative cry: "Return, O Lord! How long? / Have pity on your servants! / Satisfy us in the morning with your steadfast love, / that we may rejoice and be glad all our days. / Make us glad for as many days as you have afflicted us, / and for as many years as we have seen evil" (Ps 90:13-15).[4] In the context of the psalm's original *composition*, this was a clear appeal for the end of the wilderness wanderings, and the beginning of their anticipated new life in the Promised Land.

It is easy to plot Psalm 90 on our timeline of redemptive history: its original setting was between Abraham and David, likely around 1400 BC, just after the exodus from Egypt. However, in light of its new context in the book of Psalms, we can also plot Psalm 90 in a second place on our timeline. We may recall from part one of this book that Psalm 90 is the first psalm in book 4, and this section reflects on the life of the exiled people of God. Book 4 begins with

---

[4]Note that the psalm continues with a few more verses, but vv. 13-15 offer a helpful summary of their content.

Psalm 90 and its reflection on the first wilderness wanderings. This psalm of Moses was, therefore, reappropriated for a new situation of a second wilderness period for the people of God. So Psalm 90 can also be plotted on our timeline somewhere between the prophets and the time of Christ.

As we move from Psalm 90 to our "knee-jerk" reaction of thinking about its fulfillment in Christ, we can notice that Jesus embodied Israel. And Jesus' forty days of fasting in the wilderness—which corresponded to Israel's forty years of wandering in the wilderness—were capped off by overcoming temptation (cf. Mt 4:1-11 and parallels). Where Israel failed, Jesus was tested and found faithful. While Israel deserved *eternal* wilderness, Jesus chose to endure the *ultimate* wilderness *for them*, so that they could be eternally delivered to the new heavens and new earth.[5] This was accomplished because after proving himself faithful at the beginning of his ministry with a brutal wilderness experience (cf. Mt 4:1-11), Jesus endured the ultimate wilderness experience (outside the gates of the city, Heb 13:12) in his crucifixion and burial. While he was bearing the Father's wrath that our sins deserved (cf. Is 53:4-6), he was purchasing forgiveness for all who would turn from their sin and trust his redeeming work for them.

The wilderness experience of Christ (on the cross and in the grave) then leads us to powerful Christian application. Although in this life we are called to take up our cross (an instrument of shameful capital punishment) and follow Jesus—implying that the Christian life will not be easy—and although the Christian's life will be one of

---

[5]Admittedly, there is some overlap here, as I employ typology in places. However, as Sidney Greidanus argues, the various categories for moving from the Old Testament to Christ and Christian application are not meant to be isolated from one another. Instead, the overlap between the categories should be noticed, employed, and celebrated. For example, he explicitly states that redemptive-historical progression is "the foundational and most general of the seven ways of preaching Christ from the Old Testament," and that "it can frequently be explicated more precisely in one of the other ways such as promise-fulfilment, typology, or longitudinal themes" (Greidanus, *Preaching Christ from the Old Testament*, 308).

simultaneous tears (because they live in a fallen world and because the world will not like their allegiance to Christ) and joy (because they live under the favor of God and because their eternity is sure), the outcome of the Christian life will be the opposite of wilderness:

> Then I saw a new heaven and a new earth, for the first heaven and the first earth had passed away, and the sea was no more. And I saw the holy city, new Jerusalem, coming down out of heaven from God, prepared as a bride adorned for her husband. And I heard a loud voice from the throne saying, "Behold, the dwelling place of God is with man. He will dwell with them, and they will be his people, and God himself will be with them as their God. He will wipe away every tear from their eyes, and death shall be no more, neither shall there be mourning, nor crying, nor pain anymore, for the former things have passed away." And he who was seated on the throne said, "Behold, I am making all things new." (Rev 21:1-5a)

What a hope!

More briefly, there is a particular type of psalm that actually *re-hearses* redemptive history. For example, after its opening call to "Give thanks to the LORD, for he is good, / for his steadfast love endures forever" (Ps 136:1), Psalm 136 reflects on the eternal *hesed* of YHWH from creation, through the exodus and wilderness wanderings, to the early conquest of the Promised Land:

> 5 to him who by understanding made the heavens,
>> for his steadfast love endures forever;
> 6 to him who spread out the earth above the waters,
>> for his steadfast love endures forever;
> 7 to him who made the great lights,
>> for his steadfast love endures forever;
> 8 the sun to rule over the day,
>> for his steadfast love endures forever;
> 9 the moon and stars to rule over the night,
>> for his steadfast love endures forever;

10 to him who struck down the firstborn of Egypt,
   for his steadfast love endures forever;
11 and brought Israel out from among them,
   for his steadfast love endures forever;
12 with a strong hand and an outstretched arm,
   for his steadfast love endures forever;
13 to him who divided the Red Sea in two,
   for his steadfast love endures forever;
14 and made Israel pass through the midst of it,
   for his steadfast love endures forever;
15 but overthrew Pharaoh and his host in the Red Sea,
   for his steadfast love endures forever;
16 to him who led his people through the wilderness,
   for his steadfast love endures forever;
17 to him who struck down great kings,
   for his steadfast love endures forever;
18 and killed mighty kings,
   for his steadfast love endures forever;
19 Sihon, king of the Amorites,
   for his steadfast love endures forever;
20 and Og, king of Bashan,
   for his steadfast love endures forever;
21 and gave their land as a heritage,
   for his steadfast love endures forever;
22 a heritage to Israel his servant,
   for his steadfast love endures forever.
23 It is he who remembered us in our low estate,
   for his steadfast love endures forever;
24 and rescued us from our foes,
   for his steadfast love endures forever;
25 he who gives food to all flesh,
   for his steadfast love endures forever.
26 Give thanks to the God of heaven,
   for his steadfast love endures forever. (Ps 136:5-26)

We can apply this in a similar manner as Psalm 90. However, it was important to notice that various psalms actually rehearse redemptive history in this manner. These psalms also give Christians encouragement to sing and/or pray the sweep of redemptive history as they gather together.

PROMISE-FULFILLMENT

Understanding promise-fulfillment. The next way of moving from the Old Testament to Christ and Christian application is the way of promise-fulfillment. We have already noticed that the Old Testament can be summed up under the umbrella "promises made," and the New Testament can be summed up as "promises kept." This means that when we are looking at an Old Testament passage, promise-fulfillment will often be an important consideration. Baker offers a helpful definition:

> The term "promise" refers to a [divine] assurance of something to be done or not done in the future, which may be expressed in a formal announcement or agreement, or implied in an action or attitude. It includes specific predictions of the future and also more general prophecies that have implications fully worked out only in the New Testament.[6]

Building on this, Greidanus adds an important insight: God usually fills up his promises progressively, in installments.[7] Perhaps the best way to reinforce these things is to unpack an example.

---

[6]David L. Baker, *Two Testaments, One Bible: A Study of the Theological Relationship Between the Old and New Testaments*, 3rd ed. (Downers Grove, IL: InterVarsity Press, 2010), 200. More broadly, Walter Kaiser put it like this: "My definition of the promise-plan of God would be as follows: The promise-plan is God's word of declaration, beginning with Eve and continuing on through history, especially in the patriarchs and the Davidic line, that God would continually be in his person and do in his deeds and works (in and through Israel, and later the church) his redemptive plan as his means of keeping that promised word alive for Israel, and thereby for all who subsequently believed. All in that promised seed were called to act as a light for all the nations so that all the families of the earth might come to faith and to new life in the Messiah." Walter C. Kaiser Jr., *The Promise-Plan of God: A Biblical Theology of the Old and New Testaments* (Grand Rapids, MI: Zondervan, 2008), 19.

[7]See Greidanus, *Preaching Christ from the Old Testament*, 242.

Unpacking promise-fulfillment: Psalm 89. Although its fifty-two verses mean that Psalm 89 is quite lengthy, for our purposes we can summarize its contents and quote the portions most relevant to our study of promise-fulfilment in the Psalms. We have seen that in the canonical shape of the book of Psalms, Psalm 89 caps off the lament for exile in book 3 with tears over one of its greatest tragedies: the loss of a king on David's throne. But as we look carefully at this psalm as a whole, we see that it also contains great promises that will find their ultimate fulfillment in Christ.

Psalm 89 is a *maskil* of Ethan the Ezrahite, who would sing of the *hesed* of YHWH forever (v. 1). Ethan then recalled YHWH's promise to David from 2 Samuel 7: "You have said, 'I have made a covenant with my chosen one; / I have sworn to David my servant: / 'I will establish your offspring forever, / and build your throne for all generations.' *Selah*" (Ps 89:3-4). Although 2 Samuel 7 did not use the word *covenant* to describe YHWH's promise to David, these verses confirm that this is exactly what was initiated in that story. And in his context of exile, Ethan began his psalm by recalling this great covenant promise of YHWH: David's throne would be built for all generations.

After reveling in YHWH's sovereignty over creation, along with his faithful use of that power for his people and his king (vv. 5-18), Ethan reflected on the initial call of David:

19 Of old you spoke in a vision to your godly one, and said:
  "I have granted help to one who is mighty;
  I have exalted one chosen from the people.
20 I have found David, my servant;
  with my holy oil I have anointed him,
21 so that my hand shall be established with him;
  my arm also shall strengthen him.
22 The enemy shall not outwit him;
  the wicked shall not humble him.

23 I will crush his foes before him
and strike down those who hate him.

24 My faithfulness and my steadfast love shall be with him,
and in my name shall his horn be exalted." (Ps 89:19-24)

Ethan also recalled YHWH's promise that his *hesed* and his covenant would be kept for David forever, and that his offspring would be established on his throne as the days of the heavens (vv. 28-29) before addressing what YHWH would do if his successors broke the covenant:

30 If his children forsake my law
and do not walk according to my rules,

31 if they violate my statutes
and do not keep my commandments,

32 then I will punish their transgression with the rod
and their iniquity with stripes,

33 but I will not remove from him my steadfast love
or be false to my faithfulness.

34 I will not violate my covenant
or alter the word that went forth from my lips.

35 Once for all I have sworn by my holiness;
I will not lie to David.

36 His offspring shall endure forever,
his throne as long as the sun before me.

37 Like the moon it shall be established forever,
a faithful witness in the skies. *Selah* (Ps 89:30-37)

No matter what happened, YHWH would be faithful to these covenant promises.

In the context of these thirty-seven verses of reveling in YHWH's sovereignty, covenant promises, and faithfulness, Ethan turned to his context of exile, and deeply lamented the loss of a king on David's throne: "But now you have cast off and rejected; / you are full of wrath against your anointed. / You have renounced the covenant with your servant; / you have defiled his crown in the dust. . . . / You have made his splendor to cease / and cast his throne to the ground" (Ps 89:38-39, 44). This is honest, direct, and horrified language that describes the unthinkable: YHWH had cast off and rejected; YHWH was full of wrath against his anointed king; YHWH had renounced his covenant with his servant, the king; YHWH had defiled his crown in the dust; YHWH had made his splendor to cease; and YHWH had cast his throne to the ground. No wonder Ethan cried out: "How long, O Lord? Will you hide yourself forever? / How long will your wrath burn like fire? . . . / Lord, where is your steadfast love of old, / which by your faithfulness you swore to David?" (Ps 89:46, 49). Finally, the psalm concludes by calling on Adonai/YHWH to remember his people's suffering in mockery by their enemies, followed by a doxology that concludes the larger section of psalms (Ps 89:52, concluding Ps 73–89).

We have noticed that God's Old Testament promises are often filled up in installments, before they are ultimately fulfilled in Christ. From the perspective of Psalm 89 and the underlying covenant promise of a Davidic king on the throne, however, the Old Testament portion of these installments had already been accomplished, leading from David, to Solomon, to the line of kings in their descent. This psalm, therefore, looked back on a sure promise from 2 Samuel 7, and then wept over the curse for Israel's covenant breaking: "The Lord will bring you *and your king whom you set over you* to a nation that neither you nor your fathers have known. And there you shall serve other gods of wood and stone" (Deut 28:36, emphasis added). But the psalm also approached this curse for covenant breaking with hope, because David's "offspring shall endure forever, / his throne as long as the sun before me" (Ps 89:36). In other words, Psalm 89 also reflected the promise of restoration for covenant repentance (Deut 30:1-10) and its specific application to the king.

As readers of the lament section of this psalm, we see that the psalmist and subsequent generations of God's people lived in tension, because this promise hung in the air. In fact, there would be no king on David's throne until almost six hundred years later, when One was born as king of the Jews (Mt 2:2), who would later face trial as king of the Jews (Mt 27:11), and then die as king of the Jews (Mt 27:37). Far from a "this-worldly" kingship and kingdom (cf. Jn 18:36), Jesus would conquer through weakness and death. But in his resurrection, he displayed his victory over sin and death, and after his ascension he was seated on *the cosmic throne*, at the right hand of God (e.g., Heb 12:2, cf. Ps 110:1). Praise God that the promise recalled in Psalm 89 has been fulfilled by Jesus, so that the tragedy rehearsed in Psalm 89 has been reversed.

CONTRAST

Understanding contrast. As we move from any Old Testament text to Christ and Christian application, we need to notice that there is both continuity and discontinuity between the testaments. Greidanus explains: "Because of the progression in the histories of redemption and revelation, it should not come as a surprise that the message of an Old Testament text will sometimes stand in contrast to that of the New Testament."[8] One reason contrast is important is that the Messiah, Jesus Christ, is *better* than any Old Testament deliverer. To illustrate another reason contrast is important, Baker alerts us to some differences between Old Testament Israel and the New Testament church: "the former was a nation ruled by judges and kings living in a land with geographical boundaries, whereas the latter is an international spiritual community living throughout the world (and even beyond it, if the 'communion of saints' is taken to include the departed)."[9]

---

[8]Greidanus, *Preaching Christ from the Old Testament*, 271.
[9]Baker, *Two Testaments, One Bible*, 228.

In appendix E (found in an online PDF at www.ivpress.com /treasuring-the-psalms), I have included a long quote by Bruce Waltke about the imprecatory psalms—the ones in which the psalmist asks YHWH to justly exercise vengeance on his earthly oppressors. After a very thorough explanation of these "troubling psalms" in their Old Testament context, Waltke concludes:

> Though theologically sound, these petitions for retribution are nevertheless inappropriate for the church in the present dispensation for the following reasons. (1) Ultimate justice occurs in the eschaton (Rev. 20:11-15; cf. Isa. 61:1-2 with Matt. 13:30; 25:46; Luke 4:18-20; John 15:15; 2 Cor. 6:2; 2 Thess. 1:5-9). (2) Sin and sinner are now more distinctly differentiated (cf. Eph. 6:11-18), allowing the saint both to hate sin and love the sinner. (3) The saint's struggle is against spiritual powers of darkness. He conquers by turning the other cheek and by praying for the forgiveness of enemies (Matt. 5:39-48; 6:14; Luke 6:28, 35; Acts 7:60)[10]

I commend Waltke's entire quote for a more thorough explanation, but I suggest that in light of the discontinuity between the testaments in this regard, contrast is a helpful way of describing the way the imprecations were appropriately used in the life of the Old Testament saint, but should not be similarly used in the life of the New Testament Christian.

Unpacking contrast: Psalm 51. This is not the place to offer a thorough exposition of this great repentance psalm. For now, we will simply notice the setting from the psalm's superscription: "To the choirmaster. A Psalm of David, when Nathan the prophet went to him, after he had gone in to Bathsheba" (Ps 51:0). The horrible setting was David's adultery with Bathsheba, and his murder of her husband, Uriah. The psalm offers us a glorious model of repentance that is directly applicable to the believer's life (see chap. 9 and the discussion

---

[10]Bruce K. Waltke and Charles Yu, *An Old Testament Theology: An Exegetical, Canonical, and Thematic Approach* (Grand Rapids, MI: Zondervan, 2007), 880.

of direct application, along with part three of this book). But as we think first of the skinny part of our hourglass illustration—of the "knee-jerk" reaction to think in terms of Christ and the focal point of redemptive history—we need to say something glorious first: Jesus is a better covenant head than David. David was a great king, even the greatest king in Israel's history, but he was also a sinner who committed some horrible sins. And he was not merely an imperfect *model*, his sin also negatively impacted the people under his rule (cf. 2 Sam 24:10-16). But Christ is a perfect covenant head. He was tested and proved faithful (cf. Mt 4:1-10); he has been tempted, but is still without sin (cf. Heb 4:15). There is a glorious *contrast* between David and Jesus. This means that there is also a glorious *contrast* between the way God dealt with his Old Testament people, and the way he deals with New Testament believers in Jesus.

DISCUSSION QUESTIONS

1. The author suggested a key difference between a court stenographer and the authors of the biblical books. What is that difference, and how does it impact the way we read the Bible?

2. The author suggested an "elevator speech"–type summary of the entire Bible's storyline. What was that summary?

3. The author argued that a first step in moving from a psalm to Christ and Christian application, is to plot its place on a timeline of redemptive history. He then suggested that each psalm could be plotted in *two* places. Explain what he meant.

4. Explain the "knee-jerk" reaction the author argued is essential to consider *before* moving from the psalm to its application in the Christian life.

5. What is the focal point of redemptive history? Why is this "skinny part of the hourglass" so significant as we consider how to move from the Old Testament to Christ and Christian application?

6. The author illustrated the way of redemptive-historical progression by unpacking Psalm 90. Recount some of the points he made. Did you find any of these points particularly helpful?

7. In the discussion of promise-fulfillment, the author suggested (with Greidanus) that God often fills up his promises progressively, in instalments. Explain and illustrate this logic.

8. Why is contrast an essential consideration when moving from the Old Testament to Christ and Christian application? Give an example from the book of Psalms that supports your answer.

7

The Psalms and Christ, Part Two

IN THIS CHAPTER, WE CONTINUE TO explore ways to legitimately move from the book of Psalms to Christ and Christian application. So far we have explored three: redemptive-historical progression, promise-fulfillment, and contrast. Now we will look at three more: typology, direct prophecy, and typological prophecy.

TYPOLOGY

Understanding typology. The English word *typology* comes from the Greek word *typos* (τύπος), which can have the following range of meanings: "form, likeness, model, type."[1] When New Testament authors spoke of an Old Testament passage as a "type," they were affirming that God intentionally worked in patterns throughout redemptive history. Since God is sovereign (in control), he could do this. And since the Bible can be summarized as the story of his work of redeeming a people for himself, it makes sense that he would do this. By working in these patterns over past centuries, he was preparing our minds to make sense of his later actions. Jason S. DeRouchie explains further:

> The author of Hebrews said the Old Testament law was "a shadow
> of the good things to come" (Heb 10:1), and Paul spoke similarly

---

[1] No author listed, "τύπος," NIDNTTE 4:505.

(Col 2:16-17). In the New Testament, these anticipations and pointers are called "types" or "examples" (Rom 5:14; 1 Cor 10:6) that in turn find their counter in Jesus as their ultimate realization. God structured the progressive development of salvation-history in such a way that certain Old Testament characters (e.g., Adam, Melchizedek, Moses, David), events (e.g., the flood, the exodus, the return to the land), and institutions or objects (e.g., the Passover lamb, the temple, the priesthood) bear meanings that clarify and predictively anticipate the Messiah's life and work.[2]

In light of this, as we read the Old Testament we should be on the lookout for types—characters, events, and institutions or objects— that point to Christ (or even Christians).

When we speak about types (or typology), we can think in terms of the "type" (pattern from the Old Testament) and its "antitype" (New Testament fulfillment in Christ and/or Christians). But even within the Old Testament itself, God's work in history often took the same pattern as his previous work. For example, the promise of a return from Babylonian exile was set forth as a *new exodus* in the prophets (e.g., Is 11–12). However, the ultimate return from exile did not take place until the focal point of redemptive history, when Jesus won the victory over the ultimate slavery of sin, death, and hell, for us. In the New Testament, Jesus performed the new exodus; he was the new Moses, the new David, the new temple; and his work will ultimately usher in a new heavens and a new earth. We can

---

[2] Jason S. DeRouchie, "Redemptive-Historical Christocentric Approach," in *Five Views of Christ in the Old Testament: Genre, Authorial Intent, and the Nature of Scripture*, ed. Brian J. Tabb and Andrew M. King (Grand Rapids, MI: Zondervan Academic, 2022), 189. For more on typology, see especially James M. Hamilton Jr., *Typology: Understanding the Bible's Promise-Shaped Patterns* (Grand Rapids, MI: Zondervan Academic, 2022); Sidney Greidanus, *Preaching Christ from the Old Testament: A Contemporary Hermeneutical Method* (Grand Rapids, MI: Eerdmans, 1999), 90-98; 249-61. It is important to note that typology is different from allegory. Baker explains: "Typology consists in the comparison of facts. Allegory is not concerned with the facts but with the words from which it draws out useful and hidden doctrine." David L. Baker, *Two Testaments, One Bible: A Study of the Theological Relationship Between the Old and New Testaments*, 3rd ed. (Downers Grove, IL: InterVarsity Press, 2010), 180.

understand the fullness of these things (antitype) as we first understand the Old Testament pattern (type).

Although this is a bit of a mouthful, it will make more sense when we unpack typology in just a minute. Before we do that, we can make a two more observations. First—and in line with what we said in our previous chapter—this affirms that it is impossible to have an in-depth understanding of the gospel if we do not first understand the Old Testament. There is a richness that is lost if we are not whole-Bible Christians. Second, since the person and work of Jesus (the antitype) is *better* than the Old Testament pattern (the type), we will see *escalation* between the type and the antitype: the antitype is *better* than the type.

Unpacking typology: Psalm 72. Now that we have explained typology, we can unpack it with an example from the book of Psalms. In a previous chapter, we noticed that Psalm 72 is an "Of Solomon" psalm that may have been written as a prayer of David for Solomon (cf. Ps 72:20). Whatever the case, this is a psalm that celebrates and calls on YHWH to bless Israel's king (Ps 72:1-11, 15-17), as it also expresses a few reasons this ought to occur (Ps 72:12-14). It then concludes with a benediction that caps off all of book 2 (Ps 72:18-19, to conclude Ps 42–72), and a statement that summarizes all the psalms from books 1 and 2 (Ps 72:20, to conclude Ps 1–72). For our purposes, simply reading the first few and last few verses of the psalm will set us up to consider some ways that it functions typologically:

Of Solomon.
1 Give the king your justice, O God,
  and your righteousness to the royal son!
2 May he judge your people with righteousness,
  and your poor with justice! . . .
18 Blessed be the LORD, the God of Israel,
  who alone does wondrous things.
19 Blessed be his glorious name forever;

may the whole earth be filled with his glory!

Amen and Amen!

20 The prayers of David, the son of Jesse, are ended.

(Ps 72:0-2, 18-20)

If we are thinking in terms of direct correspondence to our lives, Psalm 72 has little to no relevance: it is about an ancient king who no longer rules over the covenant people of Israel. However, as we noticed in our earlier discussion of Psalm 89, the *promise* of a perpetual king on David's throne was fulfilled by Jesus. Therefore, the celebration of Israel's king in Psalm 72 should be *typologically* applied to Jesus.

In fact, as Christians we can legitimately insert the name *Jesus* beside *king* in the psalm, as we reflect on the various ways its statements have been typologically fulfilled in our Lord. Although I will leave it to readers to do this for the psalm as a whole, as we make a few connections we notice that its fulfillment in our Savior puts the psalm into a higher key. What I mean is this: since Jesus is much *better* than David, Solomon, or any of their successors, many of the lines of the psalm will need to be put in a higher key as we reflect on their fulfillment. For example, the various prayers in the psalm can be replaced with words of thanksgiving for their greater fulfillment in King Jesus: "Thank you that you have given King Jesus your justice, O God, and your righteousness to the royal Son!" (v. 1). At the same time, these prayers for the Old Testament king can also be addressed to YHWH about King Jesus with a greater surety, because while the Old Testament king was a sinful Israelite, Jesus is the sinless Son of God who never makes mistakes in his reign: "May King Jesus judge your people with righteousness, and your poor with justice!" (v. 2). Again, the confidence in those who pray this psalm is heightened in correspondence with the absolute perfection of Jesus and his reign. Psalm 72 is a prayer for the ancient king, and it is also typologically fulfilled by King Jesus.

DIRECT PROPHECY

Understanding direct prophecy in the book of Psalms. While the Old Testament could be summarized under the heading *promises made,* sometimes those promises were communicated through prophets. Wayne Grudem helpfully summarizes what the Bible teaches about prophecy and prophets:

> Prophecy is the most common means God used to communicate with people throughout biblical history. The story of prophecy, from Genesis to Revelation, is the story of God speaking to people through human messengers, and thus it is the story of God's varying relationships with his people and with others. Speaking through the prophets, God guided kings and people by telling them how to act in specific situations, warned people when they disobeyed him, predicted events that he would bring about, interpreted events when they came about, and demonstrated that he alone was both ruler of history and a God who relates personally to his people.[3]

When most of us think about prophecy, we think first of predictions about the future, but with Grudem we can observe that this is only one element of prophecy. Old Testament prophets did so much more than simply predict. They were *forth-tellers* of the Word of God, even more often than they were *foretellers* of what was to come in the future. As we come to the book of Psalms, I can only see one clear prophetic passage, and we will unpack it in detail next. In this case, it is a future-predictive *foretelling* of a glorious Coming One.

Unpacking direct prophecy: Psalm 110. In this section, I will explain why I believe that Psalm 110 is the only direct prophecy in the entire book of Psalms. For now, let's read it together:

A Psalm of David.

1 The LORD says to my Lord:

---

[3]Wayne Grudem, "Prophecy, Prophets," in *New Dictionary of Biblical Theology* (Downers Grove, IL: InterVarsity, 2000), 701.

"Sit at my right hand,
  until I make your enemies your footstool."
2 The LORD sends forth from Zion
  your mighty scepter.
  Rule in the midst of your enemies!
3 Your people will offer themselves freely
  on the day of your power,
  in holy garments;
  from the womb of the morning,
  the dew of your youth will be yours.
4 The LORD has sworn
  and will not change his mind,
  "You are a priest forever
  after the order of Melchizedek."
5 The Lord is at your right hand;
  he will shatter kings on the day of his wrath.
6 He will execute judgment among the nations,
  filling them with corpses;
  he will shatter chiefs
  over the wide earth.
7 He will drink from the brook by the way;
  therefore he will lift up his head. (Ps 110:0-7)

Why do I say this is the only direct prophecy in the entire book of Psalms? Because of the specific language used in verse 1. This doesn't come out clearly in English translations, but it is absolutely clear in the Hebrew. Let's walk through the entire psalm together and notice who the prophet is, why it is a prophecy, and what the prophecy is about.

First, notice who the prophet is: David. This is an "Of David" psalm. This may sound obvious at first, but as we read Psalm 110, it is very important to remember that its speaker is David. As we saw in chapter two, this transforms our reading of the entire psalm.

Second, after the superscription, the first three words of the psalm (in Hebrew) are most often translated, "The LORD says to my Lord." However, there is a precision in the wording of the Hebrew that must be *explained* in English; it is hard to bring into translation. The very first word in Hebrew is the noun *ne'um* (נְאֻם). This noun is most often translated with the English verb *says* in Psalm 110:1, but it is a noun that means something more than "to say." When coupled with the next word *YHWH*, this phrase means "a (prophetic) declaration of YHWH." In fact, the Hebrew phrase *ne'um* YHWH is used 268 times in the prophetic books, most often at the end of a prophetic announcement. The old King James Bible translated this phrase as: "thus saith the LORD." The sense of the term is this: "I, the prophet (e.g., Isaiah) have just spoken, but what I have just uttered was a prophetic declaration of YHWH. I was the mouthpiece, but he was the ultimate speaker." If David wanted to report a simple saying of YHWH, he could have used the more common Hebrew verb for "to say," but he chose this word because he was acting as a prophet, reporting a prophetic declaration of YHWH.

Now we can see why our earlier observation—that David was the speaker in the psalm—is so important. In this case, David was acting as a prophet. This is not unprecedented: in 2 Samuel 23:1, the last words of David are said to be a *ne'um* (נְאֻם, prophetic declaration) of David. Therefore, near the end of his life, David was cast in a prophetic role in 2 Samuel, and here in Psalm 110 he assumed the same role. If Saul could be numbered among the prophets prior to his rejection by YHWH (cf. 1 Sam 10:11), the great King David—who, unlike Saul, was *not* rejected by YHWH (cf. 2 Sam 7:15)—acted as a prophet on at least these two occasions.

We have noticed that David was the speaker and that he was acting as a prophet, reporting the prophetic declaration (*ne'um* [נְאֻם]) of YHWH. Now let's notice that YHWH's prophetic declaration was directed to someone. The Hebrew literally reads "to my lord." The word *to* tells us that the prophetic declaration was directed toward this person; the word *my* tells us that this person was specifically *David's* lord; and the word *lord* tells us something more. The Hebrew root *adon* (אָדוֹן) means "Lord, or master." This is a versatile Hebrew root that can be used for God as the Lord or master in relation to his people, and it can also be used of a human (or even angelic) lord or master. Whenever this word refers to God as divine Lord, it is spelled *adonay* (אֲדֹנָי), with an *ay* ending. And whenever this word refers to a human (or sometimes, angelic) lord, it is spelled with an *i* ending. So which is it? In Psalm 110:1, the prophetic declaration was made to David's *lord* (long *i* ending). So this psalm is clearly emphasizing the humanity of David's *lord*.[4]

As Christians who know how often the New Testament quotes this verse, and who know that it is speaking directly about Jesus, we may be tempted to panic, but there is no need. In fact, our careful reading of the Hebrew has significantly deepened our understanding. We would not have known that it was a clear prophetic declaration if not for a careful reading of the Hebrew. And the fact that the prophetic declaration was directed toward David's *human* lord is also not a problem, because the New Testament clearly teaches that Jesus is *both* fully human *and* fully divine. In fact, we'll see that David's (human) lord would also be exalted to the right hand of YHWH in Psalm 110—perhaps a hint at his *divine* status. Also, a quotation of Psalm 110:1 in the New Testament is often joined with a quotation of Daniel 7:13-14 and its vision of the Son of Man—one who comes with the clouds of heaven. I suggest that the vision of the fully human *and* fully divine Messiah is hinted at in both of these Old Testament texts and that it is clearly affirmed as New Testament authors employ them together.[5]

---

[4]For a more thorough explanation of this term, see Ian J. Vaillancourt, *The Multifaceted Saviour of Psalms 110 and 118: A Canonical Exegesis*, Hebrew Bible Monographs 86 (Sheffield, UK: Sheffield Phoenix, 2019), 95-98.

[5]For a thorough treatment of Jesus' use of Psalm 110:1 in one key New Testament passage, see Murray J. Smith and Ian J. Vaillancourt, "Enthroned and Coming to Reign: Jesus's Eschatological Use of Psalm 110:1 in Mark 14:62," *Journal of Biblical Literature* 141, no. 3 (2022): 513-31.

As we read on in the psalm, we find numerous indications that this human figure was also highly exalted. For starters, he was the lord of the greatest king in Israel's history. David bowed to him as master. Next, he would sit at the right hand of YHWH until YHWH made his enemies a footstool for his feet (v. 1b). Therefore, this lord was a cosmic king who would sit at the right hand (i.e., the place of power) of YHWH on the throne of the cosmos. In fact, the New Testament reveals that this verse was ultimately fulfilled when the resurrected Christ ascended to heaven and sat down at the right hand of God (e.g., Heb 8:1; 10:12; 12:2).

Since our current focus is on Psalm 110 as a *direct prophecy*, the rest of the psalm can be summarized more briefly. We have seen that YHWH invited David's lord to sit at his right hand (on the throne of the cosmos). This means that he was not *merely* David's lord, but he was also the Lord (with a capital "L") over all creation. We can also observe that his reign would continue *until* YHWH made his enemies a footstool for his feet. The picture is of a future time when his enemies would be completely subjected to him—something that will be fully realized at the second coming of Jesus.

In verses 2-3, David's lord had a willing and youthful army at his disposal, and he would be victorious. Then, in verse 4, David's lord was also said to be a priest, in the manner of Melchizedek. Just like the king-priest of Genesis 14 "crushed the power of earthly kings and ruled over nations,"[6] so it was with David's lord. In fact, Peter Gentry points out that the exalted picture of David's lord as a king and priest makes him a new and better Adam figure.[7] Just like the first Adam was cast as a priest in a garden-temple and a king who ruled over the earth, David's lord would do the same. In the case of David's lord, however, his kingly and priestly ministries would be

---

[6]Peter Gentry, "A Preliminary Evaluation and Critique of Prosopological Exegesis," *The Southern Baptist Journal of Theology* 23, no. 2 (2019): 116.

[7]See Gentry, "A Preliminary Evaluation and Critique of Prosopological Exegesis," 116.

realized (not lost like Adam's), and they would be *cosmic* (not localized like Adam's).[8]

Finally, Psalm 110 closes in verses 5-7 with the divine *adonay* (Lord) at the right hand of David's lord. This switch of positions—from David's lord at the right hand of YHWH in verse 1, to *adonay* (the Lord) at the right hand of David's lord—signals an offensive strike in which David's lord would be fighting, but the ultimate power would come from his divine Lord.[9] The vision is of end-times victory.

Along the way in this explanation of Psalm 110, I have shown that it ultimately points to Jesus as David's lord, as the divine-human Messiah (cf. Dan 7:13-14 coupled with Ps 110:1 in the New Testament), who was raised from the dead, ascended to heaven, and was seated at the right hand of the throne of God (e.g., Heb 8:1; 10:12; 12:2). At this location, Jesus would also mediate between his people and God (cf. Heb 4:14-16). And his place at God's right hand would continue *until* (Ps 110:1b) God made his enemies a footstool for his feet (Ps 110:2-3; 5-7), that is, the day of end-times victory and consummation. In New Testament terms, it will continue until the second coming of Jesus.

Although there is only one directly prophetic psalm in the book of Psalms, its importance means that it deserved attention in this book. From an Old Testament perspective, this psalm was clearly prophetic and clearly about a Savior to come who would be David's lord, as well as a cosmic king, priest, and victorious warrior. In light of its New Testament fulfillment, we know that this psalm is a direct prophecy about Jesus.

TYPOLOGICALLY PROPHETIC PSALMS

Understanding typologically prophetic psalms. So far in this chapter, we have explored typological psalms, and we have looked at directly

---

[8]For a more thorough explanation of Adam as priest-king in a garden sanctuary, see especially Peter J. Gentry and Stephen J. Wellum, *Kingdom Through Covenant: A Biblical-Theological Understanding of the Covenants,* 2nd ed. (Wheaton, IL: Crossway, 2018), 246-53, 340-42.

[9]For a more thorough explanation of Psalm 110 as a whole, see Vaillancourt, *The Multifaceted Saviour of Psalms 110 and 118,* 85-129.

prophetic psalms, but there is one more class worth considering, and it combines the two. Bruce Waltke explains what is meant by typologically prophetic psalms:

> David's sufferings and glory typify Jesus Christ, but sometimes his language transcends his own experience and finds its fulfillment in Jesus Christ (e.g., Pss. 2, 22). Select psalms that are clearly predictive are "They divide my garments among them and cast lots for my clothing" (22:18) and "He protects all of his bones, not one of them will be broken" (34:20).[10]

Waltke's distinction is important. As we are scanning the book of Psalms, we know that only one of them is directly prophetic, so there is no need to look for more prophetic material. But we are certainly looking for ways that, say, David is presented as a type, a pattern of Jesus Christ. As we do this, we are also going to find examples of elevated language that clearly go beyond the experience of the historical David. The solution is this: those sections speak in a

---

[10]Bruce K. Waltke and Charles Yu, *An Old Testament Theology: An Exegetical, Canonical, and Thematic Approach* (Grand Rapids, MI: Zondervan, 2007), 894. Perhaps Delitzsch was the first to coin the term "typical-prophetic." He wrote: "But there is also a class of Psalms which we call typico-prophetically Messianic, viz., those in which David, describing his outward and inward experiences,—experiences even in themselves typical,—is carried beyond the limits of his individuality and present condition, and utters concerning himself that which, transcending human experience, is intended to become historically true only in Christ. Such psalms are typical, in as much as their contents is grounded in the individual, but typical, history of David; they are, however, at the same time prophetic, in as much as they express present individual experience in laments, hopes, and descriptions which point far forward beyond the present and are only fully realised in Christ. The psychological possibility of such psalms has been called in question; but they would only be psychologically impossible, if one were obliged to suppose that David's self-consciousness must under such circumstances pass over into that of his antitype; but it is in reality quite otherwise. As the poet in order to describe his experiences in verse, idealises them, i.e., seizes the idea of them at the very root, and, stripping off all that is adventitious and insignificant, rises into the region of the ideal: so David also in these psalms idealises his experiences, which even in itself results in the reduction of them to all that is essential to their continuance as types. This he does, however, not from his own poetic impulse, but under the inspiration of the Spirit of God; and a still further result which follows from this is, that the description of his typical fortunes and their corresponding states of feeling is moulded into the prophetic description of the fortunes and feelings of his antitype." Franz Delitzsch, *Commentary on the Psalms*, 3 vols., trans. James Martin (Grand Rapids, MI: Eerdmans, 1976), 1:69-70. I was first pointed to this excellent Delitzsch quote by Bruce Waltke (personal correspondence).

typologically prophetic manner about the greater Son of David to come. Franz Delitzsch explains further:

> Such psalms are typical, in as much as their contents [are] grounded in the individual, but typical, history of David; they are, however, at the same time prophetic, in as much as they express present individual experience in laments, hopes, and descriptions which point far forward beyond the present and are only fully realised in Christ.[11]

Delitzsch adds that in these cases, David was *consciously* speaking under the inspiration of the Holy Spirit—he was *intentionally* idealizing his experiences—so that "the description of his typical fortunes and their corresponding states of feeling is molded into the prophetic description of the fortunes and feelings of his antitype."[12] Once again, they were clearly *meant* to point beyond David, to Jesus.

Unpacking typologically prophetic psalms: Psalm 22. Perhaps the best way to clarify what we mean by typologically prophetic psalms is to unpack an important example. Since Jesus cited Psalm 22 from the cross, this clearly deserves our attention. We can begin by reading Psalm 22 in its entirety, but as we do so, let's be looking for typologically prophetic content, for ideas that clearly go beyond the experience of the historical David, and seem to clearly and intentionally point to the greater Son of David to come, Jesus Christ:

> To the Choirmaster: According to the Doe of the Dawn. A Psalm
>   of David.
> 1 My God, my God, why have you forsaken me?
>   Why are you so far from saving me, from the words of my
>   groaning?
> 2 O my God, I cry by day, but you do not answer,
>   and by night, but I find no rest.
> 3 Yet you are holy,

---

[11]Delitzsch, *Commentary on the Psalms*, 1:69.
[12]Delitzsch, *Commentary on the Psalms*, 1:70.

enthroned on the praises of Israel.

4 In you our fathers trusted;

they trusted, and you delivered them.

5 To you they cried and were rescued;

in you they trusted and were not put to shame.

6 But I am a worm and not a man,

scorned by mankind and despised by the people.

7 All who see me mock me;

they make mouths at me; they wag their heads;

8 "He trusts in the LORD; let him deliver him;

let him rescue him, for he delights in him!"

9 Yet you are he who took me from the womb;

you made me trust you at my mother's breasts.

10 On you was I cast from my birth,

and from my mother's womb you have been my God.

11 Be not far from me,

for trouble is near,

and there is none to help.

12 Many bulls encompass me;

strong bulls of Bashan surround me;

13 they open wide their mouths at me,

like a ravening and roaring lion.

14 I am poured out like water,

and all my bones are out of joint;

my heart is like wax;

it is melted within my breast;

15 my strength is dried up like a potsherd,

and my tongue sticks to my jaws;

you lay me in the dust of death.

16 For dogs encompass me;

a company of evildoers encircles me;

they have pierced my hands and feet—

17 I can count all my bones—

they stare and gloat over me;

18 they divide my garments among them,

and for my clothing they cast lots.

19 But you, O LORD, do not be far off!

O you my help, come quickly to my aid!

20 Deliver my soul from the sword,

my precious life from the power of the dog!

21 Save me from the mouth of the lion!

You have rescued me from the horns of the wild oxen!

22 I will tell of your name to my brothers;

in the midst of the congregation I will praise you:

23 You who fear the LORD, praise him!

All you offspring of Jacob, glorify him,

and stand in awe of him, all you offspring of Israel!

24 For he has not despised or abhorred

the affliction of the afflicted,

and he has not hidden his face from him,

but has heard, when he cried to him.

25 From you comes my praise in the great congregation;

my vows I will perform before those who fear him.

26 The afflicted shall eat and be satisfied;

those who seek him shall praise the LORD!

May your hearts live forever!

27 All the ends of the earth shall remember

and turn to the LORD,

and all the families of the nations

shall worship before you.

28 For kingship belongs to the LORD,

and he rules over the nations.

29 All the prosperous of the earth eat and worship;

before him shall bow all who go down to the dust,

even the one who could not keep himself alive.

30 Posterity shall serve him;

it shall be told of the Lord to the coming generation;

31 they shall come and proclaim his righteousness to a people yet
    unborn,
  that he has done it. (Ps 22:0-31)

Did you pick out some phrases? There is a lot of material in this psalm that could be taken as simply typological. For example, it is entirely possible that David experienced what he described in verse 6: "But I am a worm and not a man, / scorned by mankind and despised by the people." At one and the same time, this verse portrays the experiences of historical David (the type), *and* it points to the greater Son of David to come (the antitype).

However, there is other material in Psalm 22 that seems to clearly go beyond the experience of the historical David. I suggest that verses 1, 14, and 16-18 fall into the category of typologically prophetic material. The following quote gathers all of this content into one place:

1 My God, my God, why have you forsaken me?
  Why are you so far from saving me, from the words of my
    groaning? . . .
14 I am poured out like water,
  and all my bones are out of joint;
  my heart is like wax;
  it is melted within my breast; . . .
16 For dogs encompass me;
  a company of evildoers encircles me;
  they have pierced my hands and feet—
17 I can count all my bones—
  they stare and gloat over me;
18 they divide my garments among them,
  and for my clothing they cast lots. (Ps 22:1, 14, 16-18)

I suggest that although David may have *felt* abandoned by God, as he opened this psalm he *consciously*, under the inspiration of the Holy Spirit, pointed beyond himself in a typologically prophetic manner.

This was confirmed when Jesus quoted Psalm 22:1 from the cross: "And about the ninth hour Jesus cried out with a loud voice, saying, 'Eli, Eli, lema sabachthani?' that is, 'My God, my God, why have you forsaken me?'" (Mt 27:46; cf. Mk 15:34). Although it seems very level-headed to suggest that David did not experience being forsaken by God in its fullness, no one would accuse Jesus of overstating his experience. It seems as though David was *consciously* speaking beyond his experience, in order to point to the day when Jesus *would* be forsaken by God as he bore our sin on the cross. Under the inspiration of the Holy Spirit, David wrote in a typologically prophetic manner.

The next example comes in verses 14 and 17. Although there is no explicit New Testament passage that cites these in reference to Jesus, I suggest that Jesus, not David, experienced the following: "I am poured out like water, / and all my bones are out of joint; / my heart is like wax; / it is melted within my breast. . . . / I can count all my bones—/ they stare and gloat over me" (Ps 22:14, 17). We can imagine that on the cross, Jesus' bones would have come out of joint, and when his side was pierced, they would have been exposed.

Next, verse 16 speaks of the piercing of David's hands and feet. While it is possible that David experienced this in hand-to-hand combat, it is more likely that he was consciously pointing to the experience of the coming Messiah. This is confirmed by various New Testament passages that speak of the crucifixion of Jesus (e.g., Lk 23:33), specifically of his piercing. For example: "And again another Scripture says, 'They will look on him whom they have pierced'" (Jn 19:37; cf. Lk 24:40; Jn 20:25). Although John 19:37 is a fulfillment of the prophecy recorded in Zechariah 12:10 (cf. Rev 1:7), the image also clearly comes from the typologically prophetic Psalm 22:16.

Finally, verse 18 speaks of the casting of lots for David's clothes. Although it is possible that this happened to David in his life, when the author of the fourth Gospel reported on this happening to Jesus while he hung on the cross, he called it a fulfillment of Scripture: "'Let us not tear it, but cast lots for it to see whose it shall be.' This was to fulfill the Scripture which says, 'They divided my garments among them, and for my clothing they cast lots'" (Jn 19:24, cf. Mt 27:35; Mk 15:24; Lk 23:34). Once again, in Psalm 22:18 David was consciously, under the inspiration of the Holy Spirit, writing of something that transcended his own experience: he was typologically-prophetically pointing to the future experience of the greater son of David to come.

In light of space restrictions, we are not able to walk through other examples. If we could, a clear candidate would be Psalm 16:8-11, which was cited by Peter on the day of Pentecost (Acts 2:25-28). In that place, Peter introduced the psalm quote with the phrase, "For David says *concerning him*" (Acts 2:25a, emphasis added). Apparently, Peter believed that David was speaking beyond his own experience (as one who *did* experience corruption; cf. Ps 16:10), and about Jesus, who did die, but who rose from the dead on the third day. In fact, I suggest that we could walk through the entire book of Psalms, looking for examples of both typology and typologically prophetic material. Although some argue that true typology or typologically prophetic material must be validated by a New Testament citation of the same material, I suggest that this need not be the case. As long as the passage from the Psalms clearly does point to an aspect of the person and work of Christ, we are meant to make the connection. Put differently, the New Testament is certainly the "answer key" to the Old Testament texts it quotes. However, it is not the *exhaustive* answer key; other connections from the Old Testament to Christ can and should be made.

DISCUSSION QUESTIONS

1. Explain what is meant by "typology."
2. Read Psalm 72 in its entirety and discuss ways each of its verses can be read typologically, with their ultimate fulfillment in Christ.

3. Summarize Grudem's definition of prophecy in your own words, and share it with your group.

4. What about Psalm 110 makes it a clear example of the only directly prophetic psalm?

5. Discuss the various ways Psalm 110 points to the person and work of Jesus Christ.

6. What is meant by "typologically prophetic" material in the book of Psalms?

7. Recount the various ways Psalm 22 can and should be read as typologically prophetic, as finding its ultimate fulfillment in Christ.

8

The Psalms and the
New Testament

IN OUR PREVIOUS TWO CHAPTERS, we noticed that on at least one occasion, Jesus taught that his suffering, death, and resurrection, along with their subsequent "good news" proclamation, were all spoken of in the Old Testament, including the book of Psalms (cf. Lk 24:25-27, 44-49). Baker moves the discussion forward:

> The Old Testament is an incomplete book. The New Testament, on the other hand, affirms the fulfillment of Old Testament hopes and promises. This affirmation does not imply that the Old Testament is obsolete, but rather that the New Testament is substantially dependent on Old Testament categories for understanding and expressing the events it records. The evidence suggests that this positive attitude to the Old Testament is not an innovation of the early church, but derives from Jesus himself.[1]

In this chapter, we will think about the way the New Testament authors cited the book of Psalms.

UNDERSTANDING THE PSALMS
IN THE NEW TESTAMENT

As we begin, we can notice something so simple it should be obvious: when a New Testament author quotes a psalm, we are given the inspired

---

[1]David L. Baker, *Two Testaments, One Bible: A Study of the Theological Relationship Between the Old and New Testaments*, 3rd ed. (Downers Grove, IL: InterVarsity Press, 2010), 267.

"answer key" for its interpretation. And this happens often. With reference to the New Testament use of the Old Testament as a whole, Sidney Greidanus points out that "depending on the criteria used, the number of quotations ranges from 250 to some 600, and the number of allusions from 650 to some 4,000."[2] Of course, this large range indicates that there is not scholarly agreement for every proposed New Testament quotation of or allusion to the Old Testament. However, since the New Testament was written as the fulfillment of the Old Testament, we can expect it to be filled with Old Testament quotes and allusions. As we noted in a previous chapter, this does not necessarily imply that the psalm's meaning will be exhausted by the New Testament citation. In fact, sometimes two different New Testament authors will quote a psalm with an emphasis on different truths that are both present in the Old Testament passage. This does mean that when we interpret the book of Psalms, it is important that we pay attention to the way a given passage is used in the New Testament.

Before we dive in, I commend using a reference Bible, or even Bible software, to help reinforce that the Scriptures are an interrelated whole. For example, reading the ESV Classic Reference Bible will provide thousands of links to other portions of God's Word. Personally, I use Accordance Bible Software for all of my academic work. This not only gives me instant access to cross-referenced Bibles (along with instant access to the verse being referenced, without having to turn a page), but it also allows me to perform my own searches of words or phrases. Whether we are reading the Bible in hard copy or harnessing the power of a digital platform, as we look up cross-references we are being led to think of the Bible as an organic whole, a book in which the various parts relate to one another.[3]

---

[2] See Sidney Greidanus, *Preaching Christ from the Old Testament: A Contemporary Hermeneutical Method* (Grand Rapids, MI: Eerdmans, 1999), 50-51.

[3] As good next steps resources for pastors and students, the following works are very important: Gregory K. Beale, *Handbook on the New Testament Use of the Old Testament: Exegesis and Interpretation* (Grand Rapids, MI: Baker Academic, 2012); Gregory K. Beale and Donald A. Carson,

UNPACKING THE PSALMS IN THE NEW TESTAMENT: PSALM 118 IN MATTHEW 21–26[4]

As a way of illustrating the New Testament use of the book of Psalms, we will focus on Psalm 118 and notice the way the Evangelist used the psalm in the latter portion of Matthew's Gospel. Psalm 118 is a good choice for our purposes: it is the most cited psalm in the New Testament. Up to eighteen of its verses are cited or alluded to in twenty to sixty New Testament passages.[5] In the Gospel of Matthew alone, Psalm 118 was shouted (*krazō* [κράζω]) by the people at the entrance narrative, cried out (*krazō* [κράζω]) by the children at the temple cleansing (Mt 21:9, 15; citing Ps 118:25-26), quoted by Jesus as a condemnation of the chief priests and elders (Mt 21:42; citing Ps 118:22-23), invoked by Jesus at the end of his lament over Jerusalem (Mt 23:39; citing Ps 118:26), and implied by the author of Matthew as the last song on the lips of Jesus before he went to the cross (Mt 26:30; referring to the whole psalm).

Psalm 118 in Its Old Testament Context. Since we have already noticed some of the initial features of Psalm 118 in previous chapters, and since we will look at it in more depth in a later chapter, we can summarize our findings and then focus on its use in the New Testament. Psalm 118 is a psalm of thanksgiving for deliverance. Its

---

eds., *Commentary on the New Testament Use of the Old Testament* (Grand Rapids, MI: Baker Academic, 2007). The first of these resources proposes a helpful method for determining and interpreting occurrences of the New Testament use of the Old Testament, and the second resource is a book-by-book commentary on the New Testament passages that employ the Old Testament.

[4]Much of the material in this section first appeared in a more academic form in Ian J. Vaillancourt, "Psalm 118 and the Eschatological Son of David," *Journal of the Evangelical Theological Society* 62, no. 4 (2019): 721-38. This chapter's summary of that article is done with the permission of Andreas Köstenberger, when he was the editor of *JETS*.

[5]Of course, differing opinions on what constitutes an allusion or an echo accounts for the large disparity between twenty and sixty references. See Frank-Lothar Hossfeld and Erich Zenger, *Psalms 3: A Commentary on Psalms 101-150*, trans. Linda M. Maloney (Minneapolis, MN: Fortress, 2011), 245; Andrew C. Brunson, *Psalm 118 in the Gospel of John: An Intertextual Study on the New Exodus Pattern in the Theology of John* (Tübingen, Germany: Mohr Siebeck, 2003), 4. In that place Brunson cites Psalm 118:5, 6, 10-12, 15-26, 28c as passages likely alluded to or directly quoted in the NT.

speaker—and main subject—was the king, and this figure experienced battlefield deliverance by YHWH before he led a procession of thanks to the temple in Jerusalem. In that locale, the speaker in the psalm led the people in singing parts of the song of the first exodus (Ex 15) as they celebrated the current deliverance. When interpreted in its immediate and broader context in the book of Psalms, we noticed that Psalm 118 portrays the ideal *torah*-steeped king of Deuteronomy 17:14-20.[6] We also noticed that it portrayed a human deliverer who was a king and who cited the words of Moses, suggesting that the deliverance he enacted was to be thought of as a second exodus. This also hints that this figure may have been associated with the new and better "prophet like Moses" to come (cf. Deut 18:15-18; 34:10-12). At a time when God's people were looking for a messiah to accomplish ultimate deliverance for them, this figure was set forth as the ideal deliverer to come.

Psalm 118 Between the Testaments. Although it is not always necessary to notice the way a given psalm is used in the intertestamental period, sometimes this can provide helpful background before we move to the New Testament use of the psalm. In this place, we will look first at one writing that used Psalm 118 in an interesting way. Although this writing is not biblical and therefore not inspired by the Holy Spirit, it will at least give us an indication about how one group of Jews viewed Psalm 118. We will also look at the use of this psalm at various Jewish festivals in the time leading up to and during the life of Jesus.

The Aramaic Targums were interpretive renderings of the Old Testament for use in synagogue worship. Rather than exact translations of the original Hebrew, the Targums *interpreted* the Hebrew

---

[6]Cf. the work of Jamie Grant. See especially Jamie A. Grant, *The King as Exemplar: The Function of Deuteronomy's Kingship Law in the Shaping of the Book of Psalms*, ed. Adele Berlin, Society of Biblical Literature Academia Biblica Series 17 (Atlanta: Society of Biblical Literature, 2004).

and sometimes added content that was meant to lead people to "proper" (to them) interpretation. Again, this is not to say the Targums were inspired and authoritative. It is to say that they witness one way that at least one group of Jews in history read particular passages. Whereas verse 22 in the Hebrew text (Masoretic text, MT) of Psalm 118 begins, "the stone that the builders rejected," the Targum of Psalm 118:22-29 reads:

22) A youth was rejected by the builders. He was among the sons of Jesse and was entitled to be appointed king and ruler.

23) "This was from Yahweh," said the builders; "This is wonderful for us," said the sons of Jesse.

24) "This day Yahweh made," said the builders; "Let us rejoice and be glad in it," said the sons of Jesse.

25) "We pray you, Yahweh, save now," said the builders; "We pray you, give success now," said Jesse and his wife.

26) "Blessed is he who comes in the name of the Word of Yahweh," said the builders; "They will bless you from the temple of Yahweh," said David.

27) "God, Yahweh, illumine us," said the tribes of the house of Judah; "Tie the lamb with chains for a festival sacrifice until you have offered it and sprinkled its blood on the horns of the altar," said Samuel the prophet.

28) "You are my God and I will give thanks before you, my God, I will praise you," said David.

29) Samuel answered and said, "Praise (him), assembly of Israel, and give thanks before Yahweh for he is good, for his goodness is eternal."[7]

---

[7] As cited in Brunson, *Psalm 118 in the Gospel of John*, 39. See also Craig A. Evans, "Praise and Prophecy in the Psalter and in the New Testament," in *The Book of Psalms: Composition and Reception*, ed. Peter W. Flint et al. (Leiden: Brill, 2005), 559; John Goldingay, *Psalms Volume 3: 90-150* (Grand Rapids, MI: Baker Academic, 2008), 361.

Notice that the Jewish community responsible for the Targum of Psalm 118 associated it with David. In the very least, this is evidence that our reading of the speaker as king has coherence with at least one early Jewish community.

Next, the entire cluster of Psalms 113–118 received special prominence in the Jewish festivals in the centuries leading up to and during the New Testament period.[8] (Jews referred to Psalms 113–118 as "The Egyptian Hallel" because of its prominent exodus and praise themes; this cluster of psalms was employed to celebrate the first exodus and to anticipate a greater second exodus to come.) Psalms 113–118 were recited by Jews between eighteen and twenty-one days every year; according to one Jewish source, these psalms were employed "on the first two days of Passover, two days of the festival of Weeks, nine days of the festival of Tabernacles and the eight days of Hanukkah."[9] Since these psalms were the only portion of the Hebrew Old Testament associated with all three main festivals, many Jews would have known them by heart.[10]

For example, the festival of Sukkoth (Booths) ended with the imperative cry, *hoshiah na* (הוֹשִׁיעָה נָּא, "save, please," Ps 118:25) and "waving and beating the ground with branches of willow and palm (cf. Mishnah Sukk. 4:3-6)."[11] In fact, another Jewish writing adds some insight about the palm branch image: when Simon Maccabeus entered Jerusalem in 1 Maccabees 13:51, the Jews celebrated with palm branches. Back to Sukkoth, since this was a festival originally associated with kingship and authority during the monarchy, Brunson

---

[8]For a more thorough discussion of Psalms 113-118, see Ian J. Vaillancourt, *The Multifaceted Saviour of Psalms 110 and 118: A Canonical Exegesis*, Hebrew Bible Monographs 86 (Sheffield, UK: Sheffield Phoenix, 2019), 167-70.

[9]Solomon Zeitlin, "The Hallel: A Historical Study of the Canonization of the Hebrew Liturgy," *Jewish Quarterly Review* 53, no. 1 (1962): 22. See also James A. Sanders, "A New Testament Hermeneutic Fabric: Psalm 118 in the Entrance Narrative," in *Early Jewish and Christian Exegesis: Studies in Memory of William Hugh Brownlee*, ed. Craig A. Evans and William F. Stinespring (Atlanta: Scholars Press, 1987), 179.

[10]See Brunson, *Psalm 118 in the Gospel of John*, 82-84.

[11]Marvin H. Pope, "Hosanna," in *Anchor Yale Bible Dictionary*, ed. David Noel Freeman (New York: Doubleday, 1992), 3:291.

suggests that the people's longing for a king would have been intensified at this time.[12]

Psalms 113–118 were also prominent at Passover. At this festival, families sang Psalms 113–114 before the meal, and Psalms 115–118 after it.[13] According to the Hillelites, this was because Psalms 113–114 recalled YHWH's saving acts in the past, and Psalms 115–118 looked forward to future redemption.[14] This means that Psalm 118 was associated with a decisive intervention by YHWH at this festival as well.

While more detail could certainly be given, for our purposes we see that Psalms 113–118 were not only known and likely memorized by most Jews of this period, they were also loved and treasured. Since many of the festivals were associated with hope for end-times deliverance by YHWH, this provides more insight into the kind of question many Jews would have been asking: would a Davidic "coming one" appear who may begin as "a rejected stone/son," but who would ultimately lead God's people in singing Psalm 118 as his thankful song of victory? The evidence certainly suggests that this reading would have made sense to the popular Jewish mind in the first century AD.

Psalm 118 in Matthew 21–26. Now that we have laid this groundwork, we can explain the use of Psalm 118 in Matthew 21–26 in an efficient manner. The first time Psalm 118 appears in this Gospel is in the entrance and temple-cleansing narratives of Matthew 21:9, 15. In the Gospel of Matthew, this was Jesus' first recorded entry into Jerusalem since his public ministry began. From the Mount of Olives, Jesus sent his disciples into the village where they would find a donkey that should be brought to him. This is said to be a fulfillment of Zechariah 9:9, where the end-times vision had the humble king riding into Zion on a donkey. This means that the royal (Davidic) tone was set from the beginning.

---

[12]See Brunson, *Psalm 118 in the Gospel of John*, 53-54.
[13]See Steven R. Swanson, "Hallel," in *Anchor Yale Bible Dictionary*, ed. David Noel Freeman (New York: Doubleday, 1992), 3:30; R. T. France, *The Gospel of Matthew*, New International Commentary on the New Testament (Grand Rapids: Eerdmans, 2007), 996.
[14]See Brunson, *Psalm 118 in the Gospel of John*, 75.

Still, since Jesus was pictured as humble, this would have tempered the revolutionary (e.g., Maccabean) associations for the reader.[15]

The disciples spread their cloaks on the donkey, and then the crowd spread their cloaks on the road, while others cut branches from the trees and spread them on the road as well. Crowds that went before and that followed Jesus shouted words from Psalm 118:26a, with the Hosanna from Psalm 118:25a bracketing the saying: "Hosanna to the Son of David! Blessed is he who comes in the name of the Lord! Hosanna in the highest!" (Mt 21:9). The addition of "Son of David" on the lips of the crowd makes sense in light of our broader study of Psalm 118 in its book of Psalms, along with its "between the testaments" contexts. In Matthew 21:11 Jesus was also called "the prophet," an obvious allusion to the prophet like Moses who was promised in Deuteronomy 18:15, 18.[16]

Next, we find that Jesus enacted the entrance into the temple from Psalm 118. However, instead of leading in a song of victory (like the figure in the psalm), he cleansed the temple. But, if with his temple-cleansing actions Jesus may have called to mind the first act of the Maccabean revolt, his later victory through suffering and death would dim the revolutionary associations of the Maccabean-style temple cleansing.[17] The victory of Jesus would come through self-sacrifice rather than revolution.

The temple cleaning was followed by some healings of the blind and lame, a likely allusion to the hope promised in Isaiah.[18] In

---

[15]See Craig S. Keener, *A Commentary on the Gospel of Matthew* (Grand Rapids, MI: Eerdmans, 1999), 494.

[16]See Dale C. Allison, *The New Moses: A Matthean Typology* (Minneapolis, MN: Fortress, 1993), 248-49.

[17]In a clear case of the student blessing the professor, I am thankful to Jonathan Cleland for his insightful comments on the possible relationship between Psalm 118, Hanukah, and Jesus' temple cleansing in Matthew. These comments were made during a seminar discussion in an upper-level "Old Testament in the New Testament" course at Heritage Theological Seminary, Cambridge, Ontario, in February 2019.

[18]These references appear in both so-called First and Second Isaiah—e.g., Isaiah 29:18; 35:5; 42:7, 16, 18.

response to the temple healings by Jesus, children (cf. Ps 8:2),[19] who would have heard the cries at the entrance into Jerusalem, and who would have known the Egyptian Hallel (which was taught to children),[20] cried out, "Hosanna to the Son of David" (Mt 21:15). This echo of Psalm 118:25a (*hoshiah nah* [הוֹשִׁיעָה נָּא]), which by the first century likely simply meant "praise,"[21] was again attached to "Son of David." By way of reminder, our discussion of Psalm 118 in its book of Psalms context found that its speaker was most likely the Davidic king. And our look at the Targum of the Psalms has confirmed that at least one community of Jews thought the same. Also of note is that Jesus let the children in the temple and the crowds at the entrance narrative speak words of praise to him, something that inflamed the religious leaders, since praise should be reserved for God. By his actions, therefore, Jesus was affirming his own deity.

Finally, both our canonical analysis and our overview of the Jewish feasts have shown that Psalm 118 had an end-times flavor in the minds of first century Jews. So even as Jesus enacted the entrance into the temple (cf. Ps 118), he showed himself as the ideal, *torah*-faithful king of Deuteronomy 17:14-20, while he cleansed the temple from the sin of the unfaithful Jewish sellers, chief priests, and scribes. Whereas these ethnic Jews had become the enemies of YHWH who were portrayed in Psalm 118, the faithful Son of David healed disease and accepted praise. According to Matthew 21:9, 15, Jesus is the Coming One, the end-times Davidic king who would accomplish victory for God's people, even as he enacted Psalm 118 in part, and even as the

---

[19]I was pointed to this link with Psalm 8 in Michael D. Goulder, *Midrash and Lection in Matthew* (London: SPCK, 1974), 413.

[20]See *t. Sota* 6.2-3 as referenced in Donald Alfred Hagner, *Matthew 14-28* (Dallas: Word, 1995), 602.

[21]See W. D. Davies and Dale C. Allison, *A Critical and Exegetical Commentary on the Gospel According to Saint Matthew*, 3 vols. (London: T&T Clark, 1997), 3:125; Craig L. Blomberg, "Matthew," in *Commentary on the New Testament Use of the Old Testament*, ed. G. K. Beale and D. A. Carson (Grand Rapids, MI: Baker Academic, 2007), 65.

workers in the temple, along with the chief priests and the scribes, were portrayed as the enemies of God's people.

Our next passage is the parable of the tenants, found in Matthew 21:33-46. In fact, the theme of the rejection of the Son by the Jewish leaders dominates the section leading up to this text—through the cursing of the fig tree, the questioning of his authority, and the parables of the two sons and the tenants. The parable of the tenants emphasizes that the ethnically Jewish leaders who were rejecting Jesus were also the enemies of YHWH, and this is reinforced by a quotation of Psalm 118:22-23 (Mt 21:42). In this text, Jesus said that "the stone the builders rejected has become the cornerstone," and that "this is the Lord's doing and it is marvelous in our eyes." Once again, these Jewish leaders were "the builders," who were the enemies of YHWH from Psalm 118. Jesus was the stone who was rejected by the enemies of YHWH, but who would become the cornerstone in the whole structure of salvation. If the Zechariah 9:9 quote began the chapter with a humble king, and the Psalm 118:25-26 reference spoke of a victorious son of David in the entrance narrative, the twin themes of humility and victory are combined in this reference to our psalm. Since the use of the psalm in Matthew presupposes the Christian belief in Jesus' death and resurrection for its first readers, the intended meaning is all the more clear.[22]

Next, Psalm 118 appears in Jesus' lament over Jerusalem. In this passage, Jesus quoted Psalm 118:26a himself: "For I tell you, you will not see me again, until you say, 'Blessed is he who comes in the name of the Lord'" (Mt 23:39). This quotation tempers the reversal motif with the reality that although the Jewish people were rejecting Jesus, there would be a day, an end-times day, when they would call him blessed. The passage, then, does double end-times duty in Matthew,

---

[22]See M. J. J. Menken, "The Psalms in Matthew's Gospel," in *The Psalms in the New Testament*, ed. M. J. J. Menken and Steve Moyise (London: T&T Clark, 2004), 73.

referring to Jesus' entrance into Jerusalem and also to his second coming, a doctrine that the first Christian readers of Matthew's Gospel would have certainly read out of the quote. It's as though Matthew was saying something akin to Romans 11:25-27 and claiming that those who welcomed Jesus in the entrance narrative, and who would subsequently reject him, would one day utter the words of Psalm 118:26 again in fullness of joy, sincerity, and understanding.[23]

Matthew's last clear reference to Psalm 118 is found in the Last Supper narrative (Mt 26:30). In light of our study of the Jewish festivals, we know that Psalms 113–118 (the Egyptian Hallel) was sung as a part of the Passover meal. Matthew's phrase "and when they had sung a hymn, they went out," is a clear reference, then, to Psalm 118, the climax of this cluster of psalms. Although our point is brief, it should not escape us that according to Matthew, the last song on the lips of Jesus before he went to the cross was this end-times song of victory—Psalm 118. Even as the humble king and the rejected Son faced the horror of the cross, he also looked ahead to resurrection victory.[24] If the Passover was a celebration of the exodus, and Psalm 118 shared imagery with the Song of the Sea, Allison notes that this "implies that [Jesus] too suffered exile, endured slavery, and celebrated freedom."[25] Praise YHWH!

How, then, can the extensive use of Psalm 118 in the New Testament be explained? Our overview of the psalm itself has shown that the speaker was likely set forth as the Davidic king, who was giving thanks to YHWH for victory in battle, and doing so publicly, leading the people in procession through the gates of the city and into the temple to sing a responsive song of thanks. Our look at the psalm in its book of Psalms context (in an earlier chapter), has shown the

---

[23]See Blomberg, "Matthew," 85.

[24]This perspective is shared by Alexander B. Grosart, "The Hallel and Jesus Singing," *Expository Times* 1 (1890): 224-26.

[25]See Allison, *The New Moses: A Matthean Typology*, 257.

extremely strong possibility that the final editors of the Psalms inter-preted Psalm 118 with reference to the end times: just as its author was mindful of the exodus event, so the shape of the Hebrew book of Psalms hints at editors who looked forward to a future "exodus-like" deliverance, with the Davidic king playing an especially prominent role. Our study of the use of the psalm in Jewish writings has shown that it was associated with both the exodus and the Davidic king. Even as its use at the festivals also brought it into an end-times milieu, the frequent singing of the Egyptian Hallel with Psalm 118 as its climax meant that this passage of Scripture was on people's minds, hearts, and even lips on a regular basis. So as the various New Tes-tament authors sought to speak meaningfully about the unique Messiah, Jesus Christ, they did not turn to obscure passages with which the people were unfamiliar but instead frequently appealed to this great psalm, which many common, illiterate people knew by heart. No wonder so many New Testament writers appealed to this psalm: they were convinced that Jesus was the "Coming One," "the rejected stone," and "the royal deliverer," and they recognized his re-flection in the "mirror" of this popular psalm.

DISCUSSION QUESTIONS

1. How often does the New Testament cite or allude to the Old Testament? What accounts for the disparity between the pro-posed number of occurrences?

2. If you have a Bible that includes cross-references, look up Psalm 118 and take note of the number of New Testament texts it points to as either citing or alluding to portions of this psalm. Share some of your findings with your group.

3. What does the rendering of Psalm 118 in the Aramaic Targum suggest about one early Jewish community's understanding of the psalm?

4. How does the use of Psalm 118 at the Jewish festivals provide background information that helps us explore this psalm's use in the New Testament more thoroughly?

5. Which of the occurrences of Psalm 118 in Matthew 21–26 stuck out to you as something you had not noticed previously? Share with your group.

9

The Psalms and
the Christian

NOW THAT WE HAVE THOUGHT ABOUT the Psalms and Christ so thoroughly, we can speak with more clarity about how this Old Testament book applies to our twenty-first century lives. We have seen the apostle Paul's bold claim that the *entire* Old Testament is "profitable for teaching, for reproof, for correction, and for training in righteousness," resulting in a Christian who is "complete, equipped for every good work" (2 Tim 3:16-17). If we want to be taught, reproved, corrected, and trained in righteousness, if we want to be complete Christians who are equipped for every good work, we *need* the Old Testament. But what does this look like? Since there is a distance between our twenty-first century *Christian* lives and the book of Psalms, we need a bit of instruction. However, as we step back we'll notice that we have actually been doing this all along in part two of this book. And we will also expand on it even more in part three.

To set up our transition from "The Savior: Reading the Psalms Christologically" (part two), to "The Soul: Reading the Psalms Personally and Corporately" (part three), we will spend some time thinking about the Psalms and the Christian. We will do this by considering two important categories to help get us out of intuitive application and on to intentional, biblically robust movements from the Psalms to the nitty gritty of the Christian life. We will call the first category "gospel application" and the second "direct application." Since we will employ Psalm 3 as a test case for each category, we'll begin by walking through it in some detail.

PSALM 3: A TEST CASE

Psalm 3 is a lament, a "tears" psalm of David. And he has invited us to listen in on his weeping. The psalm begins, though, with a historical superscription: "A Psalm of David, when he fled from Absalom his son" (Ps 3:0). As we saw in part one of this book, we encounter Psalm 3 through the lens (or gateway) of Psalms 1 and 2. The book of Psalms begins with two affirmations: (1) a *torah*-steeped life is lived under the blessing of YHWH (Ps 1); and (2) YHWH's anointed king will reign and be granted ultimate victory (Ps 2). However, as soon as the reader enters through the "gateway" of Psalms 1–2 and into the life of praise, they encounter the voice of weeping David, of the anointed king's deep lament. In this life situation, Absalom, David's son, was pursuing and trying to kill him (see 2 Sam 13–19). Ironically, the Hebrew name *Absalom* literally means "father of shalom."[1] Even more insight comes when we realize that the Hebrew word *shalom* does not simply refer to "the absence of hostility or strife," as *peace* does in English; it also refers more positively to *wholeness*, with the sense of "the most abundant life." In other words, the father of wholeness, of abundant life, of *shalom*, was pursuing his own father, the anointed king of YHWH (cf. Ps 2), and this psalm was written for the occasion.

Since the psalm's superscription (or title) invites us to read it in light of the narrative of 2 Samuel, our minds are drawn to the ultimate reason (from God's perspective) that Absalom was pursuing David: David had sinned as an adulterer and a murderer (see 2 Sam 11–12, as well as Ps 51). And in response to this sin, YHWH had

---

[1]This literal meaning comes from two Hebrew words that are joined in the name Absalom (*Abshalom* [אַבְשָׁלוֹם]): "father" (*ab* [אַב]) of "shalom" (*shalom* [שָׁלוֹם]).

punished David: there would be strife in his *household*. In other words, the horrible situation David was experiencing in Psalm 3 had been brought on, at least in part, by his own sin.

The body of Psalm 3 follows with words that expressed the tears of weeping David: "O LORD, how many are my foes! / Many are rising against me; / many are saying of my soul, / there is no salvation for him in God. *Selah*" (Ps 3:1-2). If the superscription reminded us that the author of Psalm 3 was *not* the ideal, *torah*-steeped individual from Psalm 1, the first words of Psalm 3 remind us that in Absalom and his posse, the very *Israelites* were raging against YHWH and his anointed king (cf. the *foreign* kings in Ps 2:2). And isn't it telling that the very first word of David's lament was the direct address "O YHWH!"[2] In the midst of his tears, which had ultimately been brought on by his own sin, David could still approach his God directly and boldly, and he could still call him by his personal, intimate, covenant name, the name that recalls God's redemption of his people.[3]

Through tears, David boldly came to his covenant God, to YHWH. And he specified: my foes are so many, many are rising up (in violence) against me, many are using taunts of mockery, "God won't save you!" It was not by accident that the foes of David used God's generic name instead of YHWH. By recounting this, David was basically saying, "Look at the mockery, O YHWH! I am the king of Israel, the leader of your covenant people. When they mock me, they mock you, and when my life is on the line, your blessing of your people as a whole is on the line." The implied exhortation from David to YHWH was, "Now, act! Intercede! Help!"

---

[2]In Hebrew, the first word of the psalm is indeed "YHWH," but the context supplies a vocative sense of the term; thus "O YHWH" is an appropriate English translation choice.
[3]In light of this direct address, Rolf Jacobson helpfully titles his own chapter on the lament psalms, "Mourning into Dancing, or How to Get in God's Face." See Rolf A. Jacobson, *The Homebrewed Christianity Guide to the Old Testament: Israel's In-Your-Face, Holy God* (Minneapolis, MN: Fortress, 2018), 173-94.

But David didn't end there.[4] His next words transitioned to a description, not simply of the character of YHWH *in general*, but of the character of YHWH and its application *to this particular situation*:[5] "But you, O LORD, are a shield about me, / my glory, and the lifter of my head" (Ps 3:3). If the words of verses 1-2 could easily be interpreted as the unchecked, emotive, shouting of David as his life rocked in turbulent waters, in the words of verse 3 David set himself on the granite foundation of the character of YHWH, who would act *for him in this particular, horrible situation*. He began with, "But you, O YHWH."[6] In other words, "in contrast to my horrible situation, and in direct words to my covenant God, I will personally and directly call to mind his attributes!" So who was YHWH in these times? He was a shield around David, he was David's glory, and he was the lifter of David's head. To summarize, YHWH was David's protector (shield), the object of his delight (glory), and the one who would lift his chin from sorrow to joy (lifter of his head).

The next section of the psalm does something amazing: David stepped out of the current situation and *anticipated* YHWH hearing and answering his cries: "I cried aloud to the LORD, / and he answered me from his holy hill. *Selah*" (Ps 3:4). *As David was weeping* (vv. 1-2), he was also drawing a direct line from his tears to YHWH's character (v. 3). *But then he looked ahead* to a time when his cry would have been in the past, and YHWH would have answered him (v. 4). In

---

[4]The only lament psalm that ends with words of darkness is Psalm 88, a likely reflection on the exile of Israel. However, even this psalm is followed by the words of faith at the beginning of Psalm 89, and so in the structure of the book of Psalms, lament still always leads to faith. I first learned this insight from Michael Kolarcik, who was one of my PhD professors at the University of Toronto (personal correspondence).

[5]Note that the word *Selah* follows verse 2. While there is not scholarly consensus on this word's meaning, a case can be made for "pause," in the sense of telling the reader to pause and reflect on what has just been said, before moving on to the next part of the psalm. In this way, the various occurrences of *Selah* in the psalms break up the content for the reader.

[6]The Hebrew *weattah* (וְאַתָּה) can be translated as "and you" or "but you." In this case, since there is clearly a contrast between David's horrible life situation and the character of his God, I suggest "but you" as the better translation option.

other words, in verse 4 King David began to look ahead to YHWH intervening for him.

The psalm then transitions from the (future) intervention of YHWH (Ps 3:4) to the new, current disposition of David in light of YHWH's future work for him:[7] "I lay down and slept; / I woke again, for the LORD sustained me. / I will not be afraid of many thousands of people / who have set themselves against me all around" (Ps 3:5-6). Now that David had honestly cried to YHWH, what happened to his heart disposition? He had so much inner peace that he *slept*! And the best part is this: nothing about David's external life circumstances had changed.

As David woke up from sleep, he took nothing for granted: he even attributed that waking to the sustaining grace of YHWH. And he emerged without fear: far from fearing one person (his son, the father of *shalom*) who was pursuing him in order to kill him, David would not fear many thousands of people who were set against him. Why? Because of verses 3-4, because of the coming intervention of his covenant God.

The psalm then ends by exhorting YHWH to intervene. David had already anticipated a future time when YHWH would do so, and at the end of the psalm he directly called on him to act: "Arise, O LORD! / Save me, O my God! / For you strike all my enemies on the cheek; / you break the teeth of the wicked. / Salvation belongs to the LORD; / your blessing be on your people! *Selah*" (Ps 3:7-8). David called on YHWH to act *now*, and this was grounded in the fact that YHWH would ultimately fight David's battles. Just as YHWH's work in Psalm 2 was through the agency of his anointed king, so in Psalm 3 the future deliverance of King David would be a result of YHWH's work for him. And if opposition to YHWH's anointed king was

---

[7]Note that between verses four and five another *Selah* occurs, once again marking a transition in the psalm, in this case from YHWH's answer to David's new heart disposition.

tantamount to opposition to YHWH and his people as a whole (cf. Ps 2), YHWH would counter David's violent enemy with a violent end: he would strike his enemies on the cheek and break the teeth of the wicked. Then to conclude, David attributed salvation to YHWH, his people's blessing from him alone.

GOSPEL APPLICATION: DAVID IS MORE THAN JUST "LIKE US"

I am calling this first way of moving from the book of Psalms to the Christian "gospel application." Here is what I mean: as we develop our "knee-jerk" reaction to think of the way Christ fulfills a given passage from the book of Psalms, we are actually making a gospel move. We have seen that this move to Christ usually finds its fulfillment during the focal point of redemptive history—in the death, burial, resurrection, and ascension of Jesus, along with the gift of the Holy Spirit on the day of Pentecost. Since Jesus fulfilled the Old Testament hope, and since these five events at the focal point of redemptive history are the climax of the Old Testament hope, then the entire time we are moving from the Old Testament to Christ, we are also soaking in the gospel. By doing this, we are taking our cues from Jesus himself. Remember, on the road to Emmaus we found Jesus speaking from the book of Psalms (along with the rest of the Old Testament) about the following: "Thus it is written, that the Christ should suffer and on the third day rise from the dead, and that repentance for the forgiveness of sins should be proclaimed in his name to all nations, beginning from Jerusalem" (Lk 24:46-47). The book of Psalms was ultimately written about the gospel.

Put another way, although we can see many similarities between our own lives and the life and words of David, this gospel move also teaches us that David is more than just "like us." As we read through the seventy-three "Of David" psalms, we can definitely notice similarities between David's experiences and our own. As we discuss "direct application" later in this chapter, we will see that this intuition is healthy and biblically warranted. But as we think about the fulfillment of the Old Testament hope in the person and work of Jesus Christ, we also need to notice that the Bible presents David as more than just "like us"—he points us to the greater Son of David to come, Jesus Christ. As we move from the Old Testament to a Christ-centered application—by thinking in categories such as redemptive-historical progression, promise-fulfillment, contrast, typology, direct prophecy, typological prophecy, or the New Testament use of the Old Testament—we are constantly soaking in the gospel. We are constantly reminding ourselves that more than being "just like us," David was also different from us: he was the covenant head of God's people, and his life points us to the person and work of Jesus Christ.

UNPACKING GOSPEL APPLICATION: WEEPING DAVID AND WEEPING JESUS

What does this look like, practically speaking? When we soak in a lament psalm of "weeping David," and then move to the tears of Christ throughout his life and the culmination of those tears as he faced the horror of the cross, we are being led to reflect on the depth of Christ's sacrifice *for us*. We are also being led to reflect on how much *better* Christ's headship is than that of any Old Testament saint. As we read in the book of Psalms with an instinct, a "knee-jerk" reaction to think about how our passage is fulfilled in Christ, we find that so much of the book clearly points to the suffering of Christ (e.g., Ps 3, typologically), the death of Christ (e.g., Ps 22, as a typological prophecy), the resurrection of Christ (e.g., Ps 16:10-11, as a typological prophecy), the ascension of Christ to the right hand of the throne of God (e.g., Ps 110:1, through direct prophecy), the priesthood of Christ as our perfect mediator (e.g., Ps 110:4, through direct prophecy), and the gift of the Holy Spirit (e.g., Ps 51:11, through contrast between the

Old Testament ability to have the Holy Spirit taken from "me" and the New Testament promise of the Spirit's permanent indwelling of the believer in Jesus).

However, more than simply offering us a springboard to spend the bulk of our time in the New Testament, we find the opposite to be most helpful. If we are reading an Old Testament text in personal Bible reading or Bible study/sermon preparation, we should seek to thoroughly understand it in its original context, so that our subsequent move to reveling in its fulfilment in Christ will be all the more fruitful.

To illustrate this, let's scan Psalm 3 with the categories from our "Psalms and Christ" chapters in mind. Immediately, we settle on typology. How is Psalm 3 typological? First and foremost, the New Testament makes clear that Jesus is the greater son of David to come (e.g., Mt 22:42). If 2 Samuel 7 had promised that a son of David would always reign, according to the New Testament Jesus reigns today at the right hand of the Father on the throne of the cosmos (cf. Ps 110:1; Heb 12:2). While David's reign was local, Jesus' reign is *cosmic*. From this we learn to look for typology in a psalm's authorship. When a psalm lists its author (101 times out of 150 psalms), we can ask if there is a legitimate typological relationship between that author and Christ.

Moving from the general to the specific, we need to move from the author of the psalm to its content. Psalm 3 is also a *lament* of David as he suffered at the hands of his own son. Typologically, we can ask whether Jesus ever suffered in his life. Our answer would be that throughout his ministry, he was a man of sorrows and acquainted with grief (Is 53:3): as he was rejected (e.g., Jn 6:66), betrayed to death by his own people (Mt 27:1), abandoned at his greatest moment of need (Mt 26:56), and bore our sins upon himself on the cross (Is 53:4-6), the Father turned his face away (Mt 27:46; cf. Ps 22:1). On the cross, for the first time in all of eternity, God the Father abandoned his beloved Son. Therefore, after we have soaked in the anguish of suffering found in the psalm, we can exclaim, "How much more were the sufferings of Jesus *for me!*"

There is one more important observation we can make as we consider Psalm 3 as typological: there is also an element of *contrast* present. Consider the sin of David versus the sinlessness of Christ. Recall again that in Psalm 3, David's sufferings were ultimately prompted by his own sin (see 2 Sam 11–19). This reminds us that the categories we are working in are not always (or even usually) neatly separated out from one another. Instead, they are starting points from which we can brainstorm. Most often, they will work together. In this case, Jesus is the king greater than David, and he experienced ultimate suffering. There is escalation in the typology. And now, in *contrast* to David, Jesus is the *sinless* Son of God (Heb 4:15). Because of this, we can revel in Jesus as the better covenant head than the greatest king in Israel's history.

As we finish and then look ahead on our timeline of redemptive history, we find that in contrast to David, Jesus was sinless and so was suffering in perfect innocence. And just like David was mocked in his time of great vulnerability, as Jesus was being sentenced to the cross, he was mocked (Mt 26:67-68), and this mockery happened again as he was hanging on the cross:

> And those who passed by derided him, wagging their heads and saying, "You who would destroy the temple and rebuild it in three days, save yourself! If you are the Son of God, come down from the cross." So also the chief priests, with the scribes and elders, mocked him, saying, "He saved others; he cannot save himself. He is the King of Israel; let him come down now from the cross, and we will believe in him. He trusts in God; let God deliver him now, if he desires him. For he said, 'I am the Son of God.'" And the robbers who were crucified with him also reviled him in the same way. (Mt 27:39-44)

While David was not powerful enough to save himself, Jesus was. While David sometimes suffered because of his own sin (e.g., Ps 3), Jesus *chose* to suffer for *our sin*. While David was indignant at mockery that called his God into question, part of Jesus' suffering was the temporary assault on the glory of God. While the New Testament passage vividly tells us what happened, Psalm 3 shows us *how it felt* for David, and typologically, for Jesus, as he endured such suffering. One of the great blessings of developing a "knee-jerk" reaction of moving from the book of Psalms to Christ is that we soak in the gospel. Much more could be said about this, but I hope we have been given a taste of the benefit of reading, leading Bible studies on, and preaching the book of Psalms as a witness to Christ.

DIRECT APPLICATION: IN MANY WAYS, DAVID IS "LIKE US"

Throughout part two of this book, I have been advocating a Christ-as-fulfillment reading of the book of Psalms. However, if we left things there, we would be missing out on some other precious application. Not only does the book of Psalms lead us to soak in the gospel, it also applies to our lives by way of direct application. As we apply the psalms directly, we are making them our very own, letting their words become our words.

In my view, direct application is a very important "tool in our tool-belts" for applying the book of Psalms to our lives, but it also comes with some challenges. Direct application puts us in the front seat of the roller coaster, making a direct connection between the psalm and our own lives, but direct application can also be done poorly. I can't emphasize this enough: in order to do this well, we need to make the connection to Christ-as-fulfillment *as well as* direct application. In other words, we need to soak in the gospel at least as much as we think about how our experiences may have similarities to the experiences of David. In fact, we need to train ourselves to think of Christ and the gospel *more* than we think about ourselves. But as we develop this reflex, if we are going to do the Psalms passage justice, we also need to apply it by means of direct application.

When we employ direct application, we affirm with Achtemeier that "the church has . . . inherited the role of Israel, and in Christ it has become the recipient of the promises given to Israel in the Old Testament."[8] Another author illustrates this concept well:

> [In] 1 Corinthians 10:6, the Apostle Paul says that Israel's wilderness experiences are a "type" of the events in the Corinthian Church. . . . Paul uses this term (likewise τυπικῶς in v. 11) to interpret the events in the Corinthian church in the light of Israel's experiences in the wilderness. The punishment of God's ancient people, following their disgraceful practices, is seen as a prefiguration of judgment on those who conduct themselves in similar fashion.[9]

According to 1 Corinthians 10:6, Israel's *Old Testament* experiences are a type of the Christians in the *New Testament* Corinthian church. Put another way, as the new Israel (Gal 6:16), each believer in Jesus is *similar* to a member of Old Testament Israel.

When we move from the passage in the book of Psalms to the life of the believer, we are asking with Greidanus "[whether] Israel's situation in relation to God . . . is analogous to ours."[10] This allows us to make an immediate and direct connection between a psalm and our own lives. In my own preaching on the Psalms, for example, I like to show the interplay between gospel application and direct application by unpacking two statements near the end of each sermon: (1) in many ways, David is like us (direct application); (2) but we also need

---

[8]Elizabeth Achtemeier, *The Old Testament and the Proclamation of the Gospel* (Philadelphia, PA: Westminster, 1973), 117. Whereas Achtemeier and Greidanus employ the term "analogy," I find "direct application" to be a more helpful description of the same concept, especially when dealing with the Psalms.

[9]No author listed, "τύπος," NIDNTTE 4:507.

[10]Sidney Greidanus, *Preaching Christ from the Old Testament: A Contemporary Hermeneutical Method* (Grand Rapids, MI: Eerdmans, 1999), 262.

to remember that David is more than just like us: he points us to Jesus (gospel application). Each of these statements gives me an opportunity to move from the Old Testament passage to Christ and the Christian life.

UNPACKING DIRECT APPLICATION: WEEPING DAVID AND THE WEEPING CHRISTIAN

We have noticed that the tears of David lead us to soak in the gospel. However, as we employ direct application, we say something in addition to this: because of the measure of continuity between the Old Testament people of God and New Testament believers in Jesus, there will be a measure of continuity between the experiences of David and the experiences of the Christian. On the one hand, as the royal corporate head over God's people, weeping David is more than just like us: he is a type of Christ. But on the other hand, as a member of the people of God who experienced the nitty gritty of real life in covenant with the same God we worship, in a lot of ways David is also just like us: he is a type of the Christian.

So what about a connection between the tears of weeping David and the tears of a weeping believer in Jesus? If Hebrew poetry *emotes* by definition (keep reading on in this chapter for more on this), and if there is a measure of continuity between weeping David and the weeping believer in Jesus, then weeping believers should employ the tears of David in their own laments. As we do this, our radar should be up for times when a particular line would not apply to a believer in Jesus today (because of contrast, or because of a typologically prophetic text, etc.). However, even as differences are recognized, these should be offered as qualifications while the rest of the words are still applied by way of direct application.

Let's return to Psalm 3 and see how this works in our specific test case. This time, we will listen in on weeping David so we can employ his tears in our own night of weeping. The psalm begins with a superscription:

"A Psalm of David" (whose experiences were a lot like the experiences of believes in Jesus today), "when he fled from Absalom his son" (Ps 3:0). In Psalm 3, we are reminded that as we enter through the gateway of Psalms 1 and 2 and into the life of praise (*Tehillim*), the very first thing we encounter is lament, *because we live in a world in which we sin, we are sinned against, and that is generally a mess.* And so David weeps, he *laments.* So ought we, as believers in Jesus today. And then we remember that David's suffering had been brought on, at least in part, by his own sin. Have you ever committed a sin that makes you wonder whether God would ever be gracious to you again? The book of Psalms is a gift to Christians in these moments. Perhaps it is instinctive for us to re-member that a believer's groaning in this fallen world is often the result of their being sinned against, but Psalm 3 also reminds us that some-times our groaning is a result of our own sin. In fact, Psalm 3 teaches us to sing/pray our tears when the horrible situation is ultimately our own fault. Then later, Psalm 51 (a psalm of repentance) will give us words to help us turn from our sin when it has been first exposed.

The psalm then continues with David's tears in verses 1 and 2: "O LORD, how many are my foes! / Many are rising against me; / many are saying of my soul, / 'There is no salvation for him in God.' *Selah.*" How directly do these emotive words help the believer in Jesus to emote in the midst of opposition! When unbelievers oppose, and when unbelievers mock, Psalm 3:1-2 is a gift to the Christian. It helps us to release what is going on in our souls. And it invites us to address God directly: just as David used the vocative "O" and the personal name of God "YHWH," so we can do the same—or, in line with the teaching of Jesus, to intimately call on God as "our Father" (cf. Mt 6:9).

Psalm 3 continues with a reflection on the character of God in verse 3: "But you, O LORD, are a shield about me, / my glory, and the lifter of my head." Just as YHWH was David's protector (shield) and the one who rejuvenated him (lifter of his head), these characteristics of God and this way God dealt with his Old Testament saints also apply directly and even more intensely to the new covenant believer in Jesus. Since we look back on the ultimate display of the "yes" of God to all who would trust in Christ (i.e., the gospel event at the focal point of redemptive history), how much more confidence we can have when we ask God to work for our good and for his glory in the midst of our horrible situation of opposition. When we make the words of this psalm our own—when we employ its words directly in our own singing or praying—the psalm takes us by the hand and leads us in an experience of practical theology.

Next, Psalm 3:4-5 looks ahead to a time when YHWH will have answered David's prayer: "I cried aloud to the LORD, / and he answered me from his holy hill. *Selah* / I lay down and slept; / I woke again, for the LORD sustained me." What is the first thing that leaves us when deep burdens enter in? Sleep! When we lay down, when everything is quiet and our minds have the opportunity to slip into neutral, it is so easy for our worries to get the best of us. Quiet breeds worry, and this is likely why so many people drown out quiet with headphones, earbuds, and screens. But do you notice what happened to David's heart disposition now that he had honestly cried in lament to YHWH, drawn a line from YHWH's character to his particular life situation, and anticipated a time in the future when YHWH would have answered his cries? He slept. No insomnia. Rest. Inner peace. *And the best part is this: Christians can experience this when nothing about their external life circumstances have changed.* It is so easy for us to conclude that our biggest problem is "out there" (i.e., hard life situations), but Psalm 3 models for us that our biggest problem is "in here" (i.e., in our own hearts). Therefore, when external hardships come, one of the healthiest things we can do is to pray, and even *sing*, the lament psalms.

This is followed in verse 6 with an expression of confidence: "I will not be afraid of many thousands of people / who have set themselves against me all around." Believers in Jesus do not need to fear because of who God is for us. When the situation seems impossible on a human level, our God is for us, and he is working.

Finally, weeping Christians can read Psalm 3:7-8 as a final call on their God to act, and as a final expression of trust in his work for them: "Arise, O LORD! / Save me, O my God! / For you strike all my enemies on the cheek; / you break the teeth of the wicked. / Salvation belongs to the LORD; / your blessing be on your people! *Selah*."

Returning to the disposition of David, notice again that nothing about his external life situation had changed, but through the process of his lament, YHWH faithfully changed his heart and brought him to a place of sleep at night and *shalom* in his soul as he anticipated the work of YHWH *for him*. David could hope for victory because this hope was founded not on wishful "pie in the sky" thinking but on the character and the promises of his covenant God, YHWH. And if you and I are believers in Jesus, we can do the same. I am thankful for a model of praying and/or singing my tears that first teaches me to honestly bring my tears to my covenant God, leads me to exult in the particular aspects of YHWH's character that will impact my current situation, and then anticipates future deliverance, all as a means of attaining inner *shalom* now, even before anything about my external circumstances has changed. Psalm 3 not only prompts us to move from weeping David to weeping Jesus, but it also prompts us to move from weeping David to our own seasons of weeping. The lament psalms are a precious treasure for personal or corporate direct application. In fact, they help us with the words to express our tears to our heavenly Father.

A WINDOW INTO THE SOUL

Before we close our chapter, we should notice something that makes gospel application and direct application of the Psalms especially precious.[11] In his book *Psalm and Story: Inset Hymns in Biblical Narrative*,

---

[11]A study of the nature of Hebrew poetry is outside the scope of this book. For such an introduction, the work of Robert Chisholm is brief and accessible. For his overview of five types of

James W. Watts examines Old Testament narratives that insert psalms into the flow of a story. We often don't think about it like that, but the author of Jonah, for example, chose to insert the psalm of Jonah (Jonah 2) into the middle of a book that is otherwise written in story form (Jonah 1, 3, 4). Since the author was not a court stenographer—whose job is to write down every word spoken in the court room—we can say that he chose to include the psalm for a reason. As an author who intentionally wrote "all that is needed for life and godliness" (2 Pet 1:3), the Holy Spirit led him to include the psalm for our good. Other examples of this "inset psalm" into Hebrew narrative include the Song of the Sea (Ex 15:1-21), the Song of Moses (Deut 32:1-43), the Song of Deborah (Judg 5), Hannah's Song (1 Sam 2:1-10), and David's thanksgiving (2 Sam 22), among others.[12]

Watts examines each inset psalm in turn before offering a very helpful conclusion. For our purposes, we can notice that these psalms that have been inserted into Hebrew narrative are very similar to the psalms found in the book of Psalms, and they are often placed in important and even climactic places in the larger narrative. In Watts's view, while Hebrew narrative tends to avoid offering direct commentary,[13] Hebrew poems offer vivid descriptions of feelings and emphatic statements of ideas. Therefore,

---

Hebrew parallelism, see Robert B. Chisholm, *A Workbook for Intermediate Hebrew: Grammar, Exegesis, and Commentary on Jonah and Ruth* (Grand Rapids, MI: Kregel Academic, 2006), 12-13. For two extremely helpful and brief resources that summarize linguistic terms, see Todd J. Murphy, *Pocket Dictionary for the Study of Biblical Hebrew* (Downers Grove, IL: InterVarsity, 2003); Kyle Greenwood, *Dictionary of English Grammar for Students of Biblical Languages* (Grand Rapids, MI: Zondervan Academic, 2020). Finally, more advanced students will be challenged by the following critique of Hebrew parallelism: Robert D. Holmstedt, "Hebrew Poetry and the Appositive Style: Parallelism, Requiescat in Pace," *Vetus Testamentum* 69, nos. 4-5 (2019): 617-48. This article not only sets forth Holmstedt's own contribution toward solving the problem, but it also overviews the conversation thus far and so will point readers to other key sources. For Holmstedt's in-depth analysis of Psalm 23, see page 639 of this same article.

[12]In addition to those I have listed, Watts also includes chapters on Hezekiah's psalm (Is 38:9-20), Daniel's praise (Dan 2:20-23), and a Levitical medley (1 Chron 16:8-36). See James W. Watts, *Psalm and Story: Inset Hymns in Hebrew Narrative*, Journal for the Study of the Old Testament Supplement Series 139, ed. David J. A. Clines and Philip R. Davies (Sheffield, UK: JSOT Press, 1992).

[13]A notable exception to this is found, for example, in Genesis 3:1, where the craftiness of the serpent is noted by the narrator of Genesis.

[when] writers or editors of narrative needed to make thematic emphases and emotions explicit, they did not try to reproduce the effects of poetry in prose, but simply switched modes. Explicit emotional displays and interior characterization were thus introduced into Hebrew narrative without changing its basic nature.[14]

In other words, Hebrew poetry offers insight into the emotions and inner lives of the characters in the story—a window into their soul.[15]

These principles hold true not only for psalms that are inserted into Hebrew narratives but also for the 150 psalms in the book of Psalms. This means that the psalms not only appear in a different *form* than Hebrew narrative, but they also serve a different *function* as they offer insight into the inner life of the author rather than simply their outward actions.

Brevard Childs is also helpful on this point. In his article "Psalm Titles and Midrashic Exegesis," Childs explores the thirteen psalms that contain historical superscriptions—like, for example, Psalm 51, which is said to have been written by David after he was confronted by Nathan for his adultery with Bathsheba. He suggests:

> By placing a Psalm within the setting of a particular historical incident in the life of David, the reader suddenly was given access to previously unknown information. David's inner life was now unlocked to the reader, who was allowed to hear his intimate thoughts and reflections.[16]

Once again, the inner characterization of the author of the psalm is revealed in the poem itself. While reading Hebrew narratives—such as the book of Genesis, for example—will provide a theological

---

[14]Watts, *Psalm and Story*, 194.

[15]For a more detailed summary of Watts's work, see Ian J. Vaillancourt, "The Pious Prayer of an Imperfect Prophet: The Psalm of Jonah in Its Narrative Context," *Journal for the Evangelical Study of the Old Testament* 4, no. 2 (2015): 180-82.

[16]Brevard S. Childs, "Psalm Titles and Midrashic Exegesis," *Journal of Semitic Studies* 16, no. 2 (1971): 149. Earlier in this book I devoted an entire chapter to psalm superscriptions. In this place I am simply discussing superscriptions where they help us understand the function of Hebrew poetry.

commentary on what happened, reading Hebrew poems—such as the entire book of Psalms—will give us a window into the poet's soul.

I suggest that one's doctrine of Scripture comes into play at this point. Since I believe that the Word of God is infallible (incapable of error) and inerrant (without error in the final form of the original autographs), this means that when I am reading the book of Psalms, I am receiving the *true*, accurate descriptions of the inner lives of its poets. While Hebrew narratives focus on what happened, Hebrew poems reveal the inner life, the inner world of the poet, with a focus on modeling pious, godly praying, singing, and theology, all in the midst of the nitty gritty of real life.

READING THROUGH THE WINDOW

As we apply the book of Psalms through gospel application and direct application, we are learning to "read through the window" into the psalmist's soul and apply this window to our twenty-first-century lives. As we unpacked Psalm 3 typologically, this window into David's soul led to vivid reveling in Jesus' gospel work for us. Calvin's insight about the book of Psalms as *an anatomy of all the parts of the soul* also means that we will find a psalm that is suited for direct application to every occasion of *our lives* and every emotion *we* can possibly feel. But far from merely giving us words to express our emotions, the psalms also lead us to the character of God, help us to trust him, and anticipate his work in our situation. No wonder we have exclaimed that the book of Psalms is a treasure! Although the chapters in part three will not exhaust the "every season of the soul" nature of the Psalms, they will help us along in our quest to make the words of the psalmist our own.

DISCUSSION QUESTIONS

1. Explain what the author meant by "gospel application" of a passage from the book of Psalms.

2. In your own words, restate the author's example of "gospel application" in the tears of David.

3. Explain what the author meant by "direct application" as an important way of applying the various psalms to the life of the believer.

4. Did anything stick out to you in the author's example of "direct application," from the tears of David in Psalm 3 to the tears of the Christian? Share with your group.

5. What are some key insights about the nature of Hebrew poetry, especially as taught by James W. Watts and Brevard S. Childs?

6. What one thing in this chapter did you find most helpful as you think about applying the book of Psalms to your own life as a believer in Jesus?

7. Is there one thing in this chapter that you found confusing that some group discussion might help to clarify?

PART THREE

THE
SOUL

READING THE PSALMS PERSONALLY
AND CORPORATELY

PART TWO OF THIS BOOK culminated in chapter nine, where we learned two directions we can go in order to legitimately apply the book of Psalms to the Christian life: gospel application and direct application. While the focus of part two was on gospel application, in part three we will unpack direct application in more detail. By employing direct application, we recognize that we can apply the Psalms to our individual and community lives because we worship the same God as the Old Testament saint worshiped, and because the church is the new Israel (Gal 6:16). And since the various psalms are by their very nature "windows into the soul," we are *meant* to appropriate their words in our personal and corporate prayers and songs.

In this section, we will recognize that readers need some guidance about a below-the-surface excavation of the individual psalms before they learn to adopt the psalmist's language as their own. The three chapters in this section will model how to directly apply three prominent kinds of psalms to our lives: psalms of desperation (lament), psalms of deliverance (thanksgiving), and psalms of exaltation (praise). Along the way in each of these three chapters, we will unpack a representative psalm, modeling what it looks like to apply it directly to our lives (whether as individuals or an entire local church).

DID YOU KNOW?
Major Themes in the Book of Psalms

The following three chapters in this section teach the direct application of what I refer to as three "major themes" in the book of Psalms: lament, thanksgiving, and praise.[1] It is important to understand that instead of "themes," many Psalms scholars—who employ a method of interpretation called "form criticism"—prefer to classify the various psalms according to genre. Understanding the differences between form criticism and my approach will help those who read articles, books, and commentaries—in Bible study preparation, for example—to use those works more effectively. The form-critical approach has strengths: readers are invited to get "back to the Bible," and psalms are categorized according to genre. Although we can benefit from those who follow this approach, I suggest that it is more helpful to soften our language to observe what *typical* elements are *often* present when the various themes occur in the individual psalms—instead of form criticism's *required* elements that *must* occur in each of the forms. For those who would like to dig deeper into this issue, appendix D is available as a free download on the IVP website (www.ivpress.com/treasuring-the-psalms).

---

[1]While space restrictions do not allow me to expand on the various other major themes in the book of Psalms, and while I will deal with others in other sections of the book (e.g., royal psalms), in this place simply note that lament, thanksgiving, and praise are not exhaustive of the types of psalms in the book of Psalms.

10

Direct Application of Desperation Psalms

LAMENT

In a November 2019 interview with *The Christian Post*, songwriter Keith Getty offered a stunning diagnosis: he warned that the modern worship movement is "utterly dangerous" and a cause of the "de-Christianizing of God's people."[1] These are strong words! If someone less qualified than Getty were to make this assessment, we probably wouldn't consider listening, but he is one of the great Christian songwriters of our day, with "In Christ Alone," "The Power of the Cross," "By Faith," "My Heart is Filled with Thankfulness," and "Speak, O Lord," among the hundreds he has written.[2] In fact, if we were to only focus on the prominence of "In Christ Alone," Getty would still be one of the most influential Christian songwriters of our day. If he makes this kind of shocking assessment, then we should at least evaluate his diagnosis.

The crux of Getty's warning is this: "many modern worship songs focus on emotionalism rather than sound doctrine and Scriptural

---

[1] Leah MarieAnn Klett, "Modern Worship Movement Is 'Utterly Dangerous,' Causing 'De-Christianizing of God's People,'" *The Christian Post*, November 9, 2019, www.christianpost .com/news/keith-getty-modern-worship-movement-is-utterly-dangerous-causing-de -christianizing-of-gods-people.html.

[2] Or co-written. For example, Getty has co-written many of his songs with Stuart Townend, including "In Christ Alone."

truths."[3] He continues: "over 75 percent of what are called the great hymns of the faith talk about eternity, Heaven, Hell and the fact that we have peace with God. Yet, less than 5 percent of modern worship songs talk about eternity."[4] Perhaps the best way to evaluate Getty's diagnosis would be to read a copy of the lyrics of every song our churches have sung in the last year, with an eye on the doctrine they teach. As we record the themes of our songs, we may ask ourselves: are we singing the full-orbed, well-rounded, biblical gospel, or are we indeed focusing too much on this earth, to the neglect of eternity? Getty's suggestion is that we use the themes and emphases of the great hymns of the faith as a standard against which we evaluate our contemporary song lyrics.

If the book of Psalms is indeed "the book of Praises" (*Tehillim*), "a little Bible" (Luther), and "an anatomy of all the parts of the soul" (Calvin), maybe another way to evaluate the singing and praying and even the preaching in our corporate worship services would be to test these aspects of our services against the book of Psalms. I think it likely that if we did this, one of the first differences to emerge would be in the area of lament, of *tears*. Sad songs and prayers. Groaning. Ironically, in a contemporary evangelical environment that Getty believes is too flooded with emotionalism to the neglect of doctrine, the full-orbed nature of emotions found in the psalms, along with their theological underpinning, are often neglected today. In particular, I suggest that evangelicals tend to place an inordinate emphasis on joy to the neglect of singing our tears.

To be sure, Christians have every reason to be filled with joy, to sing joy-filled songs, to pray joy-filled prayers, and to hear joy-inducing sermons. Why? Because in light of a Christian's standing in Christ, they have been *redeemed from* sin, death, and hell, *and freely given* new

---

[3]Getty, "Modern Worship Movement Is 'Utterly Dangerous.'"
[4]Getty, "Modern Worship Movement Is 'Utterly Dangerous.'"

life in Christ, peace with God, and "an inheritance that is imperishable, undefiled, and unfading, kept in heaven" for them (1 Pet 1:4). What glorious truths! Therefore, many song writers rightly conclude that Christians should be the most joy-filled people in the world.

As we scan the Bible, however, these truths are balanced with the reality that since Christians live in a fallen world, they will also experience *deep sorrow*. In this life, Christians will be sinned against and deeply hurt; they will sin against others (and ultimately, God), which will cause deep pain; they will experience trials that the apostle Paul likened to "the flaming darts of the evil one" (Eph 6:16); and they will experience the less-direct effects of living in a fallen world, such as fatigue, disease, death, and other horrible losses (cf. Rom 8:22). So on the one hand, Christians can say with the apostle Paul that "the sufferings of this present time are not worth comparing with the glory that is to be revealed to us" (Rom 8:18) and also that "we ourselves, who have the firstfruits of the Spirit, groan inwardly as we wait eagerly for adoption as sons, the redemption of our bodies" (Rom 8:23). In a fallen world, it is appropriate to *groan*, even in the midst of an abiding sense of joy, or in the words of the apostle Paul, to be "sorrowful, yet always rejoicing" (2 Cor 6:10).

This means that according to a robust biblical theology, there is a time for Christians to be sorrowful, even as deep down inside there is a disposition of joy that is rooted in the inheritance that is ours in Christ. And since, in the New Testament, the apostle Paul affirms the appropriateness of groaning and sorrow for the Christian, when we come to the book of Psalms, we find *precious words to help us sing and pray our tears.*[5] In fact, fifty (or so) out of the 150 psalms contain a theme of lament.

The lament psalms are conscious of the fact that life in the covenant community is not always easy. In these psalms, the author has been

---

[5] I first heard the turn of phrase "praying our tears" in the ministry of Timothy Keller.

in the thick of a horrible situation, *and he is not out of it yet*. So, the psalmist spends his time aching in desperation, and then moves to focus on the character of YHWH. As the psalmist does this, he begins to be encouraged. In all but one lament Psalm, by the end the author is soaking in the character of YHWH, and on this basis he is also clinging to hope for deliverance from his trial. These are great psalms to pray when life is hard, because they help us to emote, and they also focus us on the character of YHWH as they help us to ache in faith. Once again, in the lament psalms, we sing and pray our honest, heartfelt *tears* back to God. This is why the direct application of the lament psalms is a gift for Christians.

THE STRUCTURE OF LAMENT

As I explain in appendix D,[6] one way this Psalms book is different from some others is that I tend to shy away from *prescriptive* lists of what a given "type" of psalm *must* include.[7] This is because these lists were derived from a scholar's inductive comparison of the 150 psalms in the book of Psalms. The problem is not with the comparison but with the circular reasoning in concluding that a certain psalm is missing an essential element, and therefore belongs to a mixed genre. Instead, I prefer to speak of the elements that are *typically* included in a given psalm-type.

Rolf and Karl Jacobson point out that roughly one-third of the 150 psalms are laments.[8] In these psalms—also called "prayers for

---

[6]This can be found as a free online PDF on the IVP website at www.ivpress.com/treasuring-the-psalms.

[7]I introduced readers to this distinction in the "Did You Know?" text box, found in p. 166. See also Appendix D, where I more thoroughly compare my thematic study to the form-critical work of Gunkel and others.

[8]Rolf and Karl Jacobson cite the following as laments: Psalms 3, 4, 5, 7, 9, 10, 13, 17, 22, 26, 28, 31, 35, 36, 38, 39, 42, 43, 44, 51, 54, 55, 56, 57, 58, 59, 60, 61, 67, 69, 70, 71, 74, 77, 79, 80, 82, 83, 85, 86, 88, 89, 90, 94, 102, 108, 109, 120, 123, 126, 130, 137, 139, 140, 141, 142, 143, 144. See Rolf A. Jacobson and Karl N. Jacobson, *Invitation to the Psalms: A Reader's Guide for Discovery and Engagement* (Grand Rapids, MI: Baker Academic, 2013), 40n3. In this list, notice that forty-two of these occur in books 1-3, and the remaining sixteen occur in books 4-5. This confirms that

help"[9]—the psalmist cries out on behalf of himself (individual laments) or the community (community laments), and the following elements are often present: an address to God, a complaint/expression of agony in light of oppression, a request for deliverance (with supporting reasons YHWH *should* answer), words of confidence or trust in YHWH, and a promise to praise YHWH in the future (after deliverance).[10] This general structure should help orient us to the psalms of lament, the psalms written for occasions of personal or community *desperation*.

DID YOU KNOW?
Imprecatory Psalms

Under the umbrella of lament psalms are the so-called imprecatory psalms—also referred to as "vengeance psalms." In these, the psalmist calls on YHWH to destroy his earthly enemies. Twenty-first century readers often find them confusing because the language in these psalms seems out of step with the call for Christians to love their enemies (cf. Mt 5:44). Since these warrant a lengthy explanation, and since Bruce Waltke has done so in a clear and understandable way, I cite him at length in the bonus material. For those who would like to dig deeper into this issue, appendix E is available as a free download on the IVP website (www.ivpress.com/treasuring-the-psalms).

DIRECT APPLICATION OF LAMENT PSALMS: PSALM 42

What do these "tears" psalms sound like? As we look at one together, we will be helped with how to employ it and others in our own night

---

lament psalms are more heavily clustered at the beginning of the book of Psalms and are less frequent in the latter portion of the book.

[9]See Jacobson and Jacobson, *Invitation to the Psalms*, 40.

[10]See Nancy L. deClaissé-Walford, Rolf A. Jacobson, and Beth Laneel Tanner, *The Book of Psalms*, New International Commentary on the Old Testament (Grand Rapids, MI: Eerdmans, 2014), 19.

of weeping. In the following example, I will read Psalm 42 chunk by chunk, and then comment on the way its words can be directly employed by the believer in Jesus. It begins with a superscription, and then a note of yearning: "To the choirmaster. A Maskil of the Sons of Korah. / As a deer pants for flowing streams, / so pants my soul for you, O God" (Ps 42:0-1). Since every psalm was to be employed in singing and/or praying in temple worship, we remember that Psalm 42 is appropriate for our personal or corporate singing or praying. As will be the case every time we directly employ the words of a psalm in our lives as Christians, we need to ask how the Old Testament saint's situation was different from ours (for example, in appendix E in the online bonus material, I argue with Waltke that imprecations are not appropriate for believes in Jesus to pray against their earthly enemies). However, much of the language will carry over directly to our lives. In this case, the tone of yearning—comparing our yearning for God's presence to the yearning of a thirsty deer—is something that Christians today can and should directly employ in private or public worship.

Psalm 42 then transitions to lament, crying out to God in the midst of a very difficult life situation: "My soul thirsts for God, / for the living God. / When shall I come and appear before God? / My tears have been my food / day and night, / while they say to me all the day long, / 'Where is your God?'" (Ps 42:2-3). In the context of the psalmist's thirsting for God, he asks when he will come and appear before God. And in the absence of God, he reveals day-and-night tears and the taunts of outsiders: "Where is your God?"

As we directly apply these words, we remember that we no longer need a pilgrimage to Jerusalem and its temple in order to appear before God: Jesus told us that he will be with us always as we go to the ends of the earth with his gospel (Mt 28:19-20)! However, there are many life situations in which Christians will be kept from places "where two or three gather with Christ present among them" (cf. Mt 18:20). For example, the global Covid-19 pandemic meant that for a time, many Christians had to worship from home. And during this period, many of us found that although God was gracious to us throughout a season of online worship, nothing compares to gathering with our brothers and sisters in Christ. Apart from the unique situation of a global pandemic, there are many other trials that might result in people being unable to gather in God's presence with his people: young people get concussions and find themselves to be sound-sensitive; the elderly sometimes get to a place where they are not able to leave home; and Christians live in closed countries where secret gatherings of believers are dangerous to attend and hard to locate. In other words, there are countless reasons for weeping Christians to employ the words of Psalm 42 in their singing and praying.

Next, the psalmist looks back: "These things I remember, / as I pour out my soul: / how I would go with the throng / and lead them in procession to the house of God / with glad shouts and songs of praise, / a multitude keeping festival" (Ps 42:4). The psalmist's yearning for God comes from a recollection of past experiences in his presence.

It is what comes next, though, that may surprise us: the psalmist addresses himself: "Why are you cast down, O my soul, / and why are you in turmoil within me? / Hope in God; for I shall again praise him, / my salvation and my God. / My soul is cast down within me; / therefore I remember you / from the land of Jordan and of Hermon, / from Mount Mizar" (Ps 42:5-6). As is often the case in the psalms of lament, the psalmist models truth-telling to himself, but he also does something unique: he actively speaks, even preaches, this truth to his own soul. Martyn Lloyd-Jones put it like this:

> [The psalmist] was not content just to lie down and commiserate with himself. . . . Have you realised that most of your unhappiness in life is

due to the fact that you are listening to yourself instead of talking to yourself? . . . The main art in the matter of spiritual living is to know how to handle yourself. You have to take yourself in hand, you have to address yourself, preach to yourself, question yourself. You must say to your soul: "Why art thou cast down"—what business have you to be disquieted? You must turn on yourself, upbraid yourself, condemn yourself, exhort yourself, and say to yourself: "Hope thou in God"—instead of muttering in this depressed, unhappy way. And then you must go on to remind yourself of God, Who God is, and what God is and what God has done, and what God has pledged Himself to do. Then having done that, end on this great note: defy yourself, and defy other people, and defy the devil and the whole world, and say with this man: "I shall yet praise Him for the help of His countenance, who is also the health of my countenance and my God."[11]

This psalm offers a rallying cry against passively letting our minds get overcome with sorrow or regret or hopelessness, and to remember past blessing while we anticipate God's future work in our lives.

For the sake of efficiency, we can read the rest of the psalm in a single chunk:

7 Deep calls to deep
    at the roar of your waterfalls;
    all your breakers and your waves
    have gone over me.
8 By day the LORD commands his steadfast love,
    and at night his song is with me,
    a prayer to the God of my life.
9 I say to God, my rock:
    "Why have you forgotten me?
    Why do I go mourning
    because of the oppression of the enemy?"

---

[11]Martyn Lloyd-Jones, *Spiritual Depression: Its Causes and Cure* (Grand Rapids, MI: Eerdmans, 1965), 20-21.

> 10 As with a deadly wound in my bones,
>   my adversaries taunt me,
>   while they say to me all the day long,
>   "Where is your God?"
> 11 Why are you cast down, O my soul,
>   and why are you in turmoil within me?
>   Hope in God; for I shall again praise him,
>   my salvation and my God. (Ps 42:7-11)

Notice that preaching to ourselves is not the end of the story: it will most often lead to more lament and more recollections of YHWH's faithfulness and goodness as well as more direct questions ("Why have you forgotten me?"), and these ultimately lead to more preaching to ourselves. To sum up, when we make the words of a lament psalm our own—when we employ its words directly in our own singing or praying—the psalm takes us by the hand and leads us in an experience of practical theology: it helps us to come to YHWH with our tears.

LAMENT AS SANCTIFIED COMPLAINING

Now that we have unpacked lament, we can step back and notice a frequently occurring element in lament psalms that I called "puzzling" in this book's introduction: the language of forthright *complaining* to God. In Psalm 3, for example, this directness is comparatively tame: "O LORD, how many are my foes! / Many are rising against me; / many are saying of my soul, / 'There is no salvation for him in God'" (Ps 3:1-2). However, in other psalms of lament this language of complaint is much more direct, and much stronger. For example, "Why, O LORD, do you stand far away? / Why do you hide yourself in times of trouble?" (Ps 10:1); "How long, O LORD? Will you forget me forever? / How long will you hide your face from me? / How long must I take counsel in my soul / and have sorrow in my heart all the day? / How long shall my enemy be exalted over me?" (Ps 13:1-2). We could go on.

In the complaint sections of many lament psalms, the psalmist very forcefully and directly complains to YHWH, his covenant God. Needless to say, this is an especially relevant issue as we seek to directly sing or pray these psalms back to God. Those who have read the extended Waltke quote in appendix E noticed that the psalmist's language of vengeance should be tempered with New Testament theology, and not employed against a Christian's earthly enemies. What about the language of complaining? Should we employ *it* today?

As I seek to answer this important question, I'll begin with a story about my own initial, culturally conditioned instinct. A number of years ago, I shaped my morning time of prayer and Bible reading with the book of Psalms. During that season, I would simply read a line of a psalm and then pray it in my own words back to God. In other words, I was practicing exactly what I am advocating in part three this book. I would go line by line, as I sought to allow the language and the ethos of the book of Psalms to shape my practice of prayer. As I came to phrases of direct complaint to YHWH, though, I instinctively qualified the directness. I read a phrase, such as, "How long, O LORD? Will you forget me forever? / How long will you hide your face from me?" (Ps 13:1), and went on to pray something like, "Lord, it sometimes *feels* like you are far off, *but I know* you are always with your children; it sometimes *feels* like you forget me and hide your face from me, *but I know* you never leave nor forsake your children." On the one hand, my prayer was theologically accurate. On the other hand, however, it lacked the directness, the urgency, and the desperation of the psalm. As a polite Canadian who was appropriately reverencing the God who is a consuming fire (Deut 4:24; Heb 12:29), I was reticent to pray with the directness of the psalmist.

Throughout this book, we have affirmed that Christians ought to apply Old Testament content through the lens of its New Testament fulfillment. The crucial question, then, is this: since Jesus fulfilled the

Old Testament hope, is it still appropriate for Christians to pray with the directness and forthrightness that is witnessed in some of the lament psalms? As we turn to the New Testament, we remember that Jesus himself prayed the words of Psalm 22:1 at his crucifixion: "And about the ninth hour Jesus cried out with a loud voice, saying, 'Eli, Eli, lema sabachthani?' that is, 'My God, my God, why have you forsaken me?'" (Mt 27:46, citing Ps 22:1; cf. Mk 15:34). In the very least, then, we can conclude that it is *sometimes* appropriate for believers in Jesus to offer direct complaints to God.

In light of this, a question we might face as we pray through the book of Psalms is, "How do we employ the language when our situation doesn't quite fit that of the psalmist?" I suggest that this is the crux of the matter. As David was experiencing desperation on the front lines of battle, he *felt* abandoned by God, and so he cried out in desperation. As the sinless Son of God was bearing the wrath of God that our sins deserved, he *was* forsaken by God, and so he cried out in desperation. As we have seen, by citing the words of David in this way, Jesus was implicitly claiming to be the greater Son of David to come.[12] In other words, as David witnessed death and the seeming chaos of the battlefield around him, it was appropriate for him to cry out with this type of forthrightness. And as Jesus—who fulfilled this psalm in a typologically prophetic manner—was experiencing the horror of the cross, it was appropriate for him to cry out with an even more intense forthrightness.

The further question we could ask, then, is, "Are there certain seasons in our lives when this type of directness, this type of sanctified complaining, is appropriate?" The answer is, "Sometimes, but not always." In the middle-class West, people may be tempted to pray with this kind of gusto when their minivan breaks down, when they

---

[12]In fact, in an earlier chapter we unpacked Psalm 22 as an example of a psalm which I suggest is inherently typologically prophetic.

can't find a parking spot, or when traffic is making them late for a job
interview and so ruining their chance at climbing the corporate
ladder. But this would cheapen the psalm and reveal a lack of rev-
erence for God. However, in the midst of *real desperation*—at a hospital bed, in the midst of financial crisis, when suffering for the sake
of righteousness—a Christian can and ought to pray with this tone
of desperate directness.

Perhaps a theological litmus test is this: does your situation warrant
the type of deep *groaning* that Romans 8 speaks about, when our
standing in Christ is out of step with the impact a fallen world is
having on us? Further to this, we should recognize that when we pray
our honest prayers directly and forthrightly to the Lord, we are implicitly doing so in faith, because we believe that we approach a God
who will listen to our complaints. Finally, our prayers should not stop
at the direct complaint, but they should move to the other elements
of lament, including recounting the character of God and antici-
pating deliverance by God. Since God knows our hearts, one of the
functions of beginning prayer with the language of complaint is to
simply express with our mouths what our hearts already feel, but then
to move to the other elements of lament.

The goal, brothers and sisters, is for the Lord to work *in us* as we
pray our tears, to assure us of his love for us in Christ, and to give us
the gift of his presence in the midst of our trial. Our outside circumstances may not change, but as we ache in faith using the language of
the lament psalms, God may change our hearts. The next time you
are praying the psalms and come to a forthright line of complaint, I
encourage you to lighten the language to fit the comparative lightness
of your current trial, or if your situation does match the seriousness
of the lament, that you allow the language of lament psalms as a
whole to shape your prayer as a whole. In so doing, you will be aching
in faith as God draws you near to himself. You will be *groaning* toward

the day of Christ, when you will live in a new heavens and a new earth where righteousness dwells.

THE FLOW OF THE PSALMS:
FROM LAMENT TO PRAISE

In part one of this book, I argued that although the various psalms were written as individual compositions in the midst of particular life situations, they were also purposefully gathered into a book and meant to be read in the context of that book's structure. Building on this insight, as we survey the flow of the Psalms, we witness a pattern: just like the book of Isaiah exhibits a greater concentration of oracles of judgment near the beginning of the book, and a greater concentration of oracles of salvation later in the book, the book of Psalms exhibits a greater concentration of lament psalms early in the book, and a greater concentration of praise psalms later in the book.

This observation results in rich application to the Christian life: in the believer's life of praise (*Tehillim*), there is a general movement from lament to praise. Even as praise psalms are also found early in the book (e.g., Ps 8) and lament psalms are also found later in the book (e.g., Ps 137), the *general* movement in the life of praise is from lament to praise. As long as we live in a fallen world, there will be occasions to sing and pray our tears, but the deeper we go in our walk with the Lord—the more we learn and experience the blessings that our ours in Christ—there will be more reasons for praise, until that great day when every tear will be wiped away forever (cf. Is 25:8; Rev 21:4). To qualify, this general movement is not because a Christian's life will tend to get easier as they grow older. Actually, the opposite is most often the case: the longer we live in a world of groaning, our occasions for groaning will be multiplied. But as we have seen, the more the Lord works in our hearts, what happens "out there" (as a result of living in a fallen world) will have less bearing on the *shalom* we experience "in here" (in our hearts), even as we still have many occasions to sing and pray our tears.

THE COSTLY LOSS OF LAMENT IN WORSHIP

As we close this chapter, I return to the observation I began with: in evangelical worship services today, a happy, upbeat ethos tends to abound, to the neglect of lament. The fact that fifty (or so) out of 150 psalms are laments, and the fact that the New Testament witnesses the tears of Jesus (e.g., Jn 11:35) and Christians (e.g., 2 Cor 2:4; 6:10) in the midst of a fallen world, is evidence that learning to sing and pray our tears is not an optional add-on for some Christians who happen to be more emotively wired. Learning to sing and pray our tears is an essential part of the Christian life. In an article titled, "The Costly Loss of Lament in Worship,"[13] Walter Brueggemann put it like this:

> Where lament is absent, covenant comes into being only as a celebration of joy and well-being. Or in political categories, the greater party is surrounded by subjects who are always "yes men and women" from whom "never is heard a discouraging word." Since such a celebrative, consenting silence does not square with reality, covenant minus lament is finally a practice of denial, cover-up, and pretense, which sanctions social control.[14]

For this reason, believers in Jesus need to learn the language of lament to help them in every season of their soul.

Christianity is not simply a blessing when life is going well; it is to be a granite foundation when it is not well in our souls. In fact, the lament psalms are meant to be an injection of theological iron for times when the brittle bones of our faith are under pressure. Therefore,

---

[13]I should mention that although I do not agree with everything Brueggemann writes in this article, I find the quotes I cite in this place extremely helpful, compelling, and essential correctors for Christians today.

[14]Walter Brueggemann, "The Costly Loss of Lament," *Journal for the Study of the Old Testament* 36 (1986): 60.

I agree with Brueggemann that there is a cost to our civility[15] when a "community of faith which negates laments soon concludes that the hard issues of justice are improper questions to pose at the throne, because the throne seems to be only a place of praise."[16] If you and I don't ever hear prayers from the pulpit that ache, and if we never sing songs that speak words of faith in the midst of sorrow, we actually create distance between ourselves and God because we never learn how to approach him in seasons of pain. And if those who lead in corporate prayer and singing in evangelical worship services omit lament from their language, they implicitly teach Christians that God can only be approached when "it is well with my soul."[17] Perhaps the fact that a third of the various psalms contain a prominent theme of lament should suggest to us that our worship services should include regular aspects of lament. In the psalms of lament we learn not simply that we can approach God when life is hard but also how to approach God in the midst of our aching.

LORD FROM SORROWS, DEEP I CALL (PSALM 42)

Although it is often less prominent, I thank God that the language of lament has not been omitted from the prayers and the songs of many evangelical worship services. Of the numerous examples that flood my mind, "Lord from Sorrows Deep I Call (Psalm 42)," by Matt Boswell and Matt Papa is an especially powerful expression of contemporary Christian lament.[18] Structured around Psalm 42, the song begins with honesty as the singer cries out to the Lord from deepest sorrows. Because their hope is shaken, they are feeling the effects of the fall into sin (Gen 3), and they feel desperate. The first

---

[15]Brueggemann, "The Costly Loss of Lament," 66-67.

[16]Brueggemann, "The Costly Loss of Lament," 64.

[17]As one of my friends used to put it, "theology is often caught, more than taught."

[18]Readers can access a lyric video of the song, along with free downloads of the sheet music, audio MP3, and choir and orchestra music here: www.challies.com/resources/lord-from -sorrow-deep-i-call-free-downloads/.

verse continues with the recognition that the singer has long pled that the Lord would come to their rescue, but the difficult life situation has not gone away.

In verse two the theme of lament continues, this time by listing broad reasons for the singer's tears: they have storms within their soul and questions that go unanswered, and their faith seems to be riding in a storm on the sea. And then, mid-verse the singer transitions to call on God to be their shelter *now*. They then cite the refrain from Psalm 42, asking why their soul is cast down, and preaching to themselves to hope in the One who saves them. The verse closes with the singer asking the Lord to cause their heart to praise him, even when the fires have all grown cold. This new disposition of heart is reinforced by the song's chorus—a refrain that will be repeated multiple times before the song concludes:

> And, oh, my soul, put your hope in God
> My help, my Rock, I will praise Him
> Sing, oh, sing through the raging storm
> You're still my God, my salvation

The third and final verse recognizes that it is possible to praise God even if the trials do not go away: even if the singer's life is taken from them, even if every pleasure they enjoy in this world is gone, and even if they only possess grief, they ask God to be their treasure, their vision in the night, and their hope and refuge. In this verse the singer also recognizes that there will come a time when their faith will be sight, but until that great day, they are resolved to praise the Lord. The song then concludes by repeating the chorus twice more, and this is especially powerful: now that the singer has rehearsed their lament *and* their hope, they call on their soul to hope in God who is their help, rock, and object of their praise; even throughout the raging storms that life can bring, the singer affirms that they can continue to sing because he is still their God and their salvation.

DISCUSSION QUESTIONS

1. Do you agree or disagree with Keith Getty's assessment of the modern worship movement? Give some examples of ways his critique is accurate and/or inaccurate, depending on your assessment.

2. Early in this chapter, the author listed various biblical reasons for lament (from both the Old Testament and the New Testament). Which of them resonated with you most? Why?

3. In Psalm 42, the Sons of Korah model for us that lamenting should include honest, emotive expressions of sorrow, but it should also have other aspects. What are some of these other aspects, and why are they so important?

4. Discuss the idea of sanctified complaining to God. Can you think of seasons in life when these types of words have helped you to express your aching and moved you to pray with faith? If you are comfortable, share such a story with your group.

5. Do you agree with Walter Brueggemann that a complete loss of lament in corporate worship (i.e., songs and prayers) would be very costly? Explain the reasons for your answer.

6. Recall some ways your particular local church has modeled corporate prayers of lament for particular difficult world and local life situations.

7. The author provided one example of a recent song of lament that was written for corporate worship. Can you think of some other songs or portions of songs that we as Christians should sing together during our own seasons of lament?

11

Direct Application of Deliverance Psalms

THANKSGIVING

IN HIS BOOK-LENGTH STUDY OF THANKSGIVING, David W. Pao reveals a contrast. He points out first, "Modern Western conceptions of thanksgiving are dominated by the model that privileges the emotional sense of gratefulness in response to a certain act of kindness and the need to fulfill the 'debt' to achieve the balance of personal relationship."[1] However, Pao explains that the biblical concept is quite different:

> [The apostle] Paul is not concerned with teaching his churches proper etiquette. It is the proper response to the salvific acts of God that is at the centre of both his "theology" and "ethics." Thanksgiving in Paul is an act of worship. It is not focused primarily on the benefits received or the blessed condition of a person; instead, God is the centre of thanksgiving. This understanding of thanksgiving as worship is shared by other New Testament authors. In Hebrews, for example, one reads: "since we are receiving a kingdom that cannot be shaken, let us be thankful, and so worship God acceptably with reverence and awe" (12:28). In thanksgiving, God is being honoured.[2]

[1] David W. Pao, *Thanksgiving: An Investigation of a Pauline Theme*, New Studies in Biblical Theology 13 (Downers Grove, IL: InterVarsity, 2003), 19-20.
[2] Pao, *Thanksgiving*, 28-29.

We can conclude that while thanksgiving may be prompted by something we have experienced in our lives, its focus is to be on the God who brought that deliverance about; biblical thanksgiving is Godward.

While Pao's study is focused more heavily on thanksgiving in the writings of the apostle Paul, this chapter will focus on the same theme as it appears in the book of Psalms.[3] However, as we remember Paul's elite training in the (Old Testament) Scriptures as a Pharisee, and then as a Christian who confessed Jesus as the fulfillment of the Old Testament hope, we should not be surprised that his understanding of thanksgiving was shaped by the Old Testament. In line with this, the apostle Paul "mentions the subject of thanksgiving more frequently per page than any other Hellenistic author, pagan or Christian."[4] In addition to the writings of Paul, we find mentions of thanksgiving throughout the New Testament, with a special emphasis found in the narratives of Jesus feeding the crowds, and in the accounts of the Last Supper.[5] Pao's study reveals that biblical thanksgiving ought to characterize the behavior of God's people.[6] Alternatively, ingratitude is said to be one of the distinguishing marks of unbelievers (e.g., Rom 1:21).[7]

---

[3]Waltke's list of thanksgiving psalms is as follows: Psalms 18, 21, 30, 32, 34, 92, 103, 107, 116, 118, 124, 138. See Bruce K. Waltke and Charles Yu, *An Old Testament Theology: An Exegetical, Canonical, and Thematic Approach* (Grand Rapids, MI: Zondervan, 2007), 881. For Bellinger, the following are listed as thanksgiving psalms: "1. Individual Psalms 30, 34, 41, 66, 92, 116, 118, 138. . . . 2. Community Psalms 67, 75, 107, 124, 129, 136." See William H. Bellinger Jr., *Psalms: A Guide to Studying the Psalter*, 2nd ed. (Grand Rapids, MI: Baker Academic, 2012), 23-24.

[4]Paul Schubert, *Form and Function of the Pauline Thanksgivings* (Berlin: Alfred Töpelmann, 1939), 41, as cited in Pao, *Thanksgiving*, 15.

[5]Pao, *Thanksgiving*, 15. In footnote two on the same page, Pao specifies: "In the gospels, outside of the feeding stories and the non-Pauline Lord's Supper account, the *eucharisteō* word-group appears only in Lk 17:16; 18:11 and John 11:41. Two of such appearances are in the context of prayer. Besides the gospels' usage, this word-group appears only in Acts and Revelation. In Acts, the occurrences (24:3; 27:35; 28:15) can all be found in accounts related to Paul. In Revelation, the three occurrences (4:9; 7:12; 11:17) appear in contexts where honour is given to God. The use of *charis* as a reference to thanksgiving can be found only in Heb. 12:28, outside the Pauline epistles."

[6]This sentence summarizes the helpful summary of Paul's use of thanksgiving in Pao, *Thanksgiving*, 20.

[7]See Pao, *Thanksgiving*, 21.

As we turn back in our Bibles from the New Testament to the ultimate source that undergirded its teaching—the Old Testament, and for our purposes, the book of Psalms—we find that several psalms contain a prominent thanksgiving theme. The psalms of thanksgiving were written for times when God brought deliverance out of a period of desperation. As the psalmists looked back, they drew a line *from* this incredible deliverance *to* the God who brought it to pass. In so doing, they experienced something of the goodness of God. And they experienced it in a way that led them to trust God more, to anticipate his good and gracious working, and to invite other believers to employ their words in their own songs and prayers. This is why the direct application of thanksgiving psalms is a gift for Christians.

FROM LAMENT TO THANKSGIVING

In our previous chapter we noticed that Christians have every reason for joy, but Christians will also encounter many reasons for tears, for lament. As we turned to the psalms of lament, we found words to help us groan in faith, and in anticipation of an ultimate (and eternal) end to our current suffering. We also saw that this can and should impact our praying, our singing, and our theology.

If the lament psalms were written from the perspective of a psalmist who was in the thick of great difficulty, the psalms of thanksgiving were written by one who looked back on great difficulty but who had experienced YHWH's gracious deliverance. In fact, the psalms of thanksgiving often *necessarily* follow laments, after the trial had passed. William Bellinger explains: "The conclusion of the lament psalm often includes a vow to praise the God who delivers. The psalms of thanksgiving fulfill that vow."[8] Or, as Rolf Jacobson put it,

---

[8]Bellinger Jr., *Psalms: A Guide to Studying the Psalter,* 83. See also J. Clinton McCann Jr., "Book of Psalms: Introduction, Commentary, and Reflections," in *The New Interpreter's Bible Commentary: Introduction to Hebrew Poetry; 1 & 2 Maccabees; Psalms; Job,* ed. Leander E. Keck, 641-1280 (Nashville: Abingdon, 1996), 647; Nancy L. deClaissé-Walford, Rolf A. Jacobson, and Beth Laneel Tanner, *The Book of Psalms,* New International Commentary on the Old Testament (Grand

The reader may recall that in the prayer for help [or "lament"], the petitioner (1) is in the midst of a crisis, (2) calls on God and requests God's saving help, and (3) promises to praise God once God's help has arrived. In the song of thanksgiving (chapter 2 of the story), the singer (1) looks back on the time of crisis, (2) describes how God provided help, and (3) offers the praise that was promised.[9]

If the lament psalms teach Christians to anticipate YHWH's gracious deliverance, the psalms of thanksgiving teach Christians to look back on the end of the trial, and to give God the credit for their deliverance from it. They are the cure for entitled Christians, because they help us see that we do not deserve the gracious working of our God. They are also the cure for self-sufficient Christians because they are a constant reminder of how needy we really are, and how our current blessings are truly a gift from our gracious God. Finally, they are a cure for functionally deistic Christians who do not give God credit for his powerful and gracious working in the world.

THANKSGIVING AND PRAISE

In our next chapter we are going to focus on praise as a third prominent theme in the book of Psalms. These Godward songs of praise are similar to psalms of thanksgiving in many ways. Rolf Jacobson explains: "Similar to the hymn of praise, these songs tell who God is by telling what God has done. Also similar to the hymn of praise, the songs of thanksgiving are usually addressed both to God and to a human audience."[10] In fact, Mark D. Futato Jr. suggests that like praise psalms, the psalms of thanksgiving do celebrate God's redemptive work, but that work tends to be in the personal life of the

---

Rapids, MI: Eerdmans, 2014), 20. Allen notes the following examples of a promise to give thanks after deliverance: e.g., Psalms 7:17 [18]; 35:18; 43:4; 54:6 [8]; 56:12 [13]; 57:9 [10]; 69:30 [31]; 71:22; 109:30; 140:13 [14]; 142:8; cf. 52:9 [11]. See Leslie C. Allen, "יָדָה," NIDOTTE 2:398.

[9]Rolf A. Jacobson and Karl N. Jacobson, *Invitation to the Psalms: A Reader's Guide for Discovery and Engagement* (Grand Rapids, MI: Baker Academic, 2013), 58.

[10]Jacobson and Jacobson, *Invitation to the Psalms*, 56.

psalmist.[11] And Allen adds that thanks and praise are so related/ complementary and yet also distinct that in Chronicles, Ezra, and Nehemiah, *yadah* (יָדָה, "to thank") and *halal* (הָלַל, "to praise") often occur together as two aspects of the hymnic praise sung by the Levitical choirs.[12] I add that personal and community psalms of thanksgiving do exist, and in these psalms the poet relives the experience of desperation and deliverance.

THE LANGUAGE OF THANKSGIVING

This leads us to take a closer look at the Hebrew word our English Bibles often translate as "thanksgiving." Rather than referring to "psalms of *thanksgiving*," Claus Westermann preferred the term "psalms of *declarative praise*," because these psalms declared God's work in a specific life situation that was bleak, and from which YHWH had delivered the psalmist. As they reflect on this deliverance, these psalms are lifted up in a tone of praise.[13] Westermann went so far as to argue that the Hebrew verb *yadah* (יָדָה) should *not* be translated "to give thanks" but rather "to praise." If Westermann was right, the verb "to give thanks," and nouns like "thanks" and "thanksgiving," would simply not occur in our English translations of the Old Testament. They would be replaced with verbs like "to praise" or nouns like "praise." We should at least consider Westermann's reasoning:

> 1. In praise the one being praised is elevated . . . ; in thanks the one thanked remains in his place. 2. In praise I am directed entirely toward the one whom I praise. . . . In thanks I am expressing my thanks. 3. Freedom and spontaneity belong to the essence of praise; giving thanks can become a duty. 4. Praise has a forum and always occurs in

---

[11]See Mark David Futato, *Interpreting the Psalms: An Exegetical Handbook*, Handbooks for Old Testament Exegesis, ed. David M. Howard (Grand Rapids, MI: Kregel, 2007), 158.

[12]See, for example, 1 Chronicles 16:4; 23:30; 25:3; 2 Chronicles 5:13; 31:2; Ezra 3:11; Nehemiah 12:24, 46. See Leslie C. Allen, "יָדָה," NIDOTTE 2:399.

[13]See Claus Westermann, *Praise and Lament in the Psalms*, ed. Richard Soulen, trans. Keith Crim (Atlanta: John Knox, 1981).

a group; giving thanks is private, for it need concern no one except the one thanking and the one being thanked. 5 . . . Praise can never, but thanks must often, be commanded. 6. The most important verbal mark of difference is that thanksgiving occurs in the speaking of the words, "thank you" . . . genuine, spontaneous praise occurs in a sentence in which the one being praised is the subject: "thou hast done," or "thou art."[14]

There is a lot that is compelling about Westermann's reasoning. However, I suggest that the problem is not with the word "thanksgiving" but with the hearts of the ones doing the thanking.

Although I am ultimately not persuaded by Westermann's call to completely change our language from thanks to praise, I do think he provides an important corrector. We need to be careful to give thanks in a biblical manner: (1) elevating the One who worked for our good and his glory; (2) directing ourselves toward the One who worked in this way; (3) cultivating the habit of thanks in such a way that it freely and spontaneously springs from a joy-filled heart; (4) being both public and private as we give thanks to God; (5) thanking God without the need for constant reminder; and (6) disciplining ourselves to begin our thanks by drawing a direct line from the answered prayer to the God who brought it to pass. In short, we need to do all we can to keep our thanksgiving from lining up with the modern Western misconceptions that David W. Pao corrects in his study. Biblical thanksgiving—whether in the New Testament or the Old Testament—is God-centered.

A study of the Hebrew root *ydh* (ידה)—the one our English Bibles most often translate as "to thank" or "thanksgiving"—will help us to better understand its meaning. Leslie C. Allen notes that when this Hebrew verb occurs in the *hiphil* stem, it can be translated as "to acknowledge, give thanks, praise, confess."[15] He argues that the verb

---

[14]Westermann, *Praise and Lament in the Psalms*, 27-28.
[15]See Allen, "יָדָה," NIDOTTE 2:397.

primarily refers to an acknowledgment, in the sense of praising God, and this praise tends to be specific: giving thanks for resolution of a recent crisis.[16] In fact, Israel had a thank offering that was to be given out of a sense of divine grace.[17] When this offering is mentioned, a song of thanksgiving is often mentioned or alluded to (e.g., Ps 107:22; 116:17; Jonah 2:9), and this song attested an earlier prayer of lament that had been answered.[18]

To summarize, the Hebrew word *yadah* (יָדָה) is used in contexts where a worshiper acknowledges God as the one who brought about deliverance, often in direct answer to desperate prayers, in praise/thanks to God for his working. The object of the thanks is God, and the response of thanks is spontaneous and joy-filled. I suggest that as long as we understand this definition of "thanksgiving," we may use the traditional term in our own singing or praying of these Godward psalms of deliverance.[19]

THE STRUCTURE OF THANKSGIVING

As we saw earlier, I prefer not to speak of essential elements in each psalm genre. Instead, I prefer to notice elements that typically occur when a particular theme or emphasis is present in a psalm. In the case of psalms with a strong thanksgiving theme, certain common features often exist. Generally speaking, in these psalms there is often an interplay between the individual who is recounting the desperate circumstance, and the community whom the psalmist is summoning to join in a chorus of thanks.[20] I appreciate Rolf Jacobson's summary

---

[16]See Allen, "יָדָה," NIDOTTE 2:398.

[17]See Allen, "יָדָה," NIDOTTE 2:398.

[18]See Allen, "יָדָה," NIDOTTE 2:398.

[19]David W. Pao agrees: "Despite his questionable conclusion, Westermann does correctly remind us of the cultural gap between our understanding of thanksgiving and the ancient world of thought. Nevertheless, it is not that the idea of thanksgiving is missing in the Old Testament. It is our conception of the very notion of thanksgiving that should be re-evaluated." Pao, *Thanksgiving*, 23.

[20]See Bellinger Jr., *Psalms: A Guide to Studying the Psalter*, 84.

of what these psalms tend to include: "Call to praise . . . recollection of the past crisis . . . recollection of the past prayer for help . . . renewed call to praise, including the appeal for the community to join the psalmist in praising the Lord."[21] In another work, Rolf and Karl Jacobson add, "In these psalms, the singer's song modulates at some point from narrating what God has done to describing who God is and what God is like. That is, after reporting individual experience, the singer usually shifts gears and describes God's character."[22] Once again, these psalms are God-centered tools for worship during seasons of deliverance.

DIRECT APPLICATION OF THANKSGIVING PSALMS: PSALM 118

So what do these "deliverance" psalms sound like? As we look at one together, we will be helped with how to employ it and others in our own thanks to God. Although we looked at Psalm 118 from complementary angles in earlier chapters,[23] in this place we will simply read it in chunks as we make simple observations about how we can employ it directly in our own worship.

The psalm begins with a call to give thanks to YHWH that is grounded in his eternal *hesed*, and then it immediately moves to call three groups of people to respond with the same confession:

1 Oh give thanks to the LORD, for he is good;
    for his steadfast love endures forever!
2 Let Israel say,
    "His steadfast love endures forever."
3 Let the house of Aaron say,
    "His steadfast love endures forever."

---

[21]deClaissé-Walford, Jacobson, and Tanner, *The Book of Psalms*, 20.

[22]Jacobson and Jacobson, *Invitation to the Psalms*, 60.

[23]For a thorough canonical exegesis of Psalm 118, see Ian J. Vaillancourt, *The Multifaceted Saviour of Psalms 110 and 118: A Canonical Exegesis*, Hebrew Bible Monographs 86 (Sheffield, UK: Sheffield Phoenix, 2019), 130-76.

4 Let those who fear the LORD say,
  "His steadfast love endures forever." (Ps 118:1-4)

Note that the call to "give thanks" is an imperative verb in Hebrew
(*hodu* [הוֹדוּ]). This means that the speaker in the psalm was *summoning*
people to give thanks to YHWH, for he is good, for his *hesed* endures
forever. Also notice the identity of the people he was summoning: Israel
(v. 2), the house of Aaron (v. 3), and those who fear YHWH (v. 4).[24] It
is possible that three *different* groups of people were being summoned
here,[25] but it seems more likely that three near synonyms were being
combined to communicate that all the people of YHWH were being
addressed. The speaker in the psalm was calling all the people of YHWH
to give thanks to YHWH, for he is good, and his *hesed* is eternal. This
also means that we, the Christian readers of Psalm 118, are invited to
directly employ these words and join the chorus of thanksgiving.

After the opening call to give thanks, the speaker moved to recount
the desperate circumstances he had been in (vv. 5-18). At the outset
of this section, though, we find summary statements about what had
happened, and more confessions of YHWH's sufficiency:

5 Out of my distress I called on the LORD;
  the LORD answered me and set me free.
6 the LORD is on my side; I will not fear.
  What can man do to me?
7 the LORD is on my side as my helper;
  I shall look in triumph on those who hate me.
8 It is better to take refuge in the LORD
  than to trust in man.
9 It is better to take refuge in the LORD
  than to trust in princes. (Ps 118:5-9)

---

[24]Note that these three groups are also addressed in Psalms 115:9-13 and 135:19-20 (with the
addition of the house of Levi after that of Aaron).

[25]In this view, the last group—those who fear YHWH—could refer to Gentiles who worship
him. In support of this view, Psalm 118 is preceded by a psalm that calls all nations to praise
(*hallu* [הַלְלוּ]) YHWH (Ps 117:1).

Note first that the psalmist began with a summary statement: he was in distress, he called on YHWH, and YHWH answered him and set him free (v. 5). This is followed by four confessions of the sufficiency of YHWH: since YHWH was on his side as his helper, he would not fear because people can ultimately do nothing to him (v. 6); since YHWH was on his side as his helper, the psalmist would look in triumph on his enemies (v. 7); it is better to take refuge in YHWH than to trust in people or princes (vv. 8-9). As the psalmist looked back on the absolutely desperate circumstances he had been in, he did so in light of having experienced deliverance by YHWH. And from this vantage point, he concluded that the outcome had been sure all along.

Imagine a child who was preparing to face a bully at school. He would *feel* a sense of dread and desperation as he approached the schoolyard. But imagine that just as the bully came near, the child's tall, strong older brother stepped out from around a corner. The child could look back on that encounter and remember the sense of dread and the desperate plea for help, but as he did so, he would have a confidence that the outcome had been certain all along because his older brother was planning to come to his rescue. Although in the moment of desperation the odds may seem stacked against one of God's people, in the hindsight of having experienced God's gracious deliverance, we see that the outcome had been sure all along.

Notice that the psalmist took nine verses to recount the character of YHWH, to call on others to give thanks along with him, and to highlight the security of his life with YHWH in his corner. But then in verse 10, he finally began to recount the actual scene of desperation, and that scene was an ancient battlefield:

10 All nations surrounded me;
    in the name of the LORD I cut them off!
11 They surrounded me, surrounded me on every side;
    in the name of the LORD I cut them off!

12 They surrounded me like bees;
    they went out like a fire among thorns;
    in the name of the LORD I cut them off!
13 I was pushed hard, so that I was falling,
    but the LORD helped me. (Ps 118:10-13)

This ancient battle was not like modern warfare. Today, many aspects of war are fought from a distance, with computers and intelligence. But ancient wars were primarily fought in hand-to-hand combat. On this ancient battlefield, the psalmist had been surrounded, singled out by his enemy—likely because he was the king and so would have been a special target. And these enemies were cut off in the name of YHWH. We'll get a bit more information about what happened later in the psalm, but for now we learn that the circumstance was absolutely desperate as the psalmist was pushed hard so that he was falling, but he cut his enemies off in the name of YHWH.

As we directly apply these words, we need to make a transfer of sorts: although some of us will have been delivered in the context of war, most readers of this book will have other experiences of deliverance that occasion songs and prayers of thanks. But most importantly, we should not neglect to give thanks for the main thing: ultimate deliverance from the ultimate war with sin, death, hell, and Satan. While life will bring seasons when it is appropriate to give thanks for incidents of this-worldly deliverance, Christians should always give thanks for our eternal deliverance in Christ.

As we conclude the first main section of the psalm's body (vv. 5-18), we find more confessions of how secure the psalmist was in light of YHWH's care for him:

14 the LORD is my strength and my song;
    he has become my salvation.
15 Glad songs of salvation
    are in the tents of the righteous:
    "The right hand of the LORD does valiantly,

16 the right hand of the LORD exalts,

the right hand of the LORD does valiantly!"

17 I shall not die, but I shall live,

and recount the deeds of the LORD.

18 the LORD has disciplined me severely,

but he has not given me over to death. (Ps 118:14-18)

Significantly, the psalmist quoted Exodus 15:2a in Psalm 118:14. We may remember that Exodus 15 records the Song of the Sea, when YHWH had used Moses to lead the people of Israel out of Egypt and then to the other side of the water. After Pharaoh and his army had drowned and God's people were safely on the other side, Moses sang this song to celebrate the salvation that YHWH had accomplished. By quoting Exodus 15 in this place, the psalmist seems to have been saying, "Do you remember YHWH's miraculous redemption of his people in the exodus? Well, that same God has done it again *with me.*" This further suggests that the speaker in the psalm is to be viewed as the king over God's people: who but the king would experience a deliverance that would be a cause of national celebration (cf. vv. 1-4; 19-28)? And who but the king would be the primary target in war (vv. 10-13)? Finally, who but the king would represent the entire nation as a solitary individual?[26]

With the speaker leading the march,[27] the next section of the psalm introduces a processional from the battlefield, through the gates of the city, and then through the gates of the temple courts, where he would lead in a responsive song of thanks:

19 Open to me the gates of righteousness,

that I may enter through them

and give thanks to the LORD.

---

[26]For more on the king representing the entire nation, see the discussion of the corporate solidarity between the king and his people in chapter 5.

[27]It was the king's role in antiquity to lead the victory procession from the battlefield, and back into the city.

20 This is the gate of the LORD;
   the righteous shall enter through it.
21 I thank you that you have answered me
   and have become my salvation. (Ps 118:19-21)

The speaker in the psalm began this section by calling for the "gates of righteousness" to be opened. Later, in verse 26b we find confirmation that this referred to the gates of the Jerusalem temple. In verse 20, the psalmist wanted to enter the courts of the temple and thank YHWH, because YHWH had answered him and "become [his] salvation" (v. 21). What did he mean? Although YHWH had been his God prior to this event, when he delivered the psalmist from the trial YHWH had become his salvation, in the sense that he had directly delivered him from the horrible trial.

The psalm then concluded with a responsive song of thanks that was sung within the temple courts:

22 The stone that the builders rejected
   has become the cornerstone.
23 This is the LORD's doing;
   it is marvelous in our eyes.
24 This is the day that the LORD has made;
   let us rejoice and be glad in it.
25 Save us, we pray, O LORD!
   O LORD, we pray, give us success!
26 Blessed is he who comes in the name of the LORD!
   We bless you from the house of the LORD.
27 The LORD is God,
   and he has made his light to shine upon us.
   Bind the festal sacrifice with cords,
   up to the horns of the altar!
28 You are my God, and I will give thanks to you;
   you are my God; I will extol you.
29 Oh give thanks to the LORD, for he is good;
   for his steadfast love endures forever! (Ps 118:22-29)

If the psalmist was disregarded (rejected) by the enemies of God's people (the builders), YHWH had sent him as his primary means of effecting national deliverance (the cornerstone). The one who comes in the name of YHWH is blessed by the people as they stand in the house of YHWH (v. 26). Since the New Testament makes clear that these statements point to Christ, this leads us to direct our thanks to our Savior and our deliverance in him from the ultimate enemy. Finally, the psalm concluded exactly the way it began: with a summary statement that called all listeners to "give thanks to the LORD for he is good, for his steadfast love endures forever!" (v. 29). As was the case with the psalms of lament, when we make the words of the various thanksgiving psalms our own—when we directly employ their words in our own singing or praying—the psalm takes us by the hand and leads us in an experience of practical theology: it helps us to express our thanks to our great God.

Before we conclude, we should consider the extent to which we can directly apply the words of Psalm 118 in our personal and community songs and prayers of thanks. The short answer is this: most of it, but with a few qualifications. We have noticed that the speaker in Psalm 118 was not *simply* an "everyman" whom we can mimic in every way. Since he was the king over God's people, the existence of a community with YHWH dwelling in their midst was wrapped up in *his* deliverance. At that point in the history of God saving a people for himself, the deliverance of the king meant the preservation of the community of God's people, with YHWH dwelling in their midst, in the temple. As we keep this in mind, we can make the transition and employ this psalm in worship.

SHOULD CHRISTIANS EXPECT DELIVERANCE FROM EVERY TRIAL?

At this point we are likely left with a question: in light of the way the psalmist talked about his deliverance, should we speak in the same terms as we think about the various trials in our own lives? The short answer is that the Bible *does not* give Christians warrant to expect every situation to turn out easy, even if they desperately cry out to YHWH. Although this is a bigger discussion—about a dangerous and erroneous theology that teaches God's people to expect prosperity in every season of life—we can notice that the Bible *does* teach Christians to expect *ultimate* victory in the face of every trial. Consider the words of Jesus: "I tell you, my friends, do not fear those who kill the body, and after that have nothing more that they can do. But I will warn you whom to fear: fear him who, after he has killed, has authority to cast into hell. Yes, I tell you, fear him!" (Lk 12:4-5). There is so much we could say about this passage, but for our purposes simply notice that Christians should *not* fear the one who can kill their bodies. We could add: "just like they killed Stephen and James, and later, the other apostles." In this passage, Jesus is teaching us to fear *ultimate* and *eternal* death, rather than the trials, and even the physical death we may experience as a result. This is not to make light of death, it is simply to observe that physical death is not the worst thing that can happen to a believer in Jesus. In fact, it will usher in being present with Christ, which is far better (cf. Phil 1:23).

MY HEART IS FILLED WITH THANKFULNESS

One of my favorite examples of modern songs of thanks is by Keith Getty and Stuart Townend. In their explanation of the song's lyrics, they note that while we are often tempted to primarily focus on "health and position, family and friends, home and belongings"[28] in our prayers of thanks, the spiritual blessings that are ours in Christ are much more central in the Bible's teaching. "My Heart is Filled with Thankfulness" recounts the heart of those spiritual blessings and leads us to acknowledge our God as the gracious giver of them all.

---

[28]Keith Getty and Stuart Townend, "My Heart Is Filled with Thankfulness," Thankyou Music, 2008, https://store.gettymusic.com/us/song/my-heart-is-filled-with-thankfulness/.

Each of the three verses begin with a recognition that the singer's heart is filled with thankfulness. From this starting point, the theme of verse one is thankfulness to the One who overcame the singer's sins by bearing their pain, plumbing the depths of their disgrace, and so gave them new life, clothed them in his light, and wrote his law on their heart (cf. Jer 31). The theme of verse two is thankfulness to the One who walks beside the singer, flooding their weaknesses with strength, causing fears to fly away, whose promises are enough for every step they take in life, and who sustains them with arms of love and crowns them with grace. Verse three then concludes the song with thankfulness to him who reigns, whose wisdom is their perfect peace, and whose every thought is love. Rooted in everything they have just sung, and especially in the fact that every day the singer has on earth is given by the king, they conclude by resolving:

> So I will give my life, my all,
> To love and follow Him.

DISCUSSION QUESTIONS

1. Did any of David W. Pao's teachings on thankfulness particularly resonate with you? Share with your group.

2. How are lament psalms and thanksgiving psalms related?

3. How are thanksgiving psalms and praise psalms similar?

4. In the section on "the language of thanksgiving," we noticed the tendency to make thankfulness a duty rather than a God-centered delight. What does the Hebrew word *yadah* (יָדָה) mean, and what are some ways this meaning corrects a duty-driven, human-centered attitude toward thankful worship?

5. What common elements tend to be included in psalms of thanksgiving?

6. Were there any elements in the discussion of Psalm 118 that were particularly helpful for you?

7. Should a Christian employ the psalms of thanksgiving in a way that leads them to *expect* deliverance from every difficulty? Why or why not?

8. The author provided one example of a recent song that is particularly theologically rich, and also focuses on thankfulness. Can you think of some other songs or portions of songs that we as Christians should have in our arsenal for seasons of thankfulness?

12

Direct Application of Exaltation Psalms

PRAISE

IN HIS CLASSIC BOOK *Mere Christianity*, C. S. Lewis suggests, "If I find in myself a desire which no experience in this world can satisfy, the most probable explanation is that I was made for another world."[1] In the psalms of praise, we are given a foretaste of the self-forgetful satisfaction that will come in that other world. The lament psalms help us to emote in tears of faith, and the thanksgiving psalms lift up our hearts to give God the credit for our deliverance from a trial. The praise psalms teach us the soul-satisfying nature of Godward exaltation as we focus on who God is and what he has done for his people.

C. S. Lewis has already helped us see that our deepest longings reveal that we were made for another world. His insights continue as he reflects on why we praise and what praise looks like:

> I think we delight to praise what we enjoy because the praise not merely expresses but completes the enjoyment; it is its appointed consummation. It is not out of compliment that lovers keep on telling one another how beautiful they are; the delight is incomplete till it is expressed. It is frustrating to have discovered a new author and not to be able to tell anyone how good he is; to come suddenly, at the turn of

---

[1]C. S. Lewis, *Mere Christianity* (San Francisco: HarperCollins, 2001), 136-37.

the road, upon some mountain valley of unexpected grandeur and then to have to keep silent because the people with you care for it no more than for a tin can in the ditch; to hear a good joke and find no one to share it with. . . . The Scotch catechism says that man's chief end is "to glorify God and enjoy Him forever." But we shall then know that these are the same thing. Fully to enjoy is to glorify. In commanding us to glorify Him, God is inviting us to enjoy Him.[2]

Therefore, the praise psalms are not merely the icing on the cake. They lead us to not only *understand* who God is and what he has done in redeeming us from sin, but they also lead us to *exult* in these things. And that exultation is the apex of satisfaction in Christ.

I have stated this positively, but praise also has a dark side. Claus Westermann has pointed out that we are *hard-wired to praise*. The question, therefore, is not *whether* we will praise but *whom (or what)* we will praise. If we do not exalt God, we will exalt a less worthy object for our worship. Westermann explains:

Exalting is part of existence. It is so much a part of it, that when one has ceased to exalt God, something else must be exalted. Then God can be displaced by a man, an institution, an idea. Exalting remains a function of existence. . . . Not everywhere where God is no longer truly praised will men of necessity fall into the extremity of the deification of man. But they must surely exalt, admire, honor something. There is no real, full existence that does not in some way honor, admire, look up to something. . . . If the praise of God, as the Psalms express it, belongs to existence, then the directing of this praise to a man, an idea, or an institution must disturb and finally destroy life itself. The Psalms say that only where God is praised is there life.[3]

Have you ever been to a concert and witnessed people worshiping the performing artist? They may not be bowing down or making an

---

[2]C. S. Lewis, *Reflections on the Psalms* (San Diego: Harcourt Brace Jovanovich, 2017), 95-97.
[3]Claus Westermann, *Praise and Lament in the Psalms*, ed. Richard Soulen, trans. Keith Crim (Atlanta: John Knox, 1981), 160-61.

animal sacrifice, but their entire being is delighting and exalting and even worshiping the performer. Have you ever watched an episode of *American Idol*? Witnessed a celebrity sighting? In all of these situations and many like them, people are exalting lesser objects for praise that will not satisfy their deepest longings. It is not wrong to appreciate and honor people in this life, but they may not take the place of God. When they do, we rob God of glory and ourselves of joy.[4] In the psalms of praise, we find words to take us out of the mire of worshiping lesser gods, and we are given words to exalt the only true God—the One who is worthy of our praise. With C. S. Lewis again, in the act of employing the praise psalms in our songs and prayers, we are completing the enjoyment in our God and so are being given a foretaste of the world to come. This is why the direct application of the praise psalms is a gift for Christians.

DID YOU KNOW?
The Language of Praise

In this book's introduction we learned that the Hebrew title for the book of Psalms is *Tehillim*, "praises." This means that the entire collection of psalms—with all of its varied content—falls under the umbrella of "praises." With this in mind, we can add that certain psalms also have a specific praise theme, just like certain psalms contain a lament or a thanksgiving theme. While the title for the book of Psalms employs the Hebrew noun *Tehillim* ("praises"), the praise psalms frequently employ the Hebrew verb *halal* (הָלַל), "to praise." For those who would like to dig deeper into this issue, appendix F is available as a free download on the IVP website (www.ivpress.com/treasuring -the-psalms).

---

[4]I first learned this turn of phrase from the ministry of John Piper.

THE STRUCTURE OF PRAISE

In our previous chapters, we saw that the psalms that exhibit a lament or a thanksgiving theme often contain certain elements. This is also the case with praise (*halal* [הָלַל]) psalms.[5] While thanksgiving (*hodu* [הוֹדוּ]) psalms celebrate a specific act of deliverance in answer to a petition, praise (*halal* [הָלַל]) psalms celebrate God's person or works in general.[6] We saw in this book's introduction that the word *hesed* is a frequently occurring word in the book of Psalms, and that it speaks of God as relational and covenantal, tender and true. Therefore, "steadfast love" is a helpful way of translating the term. In the introduction, we also saw that the Hebrew name YHWH is the personal, covenantal name of God, and that it is specifically related to his work of redemption. As we put these two words together, we find that the praise psalms exalt YHWH for his *hesed*.[7] Finally, these psalms tend to refer to God in the third person ("he is," "YHWH is," and the like), instead of addressing him directly in the second person ("you").[8]

With Mark D. Futato Jr. and others, I suggest that the structure of praise is fairly simple: (1) an opening invitation that calls others to praise YHWH; (2) the reason for the praise that is rooted in who YHWH is and what he has done for his people *in general*; (3) a conclusion that often re-invites others to praise YHWH in light of the

---

[5]For Bellinger, the "general hymns" are as follows: "General Hymns 29, 33, 68, 100, 103, 105, 111, 113, 114, 115, 117, 134, 135, 139, 145, 146, 147, 149, 150." William H. Bellinger Jr., *Psalms: A Guide to Studying the Psalter*, 2nd ed. (Grand Rapids, MI: Baker Academic, 2012), 23. For Jacobson and Jacobson, "the hymns of praise may be identified as Pss. 8; 33; 47; 48; 65; 66; 67; 68; 76; 84; 87; 89; 93; 96; 97; 98; 99; 100; 103; 104; 105; 111; 112; 113; 114; 117; 135; 145; 146; 147; 148; 149; 150." Rolf A. Jacobson and Karl N. Jacobson, *Invitation to the Psalms: A Reader's Guide for Discovery and Engagement* (Grand Rapids, MI: Baker Academic, 2013), 46n6.

[6]See Bruce K. Waltke and Charles Yu, *An Old Testament Theology: An Exegetical, Canonical, and Thematic Approach* (Grand Rapids, MI: Zondervan, 2007), 881.

[7]See Waltke and Yu, *An Old Testament Theology*, 881.

[8]A notable exception to this is Psalm 8. See J. Clinton McCann Jr., "The Book of Psalms: Introduction, Commentary, and Reflections," in *The New Interpreter's Bible Commentary: Introduction to Hebrew Poetry; 1 & 2 Maccabees; Psalms; Job*, vol. 3, ed. Leander E. Keck (Nashville: Abingdon, 1996), 648.

praiseworthy focus of section two.[9] However, all of these elements will not necessarily be present in every praise psalm. For example, Psalm 150 is made up entirely of calls to praise, without a psalm body at all. I suggest, though, that the entire book of Psalms makes up the reasons for praise, and that Psalm 150 functions as a concluding call to praise in light of the entire book. The overarching point I am making here, though, is that the praise psalms tend to exhibit a *general* structure, but this is not always the case. If a psalm exhibits a praise theme or tone but does not include all of the elements I have listed above, this does not make it less a psalm of praise.

We have seen that the praise psalms tend to begin with a call to praise. This opening section invites the "community of worshipers into a celebratory expression of faith."[10] This section also sets the joyful, unrestrained, celebratory mood for praise.[11] And as we saw with Psalm 150, the call to praise is itself an act of praise. Why? Because to invite the community to celebrate God's goodness is already to begin the celebration. We have also seen that the body of the psalm lists reasons for praise. It makes sense, then, that this section often begins "with the Hebrew word [*ki*] (כִּי), which can be translated 'for' or 'because.'"[12] The ultimate reason for praise in this section can most often be summed up this way: we praise God because he has redeemed his people, thus creating a community to praise him (e.g., Ps 100; 111; 114).[13] Other reasons for praise include his sovereignty over history (e.g., Ps 33; 103; 113; 117; 145; 146; 147; 150) and his creation of the world (e.g., Ps 8; 104; 148).[14]

---

[9]See Mark David Futato, *Interpreting the Psalms: An Exegetical Handbook*, Handbooks for Old Testament Exegesis, ed. David M. Howard (Grand Rapids, MI: Kregel, 2007), 146; Tremper Longman III, *How to Read the Psalms* (Downers Grove, IL: InterVarsity, 1988), 25; Jacobson and Jacobson, *Invitation to the Psalms*, 47; McCann Jr., "The Book of Psalms," 648.

[10]Jacobson and Jacobson, *Invitation to the Psalms*, 47.

[11]Jacobson and Jacobson, *Invitation to the Psalms*, 47.

[12]Futato, *Interpreting the Psalms*, 148. See also Longman, *How to Read the Psalms*, 25; Jacobson and Jacobson, *Invitation to the Psalms*, 48.

[13]See Waltke and Yu, *An Old Testament Theology*, 881.

[14]See Waltke and Yu, *An Old Testament Theology*, 881.

DIRECT APPLICATION OF PRAISE
PSALMS: PSALMS 117 AND 150

So what do these "exaltation" psalms sound like? As we look at a few together, we will be helped with how to employ them and others in our own delight in God.

Psalm 117 begins with a typical call to praise, but from there it is anything but typical. Its two verses make it the shortest psalm in the book of Psalms, but it packs a major punch:

> 1 Praise the LORD, all nations!
>> Extol him, all peoples!
> 2 For great is his steadfast love toward us,
>> and the faithfulness of the LORD endures forever.
>> Praise the LORD! (Ps 117:1-2)

After the call to praise ("Praise YHWH"), we notice that the object of the call is not the more common "Israel," "House of Aaron," or "those who fear YHWH." No, the psalmist is calling *all the nations* to praise YHWH. Hebrew textbooks teach about a device called "parallelism" that is typical of Hebrew poetic style. For our purposes, notice that the first verse says nearly the same thing twice:[15] "Praise YHWH" has nearly the same meaning as "extol him," and "all nations" carries a very similar meaning as "all peoples." But at the same time, these two sets of parallels do not carry exactly the same meaning. One way this kind of construction works in Hebrew poetry is that the pairing of near synonyms means that the totality of the meaning of both words is being conveyed.

After the call to praise in verse 1, Psalm 117 continues with the Hebrew word *ki* (כִּי), which means "for" or "because." As we noticed earlier, the reasons for praise are often signaled by the appearance of this word. And so those reasons are stated, with two lines that are jam-packed with incredible truths: "For great is his [*hesed*] toward us,

---

[15]This is called "synonymous parallelism."

/ and the faithfulness of [YHWH] endures forever." By now we know that the word *hesed* means something along the lines of "steadfast love"—a tender and faithful love. However, in Psalm 117 the word used alongside *hesed* is not the normal Hebrew word for "great" but a verb that means "to be strong" or "to prevail." If the parallel idea in the next line is "endures forever," this verb in the first line tells us *why* YHWH's *hesed* endures forever: it is strong, it prevails. Finally, the word *hesed* is set in parallel to *emeth* (אֱמֶת), which means "faithful" or "true." Once again, the meanings overlap and complement one another, creating a bigger idea than one of the lines could have communicated on its own. The psalm then ends with a conclusion that re-invites the hearers to praise YHWH, with the typical Hebrew word *hallu-yah* (הַלְלוּ־יָה), which simply means "praise YHWH."

As we step back we notice that the two-verse Psalm 117 is filled with nuggets for direct application, especially as it summons all nations/peoples to praise/extol YHWH, and then lists YHWH's strong, prevailing, everlasting *hesed/emeth* over us as the reason (*ki*) for praise. The "us" in this verse may be easy to pass over, but do you see what was going on here? The psalmist was lumping himself in with the nations, as the people who were objects of the firm, sure, steady, covenant love and faithfulness of the covenant God, YHWH. For Christians today, especially in my native Canada, the existence of a multicultural gathering of God's people is an everyday reality. I, for one, am an active member at a church that *celebrates* its multiculturalism, and that has ministries in various languages in order to accommodate those who do not speak English. When I read the vision of a people from every tribe, tongue, people, and language worshiping the lamb in Revelation 7, it feels like a glorious extension of my everyday reality, as though my own church community is on a trajectory to take me there. But for Old Testament saints, Psalm 117 would have been revolutionary.

In the context of the Old Testament, where did the author of Psalm 117 get the audacity to include non-Jews in his call to praise? It would have begun in Genesis 3:15 and the promise that the seed of the woman would one day crush the head of the seed of the serpent. This "proto-gospel" looks ahead to a day when sin and all of its effects will be overcome. In Genesis 11:1-9, we get the account of the tower of Babel and YHWH's scattering of the nations by the creation of languages. In case one might assume, though, that the hope expressed in Genesis 3:15 would only apply to Jews, in Genesis 12—immediately after the scattering of the nations in Genesis 11—we encounter the call of Abram, who was the father of the Jewish people. Among the promised blessings was this: "in you all the families of the earth shall be blessed" (Gen 12:3). If the call of Abram signaled the beginning of the Jewish people, it also revealed hope for the nations, the very people who had been scattered at Babel (Gen 11).

What Psalm 117 anticipates, then, is not a new theology, but the fulfillment of God's promise to Abram. Psalm 47:9 is rooted in this same theology, only this time with a focus on the leaders of the nations: "the princes of the peoples gather / as the people of the God of Abraham." Beyond these psalms, we can read accounts in the prophets where the nations would stream to the presence of God en masse (e.g., Is 2) and the Great Commission in the New Testament, where Christ's followers are told to make disciples of all nations (Mt 28:16-20). And all of this anticipates the eternal hope of multicultural worship in the new heavens and earth (e.g., Rev 21:1–22:5). Psalm 117 is the shortest psalm in the book of Psalms, but it packs theological punch, even as its structure provides a brief, but typical example of a praise psalm. How appropriate, then, is this great psalm for our own corporate worship services: Psalm 117 reminds us to intentionally celebrate and specifically call people from all backgrounds to praise God in Christ. These words are glorious to sing or pray as we anticipate the eternal multicultural worship service to come!

Psalm 150, on the other hand, is atypical in its structure. I have already suggested, though, that this is not a problem, especially as we consider that the psalmists did not work from a rigid template. Instead, our general outline of what praise psalms tend to contain comes from an inductive reading across the book of Psalms. As I have also hinted, there may be another explanation for a psalm, though, that is made up entirely of calls to praise: perhaps these lines do not function as *initial* calls to praise do in most other praise psalms, but as a twelvefold re-invitation for all to praise YHWH. Why do I say this? Because Psalm 150 is the last psalm in the book of Psalms, and as such it functions as the climax of the entire book. Perhaps this book of praises (*Tehillim*) is being capped by a re-invitation to everything that has breath to make use of every possible instrument of praise in their exaltation of YHWH! Let's read together:

1 Praise the LORD!
    Praise God in his sanctuary;
    praise him in his mighty heavens!
2 Praise him for his mighty deeds;
    praise him according to his excellent greatness!
3 Praise him with trumpet sound;
    praise him with lute and harp!
4 Praise him with tambourine and dance;
    praise him with strings and pipe!
5 Praise him with sounding cymbals;
    praise him with loud clashing cymbals!
6 Let everything that has breath praise the LORD!
    Praise the LORD! (Ps 150:1-6)

What a wonderful twelvefold summons, a re-invitation to all who have journeyed through the book of Psalms to praise YHWH with their entire being. *Hallu-yah!* In line with our exploration of lament and thanksgiving, when we make the words of the praise psalms our

own—when we employ their words directly in our own singing or
praying—the psalm takes us by the hand and leads us in an experience of God's greatness: it helps us to praise YHWH.

PRAISE TO THE LORD, THE ALMIGHTY

As an example of a contemporary praise song, I turn to one that is
nearly 350 years old! However, it is still widely sung in churches, and
it is one of my favorites. Since this song is public domain, I can cite
"Praise to the Lord, the Almighty" in full:

> Praise to the Lord, the Almighty, the King of creation!
> O my soul, praise Him, for He is thy health and salvation!
> All ye who hear, now to His temple draw near;
> Praise Him in glad adoration.
>
> Praise to the Lord, who o'er all things so wondrously reigneth,
> Shelters thee under His wings, yea, so gently sustaineth!
> Hast thou not seen how thy desires e'er have been
> Granted in what He ordaineth?
>
> Praise to the Lord, who doth prosper thy work and defend thee;
> Surely His goodness and mercy here daily attend thee;
> Ponder anew what the Almighty can do,
> If with His love He befriend thee.
>
> Praise to the Lord, who, when tempests their warfare are waging,
> Who, when the elements madly around thee are raging,
> Biddeth them cease, turneth their fury to peace,
> Whirlwinds and waters assuaging.
>
> Praise to the Lord, who, when darkness of sin is abounding,
> Who, when the godless do triumph, all virtue confounding,
> Sheddeth His light, chaseth the horrors of night,
> Saints with His mercy surrounding.
>
> Praise to the Lord, oh, let all that is in me adore Him!
> All that hath life and breath, come now with praises before Him;

Let the Amen sound from His people again,
Gladly for aye we adore Him.[16]

DISCUSSION QUESTIONS

1. In the introduction to this chapter, the author cited C. S. Lewis twice and Claus Westermann once. Re-read each of these quotes and share something from each that you hadn't thought of previously.

2. How does the section on the language of praise distinguish "praise psalms" from every psalm in the book of Psalms as a *Tehillim*, a Book of Praises?

3. What is the typical structure of a praise psalm, and why is it important to guard against pressing every praise psalm into this structure?

4. What particularly stuck out to you in the discussion of Psalms 117 and 150 as examples of praise psalms?

5. What are some other praise psalms that particularly resonate with you? Take turns reading some lines together.

6. Build a playlist of praise with your group. The author cited "Praise to the Lord, the Almighty" as an example of a praise hymn that many of us sing in our churches today. As you consider the general thrust of typical praise psalms, what are some other favorite songs of this genre that you sing at your local church?

---

[16]By Joachim Neander, 1680. Translated by Catherine Winkworth, 1863. Public Domain.

Conclusion

The Treasure Hunt Has Just Begun

ALTHOUGH OUR BOOK IS DRAWING TO A CLOSE, my goal is that our study of the Psalms would last for a lifetime. In this book's introduction, we were oriented to the book of Psalms as we explored two key words—YHWH and *hesed*—and three helpful insights—that the Psalms is a book of praises (*Tehillim*), a little Bible (Luther), and an anatomy of all the parts of the soul (Calvin). Then in the book's three parts, we were led to read the Psalms in specific ways—canonically, christologically, and personally/corporately.

So where do we go from here? On the one hand, no one book could possibly teach all there is to learn about the Psalms. For this reason, I encourage you to read many others. But on the other hand, this book was not written with the goal of giving readers all the answers; it was written with the goal of equipping them to dig deeply in the bottomless gold (or treasure!) mine of the Psalms on their own. I hope we will all spend a lifetime excavating on the surface, below the surface, and deep below the surface to find soul-satisfying, God-glorifying gospel treasure in the Psalms.

We also need to remember that the entire Bible—including the book of Psalms—is indeed a bottomless gold (or treasure!) mine. This means that we can rest assured that no matter how deep we dig, we will find gospel treasure. And this frees us from perfectionism: although scholars spend entire careers studying any one of our three ways of reading the Psalms, we will hopefully find that our journey through this book has given us a few new sets of lenses that will help us to excavate deeper below the surface. There is always more learning to do, but the most important thing is that we read and re-read the Psalms on our own.

As we dig deeply in the Psalms, we can read with a sensitivity to "The Story: Reading the Psalms Canonically." Through this lens, we will remember to look at each psalm's superscription for hints about its author and time of composition, its genre, and possibly the historical occasion that led to its composition. In turn, we will remember something of the canonical process from the composition of the individual psalm to its place in the book of Psalms as we now have it. We will be able to look for themes and word choices in our psalm and ask if any surrounding psalms bear similarities—perhaps we are in a cluster that has been grouped around a particular theme. And we will be able to place our psalm in the flow of the book as a whole—does it appear early, when the emphasis is on weeping King David of history; in book three, with its strong exile theme; book four and its prominent theme that YHWH reigns even when David does not; or book five and its prominent theme of the return of a new and better David? Does our psalm cohere with the broad theme of the book it is in? Or does it add some nuance to the study? As we study the book of Psalms in more detail, perhaps we will even nuance the themes set forth in this book. Great! The key is to read the Psalms through a "canonical" lens.

We are also equipped to read with an appreciation for "The Savior: Reading the Psalms Christologically." When we read a psalm, we will remember that it points to Christ and "gospel application," and we now have categories to consider as we search for gospel links. We will remember to place our psalm in the timeline of redemptive history. We'll ask if it contains any promises Christ fulfilled, contrasts with the fullness in Christ, typology, direct prophecies, or typologically prophetic elements. And we can consult a Bible with cross-references to discover whether the New Testament cites or alludes to our psalm—if so, this will provide the Holy Spirit–inspired "answer key" for its interpretation. Developing a gospel instinct takes work, but as we discipline ourselves to read through this lens, the payoff will be enormous: we will be constantly led from the Psalms to gospel application, and in this way our lives will increasingly orbit around the life-giving and soul-refreshing gospel—the one thing that matters most.

Since the psalms offer a window into the soul of the poet, we will also remember to "read through the window" and practice direct application of the various psalms. By reading with a sensitivity to "The Soul: Reading the Psalms Personally and Corporately," we will remember that we are meant to employ the words of the psalmist as our own. Sometimes these words will have to be modified. If readers share my conviction that psalms of imprecation are not appropriate for the life of the Christian, they will point these words away from troubling people in their lives and toward Satan and ultimate things. And if a psalm contains a direct prophecy about Christ or typologically prophetic elements, readers will not employ these words directly about their own experiences. But as we read with these kinds of correctives in mind, we will find that the majority of the lines of the majority of the psalms offer fertile ground for direct application to our lives. As we read we may ask if our psalm contains a prominent lament, thanksgiving, or praise theme. Or it may contain a less prominent theme—such as, for example, repentance (e.g., Ps 51). Whatever the season of our soul, as we let the psalmist take us by the hand and lead us, his language will become our own, and we will grow in a life of full-orbed praise of God.

Bibliography

Achtemeier, Elizabeth. *The Old Testament and the Proclamation of the Gospel.* Philadelphia: Westminster, 1973.

Allison, Dale C. *The New Moses: A Matthean Typology.* Minneapolis, MN: Fortress, 1993.

Baker, David L. *Two Testaments, One Bible: A Study of the Theological Relationship Between the Old and New Testaments.* 3rd ed. Downers Grove, IL: InterVarsity Press, 2010.

Barrett, Matthew. *Canon, Covenant and Christology: Rethinking Jesus and the Scriptures of Israel.* New Studies in Biblical Theology 51. Edited by D. A. Carson. Downers Grove, IL: IVP Academic, 2020.

Bavinck, Herman. *The Wonderful Works of God: Instruction in the Christian Religion According to the Reformed Confession.* Kindle ed. Glenside, PA: Westminster Seminary Press, 2020.

Beale, Gregory K. *Handbook on the New Testament Use of the Old Testament: Exegesis and Interpretation.* Grand Rapids, MI: Baker Academic, 2012.

Beale, Gregory K., and Donald A. Carson, eds. *Commentary on the New Testament Use of the Old Testament.* Grand Rapids, MI: Baker Academic, 2007.

Bellinger, William H., Jr. *Psalms: A Guide to Studying the Psalter.* 2nd ed. Grand Rapids, MI: Baker Academic, 2012.

———. *Psalms: Reading and Studying the Book of Praises.* Peabody, MA: Hendrickson, 2009.

Blomberg, Craig L. "Matthew." In *Commentary on the New Testament Use of the Old Testament,* edited by G. K. Beale and D. A. Carson, 1-109. Grand Rapids, MI: Baker Academic, 2007.

Bock, Darrell L. "Single Meaning, Multiple Contexts and Referents: The New Testament's Legitimate, Accurate, and Multifaceted Use of the Old Testament." In *Three Views on the New Testament Use of the Old Testament,* edited by Kenneth Berding and Jonathan Lunde, 105-51. Counterpoints: Bible and Theology. Grand Rapids, MI: Zondervan, 2008.

Brueggemann, Walter. "The Costly Loss of Lament." *Journal for the Study of the Old Testament* 36 (1986): 57-71.

Brunson, Andrew C. *Psalm 118 in the Gospel of John: An Intertextual Study on the New Exodus Pattern in the Theology of John*. Tübingen, Germany: Mohr Siebeck, 2003.

Calvin, John. *Commentary on the Book of Psalms*. Vol. 1. Translated by James Anderson. Calvin's Commentaries. Grand Rapids, MI: Baker, 1979.

Challies, Tim. "Lord, from Sorrows Deep I Call." Challies.com. June 2, 2019. www .challies.com/resources/lord-from-sorrow-deep-i-call-free-downloads/.

Childs, Brevard S. "Psalm Titles and Midrashic Exegesis." *Journal of Semitic Studies* 16, no. 2 (1971): 137-50.

Chisholm, Robert B. *A Workbook for Intermediate Hebrew: Grammar, Exegesis, and Commentary on Jonah and Ruth*. Grand Rapids, MI: Kregel Academic, 2006.

CNN Editorial Research. "Boston Marathon Terror Attack Fast Facts." CNN.com. May 4, 2020. www.cnn.com/2013/06/03/us/boston-marathon-terror-attack-fast-facts /index.html.

Cole, Robert. "An Integrated Reading of Psalms 1 and 2." *Journal for the Study of the Old Testament* 26, no. 4 (2002): 75-88.

———. *Psalms 1–2: Gateway to the Psalter*. Hebrew Bible Monographs 37. Edited by David J. A. Clines, J. Cheryl Exum, and Keith W. Whitelam. Sheffield, UK: Sheffield Phoenix, 2013.

Craigie, Peter C. *Psalms 1–50*. Word Biblical Commentary. Waco, TX: Word Books, 1983.

Davies, W. D., and Dale C. Allison. *A Critical and Exegetical Commentary on the Gospel According to Saint Matthew*. International Critical Commentary. London: T&T Clark, 1997.

deClaissé-Walford, Nancy L., Rolf A. Jacobson, and Beth Laneel Tanner. *The Book of Psalms*. New International Commentary on the Old Testament. Grand Rapids, MI: Eerdmans, 2014.

Delitzsch, Franz. *Commentary on the Psalms*. 3 vols. Translated by James Martin. Keil and Delitzsch: Commentary on the Old Testament. Grand Rapids, MI: Eerdmans, 1976.

Dempster, Stephen G. *Dominion and Dynasty: A Biblical Theology of the Hebrew Bible*. New Studies in Biblical Theology 15. Edited by D. A. Carson. Downers Grove, IL: InterVarsity Press, 2003.

DeRouchie, Jason S. "Redemptive-Historical Christocentric Approach." In *Five Views of Christ in the Old Testament: Genre, Authorial Intent, and the Nature of Scripture*, edited by Brian J. Tabb and Andrew M. King, 181-211. Grand Rapids, MI: Zondervan Academic, 2022.

Evans, Craig A. "Praise and Prophecy in the Psalter and in the New Testament." In *The Book of Psalms: Composition and Reception*, edited by Peter W. Flint et al., 551-80. VTSup XCIX: Formation and Interpretation of Old Testament Literature IV. Edited by Hans M. Barstad. Leiden: Brill, 2005.

France, R. T. *The Gospel of Matthew*. New International Commentary on the New Testament. Grand Rapids, MI: Eerdmans, 2007.

Futato, Mark D. *Interpreting the Psalms: An Exegetical Handbook*. Handbooks for Old Testament Exegesis. Edited by David M. Howard. Grand Rapids, MI: Kregel, 2007.

Gentry, Peter. "A Preliminary Evaluation and Critique of Prosopological.Exegesis." *The Southern Baptist Journal of Theology* 23, no. 2 (2019): 105-22.

Gentry, Peter J., and Stephen J. Wellum. *Kingdom Through Covenant: A Biblical-Theological Understanding of the Covenants*. 2nd ed. Wheaton, IL: Crossway, 2018.

Getty, Keith, and Stewart Townend. "My Heart Is Filled with Thankfulness." Thankyou Music, 2003. https://store.gettymusic.com/us/song/my-heart-is-filled-with-thankfulness/.

Gilmore, Mikal. "The Curse of the Ramones." *Rolling Stone*. May 19, 2016. www.rollingstone.com/feature/the-curse-of-the-ramones-165741/.

Goldingay, John. *Psalms Volume 3: 90–150*. Baker Commentary on the Old Testament: Wisdom and Psalms. Grand Rapids, MI: Baker Academic, 2008.

Goldsworthy, Graeme. *Preaching the Whole Bible as Christian Scripture: The Application of Biblical Theology to Expository Preaching*. Grand Rapids, MI: Eerdmans, 2000.

Goulder, Michael D. *Midrash and Lection in Matthew*. Speaker's Lectures in Biblical Studies 1969-1971. London: SPCK, 1974.

Grant, Jamie A. *The King as Exemplar: The Function of Deuteronomy's Kingship Law in the Shaping of the Book of Psalms*. Edited by Adele Berlin. Society of Biblical Literature Academia Biblica Series, Volume 17. Atlanta: Society of Biblical Literature, 2004.

Greenwood, Kyle. *Dictionary of English Grammar for Students of Biblical Languages*. Grand Rapids, MI: Zondervan Academic, 2020.

Greidanus, Sidney. *Preaching Christ from the Old Testament: A Contemporary Hermeneutical Method*. Grand Rapids, MI: Eerdmans, 1999.

———. *Preaching Christ from Psalms: Foundations for Expository Sermons in the Christian Year*. Grand Rapids, MI: Eerdmans, 2016.

Grosart, Alexander B. "The Hallel and Jesus Singing." *The Expository Times* 1 (1890): 224-26.

Grudem, Wayne. "Prophecy, Prophets." In *New Dictionary of Biblical Theology*, 701-10. Downers Grove, IL: InterVarsity Press, 2000.

Hagner, Donald Alfred. *Matthew 14–28*. Word Biblical Commentary. Dallas: Word, 1995.

Hamilton, James M., Jr. *Psalms Volume 1: Psalms 1–72*. Evangelical Biblical Theological Commentary. Bellingham, WA: Lexham, 2021.

———. *Typology: Understanding the Bible's Promise-Shaped Patterns*. Grand Rapids, MI: Zondervan Academic, 2022.

Hensley, Adam D. *Covenant Relationships and the Editing of the Hebrew Psalter.* Library of Hebrew Bible/Old Testament Studies 666. Edited by Andrew Mein and Claudia V. Camp. London: T&T Clark, 2018.

———. "David, Once and Future King? A Closer Look at the Postscript of Psalm 72:20." *Journal for the Study of the Old Testament* 46, no. 1 (2020): 24-43.

Holmstedt, Robert D. "Hebrew Poetry and the Appositive Style: Parallelism, Requiescat in Pace." *Vetus Testamentum* 69, nos. 4-5 (2019): 617-48.

Hossfeld, Frank-Lothar, and Erich Zenger. *Psalms 3: A Commentary on Psalms 101–150.* Hermeneia. Edited by Klaus Baltzer. Translated by Linda M. Maloney. Minneapolis, MN: Fortress, 2011.

House, Paul R. *Old Testament Theology.* Downers Grove, IL: InterVarsity Press, 1998.

Howard, David M, Jr. "The Psalms and Current Study." In *Interpreting the Psalms: Issues and Approaches,* edited by David G. Firth and Philip Johnston, 23-40. Leicester: Apollos, 2005.

Jacobson, Rolf A. *The Homebrewed Christianity Guide to the Old Testament: Israel's In-Your-Face, Holy God.* Minneapolis, MN: Fortress, 2018.

Jacobson, Rolf A., and Karl N. Jacobson. *Invitation to the Psalms: A Reader's Guide for Discovery and Engagement.* Grand Rapids, MI: Baker Academic, 2013.

Johnston, Philip S. "Appendix 1: Index of Form-Critical Categorizations." In *Interpreting the Psalms: Issues and Approaches,* edited by David G. Firth and Philip S. Johnston, 295-303. Downers Grove, IL: IVP Academic, 2005.

Kaiser, Walter C., Jr. *The Christian and the Old Testament.* Pasadena, CA: William Carey Library, 2012.

———. *The Promise-Plan of God: A Biblical Theology of the Old and New Testaments.* Grand Rapids, MI: Zondervan, 2008.

Keener, Craig S. *A Commentary on the Gospel of Matthew.* Grand Rapids, MI: Eerdmans, 1999.

Klett, Leah MarieAnne. "Modern Worship Movement Is 'Utterly Dangerous,' Causing 'De-Christianizing of God's People.'" *The Christian Post.* November 9, 2019. www .christianpost.com/news/keith-getty-modern-worship-movement-is-utterly -dangerous-causing-de-christianizing-of-gods-people.html.

Kraus, Hans-Joachim. *Theology of the Psalms.* Translated by Keith R. Crim. Minneapolis, MN: Augsburg, 1986.

Kwon, Hyukjung. "The Reception of Psalm 118 in the New Testament: Application of a 'New Exodus Motif'?" PhD diss., University of Pretoria, 2007.

Lewis, C. S. *Mere Christianity.* San Francisco: HarperCollins, 2001.

———. *Reflections on the Psalms.* San Diego: Harcourt Brace Jovanovich, 2017.

Lloyd-Jones, Martyn. *Spiritual Depression: Its Causes and Cure.* Grand Rapids, MI: Eerdmans, 1965.

Longman, Tremper, III. *How to Read the Psalms.* Downers Grove, IL: InterVarsity, 1988.

Luther, Martin. *Luther's Works*. 69 vols. Edited by Jaroslav Pelikan, Helmut T. Lehmann, and Christopher Boyd Brown. St. Louis, MO: Concordia, 1955.

McCann, J. Clinton, Jr. "The Book of Psalms: Introduction, Commentary, and Reflections." In *The New Interpreter's Bible Commentary: Introduction to Hebrew Poetry; 1 & 2 Maccabees; Psalms; Job*, edited by Leander E. Keck, 641-280. Nashville: Abingdon, 1996.

McKelvey, Michael G. *Moses, David and the High Kingship of Yahweh: A Canonical Study of Book IV of the Psalter*. Piscataway, NJ: Gorgias, 2013.

Menken, M. J. J. "The Psalms in Matthew's Gospel." In *The Psalms in the New Testament*, edited by M. J. J. Menken and Steve Moyise, 61-82. London: T&T Clark, 2004.

Murphy, Todd J. *Pocket Dictionary for the Study of Biblical Hebrew*. Downers Grove, IL: InterVarsity Press, 2003.

Oss, Douglas A. "Canon as Context: The Function of *Sensus Plenior* in Evangelical Hermeneutics." *Grace Theological Journal* 9 (1988): 105-27.

Pao, David W. *Thanksgiving: An Investigation of a Pauline Theme*. New Studies in Biblical Theology 13. Downers Grove, IL: InterVarsity Press, 2003.

Piper, John. *Desiring God: Meditations of a Christian Hedonist*. Rev. and exp. ed. Colorado Springs, CO: Multnomah, 2011.

Pope, Marvin H. "Hosanna." In *The Anchor Yale Bible Dictionary, Volume 3*, edited by David Noel Freedman, 290-91. New York: Doubleday, 1992.

Robertson, O. Palmer. *The Flow of the Psalms: Discovering Their Structure and Theology*. Phillipsburg, NJ: P&R, 2015.

Sailhamer, John H. *Introduction to Old Testament Theology: A Canonical Approach*. Grand Rapids, MI: Zondervan, 1995.

———. *The Pentateuch as Narrative: A Biblical-Theological Commentary*. Library of Biblical Interpretation. Grand Rapids, MI: Zondervan, 1992.

Sanders, James A. "A New Testament Hermeneutic Fabric: Psalm 118 in the Entrance Narrative." In *Early Jewish and Christian Exegesis: Studies in Memory of William Hugh Brownlee*, edited by Craig A. Evans and William F. Stinespring, 177-90. Atlanta: Scholars Press, 1987.

Schröten, Jutta. *Entstehung, Komposition und Wirkungsgeschichte Des 118. Psalms*. Bonner Biblische Beiträge 95. Weinheim, Germany: Beltz Athenäum, 1995.

Schubert, Paul. *Form and Function of the Pauline Thanksgivings*. Berlin: Alfred Töpelmann, 1939.

Silva, Moisés, ed. *New International Dictionary of New Testament Theology and Exegesis*. 6 vols. Grand Rapids, MI: Zondervan, 2014.

Smith, Murray J., and Ian J. Vaillancourt. "Enthroned and Coming to Reign: Jesus's Eschatological Use of Psalm 110:1 in Mark 14:62." *Journal of Biblical Literature* 141, no. 3 (2022): 513-31.

Snearly, Michael K. *The Return of the King: Messianic Expectation in Book 5 of the Psalter*. Library of Hebrew Bible/Old Testament Studies 624. London: T&T Clark, 2016.

Swanson, Steven R. "Hallel." In *The Anchor Yale Bible Dictionary, Volume 3*, edited by David Noel Freedman, 30. New York: Doubleday, 1992.

Tabb, Brian J., and Andrew M. King, eds. *Five Views of Christ in the Old Testament: Genre, Authorial Intent, and the Nature of Scripture*. Grand Rapids, MI: Zondervan Academic, 2022.

Taylor, J. Glen. "Psalms 1 and 2: A Gateway into the Psalter and Messianic Images for the Restoration of David's Dynasty." In *Interpreting the Psalms for Teaching and Preaching*, edited by Herbert W. Bateman and D. Brent Sandy, 47-62. St. Louis, MO: Chalice, 2010.

Terrien, Samuel. *The Psalms: Strophic Structure and Theological Commentary*. Grand Rapids, MI: Eerdmans, 2003.

U2. "In a Little While." U2.com, n.d. www.u2.com/lyrics/68.

U2. "Live from Boston." 2001. www.youtube.com/watch?v=mcNt8oi6ETc.

Vaillancourt, Ian J. *David, Goliath, and the Gospel: Living in Light of Our Savior's Victory*. Discovery Series. Grand Rapids, MI: Our Daily Bread Ministries, 2021. https://discoveryseries.org/courses/david-goliath-and-the-gospel/.

———. *The Dawning of Redemption: The Story of the Pentateuch and the Hope of the Gospel*. Wheaton, IL: Crossway, 2022.

———. "Formed in the Crucible of Messianic Angst: The Eschatological Shape of the Hebrew Psalter's Final Form." *Scottish Bulletin of Evangelical Theology* 31, no. 2 (2013): 127-44.

———. *The Multifaceted Saviour of Psalms 110 and 118: A Canonical Exegesis*. Sheffield, UK: Sheffield Phoenix, 2019.

———. "The Pious Prayer of an Imperfect Prophet: The Psalm of Jonah in Its Narrative Context." *Journal for the Evangelical Study of the Old Testament* 4, no. 2 (2015): 171-89.

———. "Psalm 118 and the Eschatological Son of David." *Journal of the Evangelical Theological Society* 62, no. 4 (2019): 721-38.

———. "Reading Psalm Superscriptions Through the Centuries." *Themelios* (forthcoming, 2023).

Van Pelt, Miles V. "Introduction." In *A Biblical-Theological Introduction to the Old Testament: The Gospel Promised*, edited by Miles V. Van Pelt, 23-42. Wheaton, IL: Crossway, 2016.

Vangemeren, Willem A., ed. *New International Dictionary of Old Testament Theology and Exegesis*. 5 vols. Grand Rapids, MI: Zondervan, 1997.

Wallace, Robert E. *The Narrative Effect of Book 4 of the Hebrew Psalter*. Studies in Biblical Literature 112. Edited by Hemchand Gossai. New York: Peter Lang, 2007.

Waltke, Bruce K., and Charles Yu. *An Old Testament Theology: An Exegetical, Canonical, and Thematic Approach*. Grand Rapids, MI: Zondervan, 2007.

Watts, James W. *Psalm and Story: Inset Hymns in Hebrew Narrative*. Journal for the Study of the Old Testament Supplement Series 139. Edited by David J. A. Clines and Philip R. Davies. Sheffield, UK: JSOT Press, 1992.

Westermann, Claus. *Praise and Lament in the Psalms*. Edited by Richard Soulen. Translated by Keith Crim. Atlanta: John Knox, 1981.

Wilson, Gerald H. *The Editing of the Hebrew Psalter*. Society of Biblical Literature Dissertation Series 76. Chico, CA: Scholars Press, 1985.

Zeitlin, Solomon. "The Hallel: A Historical Study of the Canonization of the Hebrew Liturgy." *Jewish Quarterly Review* 53, no. 1 (1962): 22-29.

Scripture Index